Social Pedagogy and Working with Children and Young People

of related interest

Communication Skills for Working with Children and Young People
Introducing Social Pedagogy
3rd edition
Pat Petrie
ISBN 978 1 84905 137 8

Learning Through Child Observation
2nd edition
Mary Fawcett
ISBN 978 1 84310 676 0

Listening to Children
A Practitioner's Guide
Alison McLeod
ISBN 978 1 84310 549 7

Working with Children and Teenagers Using Solution Focused Approaches
Establishing Respectful and Effective Communication
Judith Milner and Jackie Bateman
ISBN 978 1 84905 082 1

Child Development for Child Care and Protection Workers
2nd edition
Brigid Daniel, Sally Wassell and Robbie Gilligan
Foreword by Professor David Howe
ISBN 978 1 84905 068 5

Child Well-Being
Understanding Children's Lives
Edited by Colette McAuley and Wendy Rose
Foreword by Dame Gillian Pugh
ISBN 978 1 84310 925 9

Improving Outcomes for Children and Families
Finding and Using International Evidence
Edited by Anthony N. Maluccio, Cinzia Canali, Tiziano Vecchiato, Anita Lightburn, Jane Aldgate and Wendy Rose
Foreword by James K. Whittaker
ISBN 978 1 84905 819 3
Child Welfare Outcomes Series

The Developing World of the Child
Edited by Jane Aldgate, David Jones, Wendy Rose and Carole Jeffery
Foreword by Maria Eagle MP
ISBN 978 1 84310 244 1

Social Pedagogy and Working with Children and Young People

Where Care and Education Meet

EDITED BY CLAIRE CAMERON AND PETER MOSS

Jessica Kingsley *Publishers*
London and Philadelphia

First published in 2011
by Jessica Kingsley Publishers
116 Pentonville Road
London N1 9JB, UK
and
400 Market Street, Suite 400
Philadelphia, PA 19106, USA

www.jkp.com

Copyright © Jessica Kingsley Publishers 2011

Library of Congress Cataloging in Publication Data
Social pedagogy and working with children and young people : where care
and education meet / edited by Claire Cameron and Peter Moss.
    p. cm.
Includes bibliographical references and index.
ISBN 978-1-84905-119-4 (alk. paper)
1. Early childhood education. 2. Child care. 3. Child care services.
4. Critical pedagogy. I. Cameron, Claire. II. Moss, Peter.
LB1139.23.S66 2010
372.21--dc22
                    2010053778

British Library Cataloguing in Publication Data
A CIP catalogue record for this book is available from the British Library

ISBN 978 1 84905 119 4

Printed and bound in Great Britain

11/7/11

Contents

CHAPTER 1

Social Pedagogy: Current Understandings and Opportunities

Claire Cameron and Peter Moss

Social pedagogy: What is it?

This book is about an approach to and profession for working with people that is widespread across Continental Europe yet little known or understood in the UK or the rest of the English-speaking world: social pedagogy. The book title talks about social pedagogy and working with children, but this approach and the profession of social pedagogue have the capacity to work not only with children but also with young people and adults of all ages – from birth to 100 years old, as some Danish pedagogues would say. They also have the capacity to work across a wide range of settings – from nurseries to residential homes for young people, from schools to services for adults with disabilities. This border-crossing potential challenges many of the divisions and specialisms we have put in place in developing our human services.

What, though, does this approach consist of? How should we understand social pedagogy? One aim of this book is to provide some answers to these questions, deepening the reader's understanding of the social pedagogic approach and the profession of social pedagogue. We avoid, however, any claim to provide the answer and definitive understanding. For what will become clear as the book unfolds is the variations – both theoretical and national – in understandings of social pedagogy and how to practise it. This diversity has led Petrie (2006) to suggest that the term 'pedagogies' might be more appropriate and has been the subject of a recent book (Kornbeck and Jensen 2009). It has also contributed to the conclusion of Walter Lorenz that social pedagogy is 'an important but widely misunderstood member of the social professions' (2008, p.625).

Things are further complicated because social pedagogy is always a political practice. As such, it can assume different political complexions, having the potential to be conservative or restorative, an agent of authoritarian government or a vehicle for democratic and emancipatory ends. It can collude with or question political regimes, seeking to maintain, modify or undermine them.

The diversity of social pedagogy in Europe makes it difficult to grasp. But this difficulty is also an opportunity. The unknown creates an uncertainty that makes one puzzle. Such curiosity is the basis of social pedagogy. The professional, known as a social pedagogue – or, in some countries, pedagogue, or variants of the term such as social educator – wants to examine, using theoretical knowledge, why something happened, what was happening to prompt its occurrence and what the consequences might be. In studies, social pedagogues often say 'it depends' in response to an interview question, because they want to take into account the context before forming a judgement or making a decision.

Social pedagogy is not only diverse and contingent but very broad in scope. It was first named as such in Germany in 1844, by Karl Mager, as the 'theory of all the personal, social and moral education in a given society, including the description of what has happened in practice' (Winkler 1988, p.41 as translated by Gabriel Thomas). It retains this breadth of action and ambition today. It can be described as where education and care meet, as being concerned with children's upbringing, as a broadly educational approach to social problems, education that takes place in everyday lives, and as 'education in its broadest sense' (Petrie *et al.* 2006). The contemporary Danish understanding adopted by Jensen and Hansen (2002, p.5) is that the aim is:

> Improving learning and developing options on behalf of ideals of individuals and society. The pedagogical theories combine
> i) ideals of a good life (philosophy), ii) understandings of individuals and groups and their resources and needs (psychology and biology) and iii) understandings of social resources, values and demands (cultural and social sciences).

Despite its diversity, its responsiveness to wider context, and its broad scope, we can identify some more specific, common components that can give some coherence to social pedagogy's identity. Research suggests that the following principles hold good across different types of pedagogic setting:

- There is a focus on the child as a whole person, and support for the child's overall development.

- The practitioner sees herself as a person, in relationship with the child or young person.

- Children and staff are seen as inhabiting the same lifespace; not as existing in separate hierarchical domains.

- As professionals, pedagogues are encouraged constantly to reflect on their practice and to apply both theoretical understandings and self-knowledge to the sometimes challenging demands with which they are confronted.

- Pedagogues are also practical, so their training prepares them to share in many aspects of the children's daily lives and activities.

- Children's lives in groups are seen as an important resource; workers should foster and make use of the group.

- Pedagogy builds on an understanding of children's rights that is not limited to procedural matters of legislated requirements.

- There is an emphasis on team work and on valuing the contribution of others in 'bringing' up children: other professionals, members of the community and, especially, parents.

- The centrality of relationship and, allied to this, the importance of listening and communicating. (Petrie *et al.* 2006, p.22)

The 'pedagogy' in social pedagogy we might take to refer to its broadly educational role, though always bearing in mind the broad, holistic understanding of education that is adopted. The 'social' emphasises several important features: the concern with the individual, the group, the community and society, their interrelationships and the good of all four levels; the commitment to inclusiveness, confronting social problems and social justice; showing solidarity with members of marginalised groups such as vulnerable families or people with disabilities by, for example, helping them set up self-help groups (Stephens 2009); overall, the centrality of relationships in working with children or any other people. 'Social' pedagogy usually refers to the pedagogic work that society undertakes, as represented in services for children and young people. Sometimes the 'social' is drawn narrowly, to refer to specialist services, such as residential care for young people or centres for people with disabilities. But in other contexts the 'social' denotes all care and education work on behalf of society and includes, for example, early childhood care and education services and free-time services.

Social pedagogy: Where is it found?

Social pedagogy is found in most countries of Continental Europe, from Russia to Portugal and from Slovenia to Norway – though, as already suggested, there is no *one* European tradition or understanding of social pedagogy (Kornbeck and Jensen 2009). There is also no single common term for social pedagogy or pedagogue, which can cause some confusion when seeking to understand its place in different countries. Thus, Petrie *et al.* (2006) describe how the Romance languages use *l'education* or variations on the term to refer to what more northern European countries call pedagogy while *la scolarité* and *l'ensignement* is used to denote formal education. In Catalonia, for example, the principal worker in residential care for children and young people is an *educador/a social*, or social educator, whose training focuses on how education can improve the quality of life and as such is within the social pedagogic tradition. The education of social pedagogues can also take place in very different contexts. For instance, the social educator programme at the University of Girona in Catalonia is situated within an Education and Psychology Faculty (Fullana 2008); while in Norway, the child welfare pedagogue, the main worker with children in care, also receives an education in the social pedagogy tradition but situated within a social work department (Stephens 2009).

Variations in terminology and context can give rise to some debate about the presence or not of social pedagogy in a country. Take the case of France. Christine Bon considers that 'the concept of social pedagogy as an intellectual discipline connecting to social work and intervention, and the technical and praxeological notion of social pedagogy as a profession do not exist in France' (2009, p.34). Certainly, there is a complex field of work with children and young people in France with over 40 different degrees and diplomas of relevance to the work of six different ministries. Of the four main areas of intervention, two come closest to social pedagogy: *éducateurs specialisés* and *animateurs socio-culturels*, the former sharing daily life in institutions and the latter working in recreation centres and summer camps and running leisure-time activities. Boddy and Statham (2009) contend that France's distinctive Bachelor programme, called *éducation spécialisé*, where the focus is on 'doing with' children and families, is social pedagogy, in contrast to the social work qualification, *assistance sociale*, which is more focused on the administrative requirements for working with children and families. In Boddy and Statham's study, social pedagogues in France were routinely employed alongside social workers as the two roles were seen as complementary.

Despite such occasional disagreements, the job title 'social pedagogue' (or its equivalent) has official recognition in Continental Europe, and, in most countries, social pedagogy is a degree-level qualification. Education as a social pedagogue typically includes study of sociology, cultural studies, psychology, pedagogics, arts and crafts as well as practice placements. For example, in Denmark, the *pædagoger* receives a three-and-a-half-year bachelor level initial education specialising in social pedagogy (Oberhuemer, Schreyer and Neuman 2010). The curriculum includes pedagogic theory and practice (drawing on a wide disciplinary base, including pedagogy, psychology and sociology); Danish culture and communication; the individual, institution and society; practical study in either health, the body and exercise, expression, music and drama, arts and crafts, or science and technology. There are also three practice placements, totalling 15 months, and students must specialise within one of three fields: children and young people, people with 'reduced functionality' or people with social problems (Danish Ministry of Education 2010).

The qualified pedagogue is usually equipped for work in a variety of settings. However, following the integration in 1992 of three separate pedagogue professions and education, the range of work open to the qualified pedagogue in Denmark is exceptional: early childhood services for children under and over three years, out of school (free-time) services, residential care for children and young people, and settings for people with disabilities or other special needs. For this reason Denmark, as we shall see, raises important questions about the scope of pedagogical work and the education of pedagogues: how broad should the former be? And how generic the latter?

Social pedagogy: Why is it so unknown in the Anglophone world?

Social pedagogy is undoubtedly becoming more familiar in Anglophone contexts, and, as Kornbeck (2009) points out, it has been discussed in British academic circles since the early 1990s. But, on the whole, social pedagogy as a discipline framing practice has remained undiscovered. Why might this be? To some extent, there is a language issue. The English-speaking world, with its language fast becoming the global *lingua franca*, has become linguistically incompetent, unable to work in and with other languages, and too ready to assume that concepts and terms in other languages can be unproblematically translated – dished up on a plate and requiring little or no effort at comprehension. Social pedagogy has taken root in countries where English is not the first language and, on encountering the Anglophone world, often gets literally lost in translation. The term of 'pedagogy' is understood in English as the 'science of teaching and learning', concerned with educational practices in classrooms or schools, which are themselves often associated with cognitive and individualistic approaches, education in its narrower sense. Confronted by the term 'social pedagogy', the English-speaker may assume that it refers to this didactic science or may be offered, unhelpfully, a translation such as 'education', which is then assumed to refer to education in its narrower sense, with a focus on cognitive learning. 'Pedagogue', similarly, can end up as 'teacher', again with strong school associations.

Then there is a wide range of concepts that are important to social pedagogy in other countries, which do not readily translate. Chapters in this book, for instance, refer to German terms such as *Bildung*, *Haltung* and *Lebensweltorientierung*, as well as to Danish terms such as *kropslighed* and *rummelighed*. To take another example, this time from Central Europe, a Hungarian researcher in an earlier study in which we were involved introduced an important social pedagogical term in her own language:

> When talking about children, most of the time we use the word *nevelés*, which does not have an English equivalent. Its meaning is close to 'upbringing', and it involves the concepts of both care and education. It expresses that care and education are inseparable concepts. When you provide care, you also teach children directly and indirectly. (Korintus 2001, p.3)

Even when the Hungarian word is translated, despite not having a ready equivalent, 'upbringing' is not a term familiar to English ears in the context of working with children; it is something we tend to think of as the function of the family. Yet it begins to capture something of the holistic nature of the social pedagogic approach: the pedagogue's acting as an 'upbringer' on behalf of society.

Gaining an understanding of social pedagogy, therefore, faces the linguistically challenged English-speaker with a dilemma. Either settle for a translation of key terms and concepts and hope not too much is lost, or recognise the centrality of language in culture and expression, and take the time and trouble to struggle to understand the meaning of important pedagogical terms and concepts.

But the reasons for the invisibility or very low visibility of social pedagogy in the Anglophone world are not confined to language. Social pedagogy, as we have already suggested, might be understood in English as 'education in its broadest sense'. On the same theme, Stephens (2009, p.344) refers to the close connection between social pedagogy and the German concept of *Bildung*, which embraces 'not just schooling, but also the cultivation and elevation of character'. Such ideas of education do not, however, relate readily to the narrower concept of education currently dominant in the Anglophone world's discourse.

If social pedagogy has difficulty relating to current Anglophone understandings of education, it also has difficulty mapping on to Anglophone understandings of social work or child welfare. Smith and Whyte (2008) argue that 'there is a limited conception of education within the Anglo-American Saxon [welfare] tradition and a consequent bifurcation of education and care' (p.15). The other side of this coin is a strong emphasis in Anglo-American traditions on individual causes and solutions, reinforced by the advance of neoliberalism:

> The location of welfare within the wider social context, apparent in Scottish and European models, is less pronounced in the Anglo-American traditions… [R]esponses to social problems tend to be located at the level of the individual, detached from social and wider community context… Over the past couple of decades case management and deficit based approaches have reinforced the focus on the individual at the expense of broader social-educational approaches… Deficit based and correctional models fit with the advance of the neo-liberal state, particularly in the Anglo-American context, but increasingly across the developed world. (Smith and Whyte 2008, pp.22–23)

From an Anglophone perspective, social pedagogy requires a reorientation, a rethinking, from a narrower individual to a broader societal focus, and from a focus on care and protection, embracing a concern with working with practical and emotional difficulties in people's lives, to thinking about practice in terms of all-round development, abilities, goals, as well as the pedagogic concept of upbringing, which is held at a societal level as well as a (substitute) parental one.

Social pedagogy struggles to make itself visible and understood in the UK and the rest of the Anglophone world because its language and sensibility are foreign. But this is not an insuperable obstacle, any more than it has proved to the spread of Italian food to the British diet. We can learn the language and gain an understanding of the social pedagogic approach: its values, its perspectives, its ways of working. And, once introduced, many find social pedagogy very appealing, a sensibility to be cultivated – and a bit resonant too. For in the process of familiarisation with social pedagogy, many in the UK find themselves reminded of rich native traditions that have been discarded but which merit revisiting and reclaiming. Social pedagogy, perhaps, is not so foreign after all.

Cameron and Petrie (2009) and Petrie and Cameron (2009) argue that while there is much about social pedagogy that is unfamiliar, there is a certain amount of historical common ground between ideas and practices in working with children in the UK and the social pedagogic approach. Hämäläinen (2003) has argued that:

> From the very beginning, the social pedagogical perspective was based on attempts to find educational solutions to social problems. Thus, the educationists who paid attention to poverty and other forms of social distress, for example, Juan Luis Vives, Johann Amos Comenius, Johann Heinrich Pestalozzi, Friedrich Fröbel, from the pedagogical point of view *and without using the term 'social pedagogy'*, are pioneers of the social pedagogical perspective. (p.71)

On this basis, Petrie (2010) has proposed Robert Owen (1771–1858), Thomas Barnardo (1845–1905), Emmeline Pethick (1867–1954) and Mary Neal (1860–1944) as prototypical pioneers of social pedagogy in the UK. A similar claim can be made for the network of Camphill-Steiner schools that specialise in the residential care and education of young people with special educational needs and whose original figurehead was an Austrian paediatrician named Karl König who brought his approach to Scotland in the late 1930s (Monteux 2006). Today the Camphill

School in Aberdeen offers degree and other courses in social pedagogy in partnership with the University of Aberdeen.

Smith and Whyte (2008) have gone further in tracing a Scottish connection, arguing that 'ideas enshrined within social pedagogy have a resonance with Scottish approaches to social welfare...[foremost amongst which] is the focus on education as the vehicle for both individual improvement and social cohesion' (p.15). The Scottish tradition of social welfare has viewed social problems as 'rooted in social context and responses...[and] education as a force for social change' (p.19). From this perspective, Scotland sits closer to Continental Europe than to either England or the United States: 'the location of welfare within the wider social context, apparent in Scottish and European models [of welfare], is less pronounced in Anglo-American traditions' (p.22). The common ground between social pedagogy and the Scottish child welfare tradition is most apparent, Smith and Whyte suggest, in the work of an official Committee established to review arrangements for dealing with young people involved in offending and those in need of care and protection. The Kilbrandon Report, published in 1994:

> was strongly educational, reflecting longstanding views that social well-being and social cohesion through education should be the ambition of the system. Children's problems were to be responded to through what was described as 'social education', which involved working in partnership with parents to strengthen 'those natural influences for good which will assist the child's development into a mature and useful member of society...' The integration of social welfare and educational services was to involve a new organisation, the Department of Social Education, located within the Department of Education and staffed mainly by social workers. (p.21)

Finally in this (not comprehensive) review of resonances between social pedagogy and UK experiences, mention should be made of what Michael Fielding in Chapter 10 calls radical democratic approaches to formal education and the common ground that he defines between this educational tradition and what Pat Petrie terms in Chapter 4 'democratic and emancipatory social pedagogy'. With this and other examples, the problem of the UK's relationship with social pedagogy appears to be not only unfamiliarity and lack of comprehension with this Continental approach to working with children (and others), but the present-day unfamiliarity and lack of comprehension in the UK itself with its rich educational and welfare traditions under the influence of neoliberalism and new public management; we have lost touch with our past and our roots. Coming closer to social pedagogy, therefore, may mean not only opening new channels of communication with our fellow Europeans, but reclaiming our relationships with British pioneers and radical traditions.

Social pedagogy: Is it coming to the UK?

As Kornbeck (2009), Stephens (2009) and Cousée *et al.* (2010) point out, there is growing interest in social pedagogy in the UK. This is most clearly shown in the English government-funded pilot programme to investigate the impact of a social pedagogic approach in children's residential care (Cameron *et al.* 2010). This programme, which began in 2008, is recruiting social pedagogues trained elsewhere, mostly in Germany, to work alongside English residential care workers to try to influence practice from the inside and from the 'bottom up'. The impact of this programme will be reported in 2011, but initial findings are that, in favourable conditions, social pedagogues are able to suggest, and make, significant changes to daily life for young people. They are also able, as unfamiliar outsiders, to throw a light on the taken-for-granted practices in and structures of residential care and identify larger changes necessary for social pedagogy to flourish in this sector.

Alongside this national project, some local authorities are also taking initiatives. Essex (a large local authority, population about 1.3 million bordering north-east London) is the best-known example. Since 2008, the local authority has employed a social enterprise company specialising in social pedagogy (ThemPra) to train their residential care and other children's sector workers in social pedagogical approaches and methods using workplace-based courses, and at the same time has worked to embed change at a local authority level by involving senior managers. Initial feedback from residential care workers was very positive and has prompted further focus on practice around improved working relationships and creative activities. One of the most significant of these changes was a rethinking of the concept of risk in relation to residential care practice (Boyce 2010).

Other local authorities and employers are also showing interest. Staffordshire (a local authority of some 830,000 people in the English Midlands) is melding the recruitment and training approaches; it has recruited social pedagogues alongside buying in training. Derbyshire

County Council (population 760,000) is using bought-in training and consultancy to raise awareness of social pedagogy among all children's services staff and to offer six days of training to residential care and some foster carers, alongside introducing changes to make staff meetings more reflective and make staff supervision more supportive to staff and children. In keeping with social pedagogic traditions, they have also focused on developing staff confidence in using expressive arts and outdoor activities with young people.

Interest is not confined to England. Children in Scotland, the national 'umbrella' agency for the whole of the children's sector in Scotland, with a membership of more than 450 statutory agencies, voluntary sector organisations, professional associations and community groups, has promoted a variant of social pedagogy known as the 'Scottish Pedagogue', blending the traditions of arts-based children's workers, rural communities and early childhood practice with the focus on building a children's workforce (Children in Scotland 2008). The Scottish Institute for Residential Child Care (SIRCC) evaluated a social pedagogy training programme based within one children's sector employer and found that residential, foster care and education workers who had undergone social pedagogy training valued the emphasis on reflective and analytic practice (Milligan 2009).

Growing interest in social pedagogy goes beyond the organisational. A grassroots Social Pedagogy Development Network holds twice-yearly meetings of practitioners and other stakeholders. The aim is to develop knowledge and ways forward in the understanding of social pedagogic practice, and there is a website dedicated to promoting social pedagogy in the UK (www.socialpedagogyuk.com).

In sum, there has been an explosion of interest in social pedagogy and its applications in children's services over the past five years, accompanied by exploration of employer-based training and education. Most focus of attention is on the potential that social pedagogy offers children's residential care, although this is clearly only one part of the work of social pedagogues in other countries. The suggestion in an English government Green Paper that 'both the "new" teacher and pedagogue models for early years' professionals have the potential to help raise the quality of early years' provision' (HM Government 2005, p.40) has so far drawn no further policy response.

The question arises as to why has this interest and activity arisen and why now? We have already argued that social pedagogy is not entirely new but resonates with some important traditions in England

and Scotland. This may account in part for the ready appeal that the approach seems to have, when put forward, among many involved in the field of child welfare.

More currently, interest in social pedagogy has arisen from deep official and public concern with the failures of the system of residential care for children and young people. The last (Labour) government recognised that this service was very expensive – costing £910 million in 2007–8 in England alone (NHS Information Centre 2009) – and offered very poor outcomes for young people in care, as we shall describe in some detail later in this chapter. Faced by this ongoing crisis in the residential care system, the English government has been open to the experience of countries with more successful systems, and in particular to the potential of social pedagogy and social pedagogues as one way to bring about fundamental reform. The potential application of social pedagogy within foster care has also been posited (Tapsfield 2010).

More broadly, the political climate of the early years of the current century created favourable conditions for interest in social pedagogy, with its potential to reconnect education and social well-being and its attention to the 'whole child'. As Smith and Whyte point out:

> The concept of 'the whole child' is re-emerging in policy directions in children's services and youth justice in the UK. In England and Wales *Every Child Matters* ([HM Government] 2004) and, in Scotland, *Getting it Right for Every Child* ([Scottish Executive] 2005), both point to the need for multi-systemic and holistic approaches to meet the individual and social needs of children… The complex needs of the whole child are easily lost in the professionalisation of distinct disciplines, despite the political zeitgeist exhorting professionals to work together. The current direction of policy and structural developments cries out for conceptual synthesis a social educational model might provide. (pp.24–25)

It remains to be seen whether a new zeitgeist is emerging in the second decade of the century, one less conducive to widespread and radical reform.

One other ingredient should be added to the mix of traditions, concerns and zeitgeist. Social pedagogy has made a strong showing in the UK in recent years because of various intermediaries – individuals, groups and organisations – who have been able to interpret and explain the social pedagogic approach to a UK audience, including providing the evidence base for giving this approach to practice and policy serious attention. In this process the Thomas Coram Research Unit (TCRU) has played a key role.

How TCRU got interested

The intermediaries who have worked to introduce the UK to the social pedagogic approach are a diverse group, working in a variety of settings in a variety of occupations. These intermediaries have not only appeared in recent years; Haydn Davies-Jones, for instance, was championing social pedagogy back in the 1980s. But what were isolated voices in the past have been replaced today by, if not a massed choir, then a substantial mixed ensemble.

Part of that ensemble has been a team of researchers who have been investigating social pedagogy for over ten years at Thomas Coram Research Unit, part of the Institute of Education, University of London. We have been privileged to be part of that team. This interest in social pedagogy and the forming of a critical mass of expertise in the area has emerged from decades of cross-national work in Europe. One of us, Peter Moss, was a coordinator of a European Commission expert group on services for young children, the European Childcare Network, from 1986 to 1996, and during the course of this and later work, including membership of review teams participating in the Organisation for Economic Cooperation and Development (OECD)'s study of early childhood policies, *Starting Strong*, became familiar with countries where social pedagogy was an important influence. Another team member, Pat Petrie, coordinated a parallel network concerned with school-age childcare (or free-time services as Nordic countries would call them) and similarly learned much about social pedagogy along the way. In the late 1990s, substantial funding became available through the English government to investigate social pedagogy in relation to children living in residential care (Petrie *et al.* 2006). Shortly afterwards, an EU-funded study of 'care work' in Europe provided further opportunities to study the potential role of social pedagogy not only in working with children but also with young people and adults; our Danish partners in this study, including the author of Chapter 8, pointed out from an early stage of the research that the concept of 'care work' was unfamiliar in Denmark, where the services we planned to study were understood to be pedagogical services (Cameron and Moss 2007).

These two major programmes of work, and subsequent studies of foster care in Europe (Petrie *et al.* 2007), interprofessional working in extended schools and children's centres (Cameron *et al.* 2008), and social work decision making (Boddy and Statham 2009), have enabled in-depth investigations and cross-country comparisons involving Denmark, Germany, France, the Netherlands, Belgium, Hungary, Spain and Sweden. Remarkable consistencies within Continental European approaches and divergences from the UK approach to care and education practice began to emerge. Further investigations, funded by the government and by the Esmée Fairbairn Foundation, took place into the possible introduction of social pedagogy into the UK (Cameron 2007; Cameron, McQuail and Petrie 2007), followed by the launch of pilot programmes to explore these possibilities in practice in residential care (DfES 2007; Bengtsson *et al.* 2008).

Not only has this sustained and substantial body of work enabled a deeper understanding of social pedagogy, but it has also provided evidence that this approach would be beneficial for working with children.

The research evidence

Overall, TCRU's research studies of children's services and professional practice in Continental Europe have painted a consistent picture. The findings regarding residential care, the focus of this work, are striking. Petrie *et al.* (2006) found, on the basis of data gathered from heads of establishments, residential care workers and young people, as well as analysis of policy documents, that young people living in residential care in Denmark and Germany, in social pedagogical regimes, were more likely to be in school, and, if over the age of 16, in employment, than their English counterparts. Moreover, young women in residential care were more likely to have had a pregnancy and young people were more likely to have a criminal record when they lived in English children's homes compared with those in Denmark and Germany. It was the characteristics of the staff that were associated with better outcomes: where, as in Denmark and Germany, staff had more in-service training, longer-term commitment to their workplace, undertook key work and conceptualised the children positively, and where they had lower staff–child ratios and looked to themselves to resolve issues in collaboration with colleagues rather than involving external agencies. All these characteristics, too, were consistent with a social pedagogic approach.

Looking at foster care, the influence of social pedagogy could be seen in the policy and practice frameworks and much less in the professional occupation of social pedagogue. Few foster carers in the countries examined – France, Germany, Denmark and Sweden – were qualified pedagogues, although there were some. Moreover, the training of foster carers, apart from in France, was on a similar model to the UK, with preparation sessions with a supervising social worker, who could also be a social pedagogue. In France, there exists a professionalised model of foster care, characterised by extensive and compulsory training, following which foster carers were seen as part of the professional team working with children and families. In both models, the social pedagogic emphasis on valuing everyday life was evident (Petrie 2007).

Turning to decision making before children come into care, Boddy *et al.* (2009) found that social pedagogues had a considerable role to play as part of multidisciplinary teams where they were considered the specialists in direct practice with children in Denmark, Germany and France and recommended the inclusion of social pedagogues and psychologists as part of child welfare teams alongside social workers in future development work in the UK.

The major theme emerging from these studies has been the importance of the professional role, supported by policy frameworks, in creating the relational environment in which children and young people can flourish.

The *Care Work in Europe* study looked in more depth at the conditions for good-quality employment in services working with children, young people and adults, and found that they were associated not just with physical conditions such as pay, important though this is, but also with the extent to which practitioners were able to exercise some autonomy and to make situated judgements at work, to be able to use knowledge and adapt it to the multiple and ever-changing situations that arise in work with children, young people and adults. The study also identified a number of key competencies for doing this work, competencies that were needed whether working with the youngest child or the oldest adult:

- communication, not just oral, with many individuals and organisations, and including listening

- contextualised judgement; the ability to make assessments and decisions specific to the individual and group and the prevailing conditions rather than simply follow laid down procedures

- analytic and reflective competencies

- understanding and valuing learning as a lifelong process

- personal competencies and experiences, such as empathy, the will to go deeper, patience, challenge (personal competencies are not about defining care work through personal characteristics but about how the worker uses the self as a resource)

- professional knowledge, about the specific group worked with, as well as social science and social psychology to support the development of the work

- working with theories and practice

- musical and aesthetic competencies

- broad cultural knowledge

- knowledge about self-protection from the physical demands of the work

- intercultural and other diversity competencies

- team work and cross-professional work.

Both conditions and competencies, as will become clear over the course of this book, are closely identified with a social pedagogical approach. The important role of the pedagogue stands out, too, in all this body of work, albeit also the considerable variations between countries in the place of the social pedagogue in the full range of services. What also have become apparent, being thrown into sharp relief by our cross-national comparative work, are the deep problems of the children's workforce in the UK, with its very hierarchical structure, headed by a professional class of teachers and social workers, followed by a fragmented and differentiated army of care workers and assistants, many poorly educated and most badly paid (Simon *et al.* 2008); the conceptual and structural split between education and care; and the reliance on the theoretically threadbare concept of 'social care'. The UK children's workforce, it has become increasingly apparent, needs both rethinking and restructuring.

What are children's lives like today?
This book is about working with children. So before embarking in detail on the book's theme, the social pedagogical approach to such work, it is

worth considering briefly the situation of children (and young people) in the UK today, as this provides the context for any future development of social pedagogical practice.

In the UK, the category 'children' is in decline: just 19 per cent of the population are children under the age of 18, compared to 25 per cent 35 years ago. But at the same time, it is also becoming ethnically richer and more diverse, as more children are born to women who were born outside the UK. In 2008, 24 per cent of live births were to mothers born outside the UK (Office for National Statistics 2009). Family formations, too, are diversifying. Again in 2008, a quarter of children were in lone-parent families; while in a fifth of two-parent families, the parents were cohabiting but not married.

Most children, too, live in homes where parents are employed. Only 5 per cent of couple families had neither parent working, while a quarter (26%) had only one parent working; most children, therefore, lived in families where both parents were employed, though in most cases this entailed the father in full-time work and the mother in part-time. Two fifths of lone-parent families (41%) were workless, and in 4 per cent the lone parent worked less than 15 hours a week (Maplethorpe *et al.* 2010).

The institutionalisation of childhood has increased in recent years, in the sense that more children and young people spend longer in some form of formal education and/or childcare, as use of pre-school and school-age childcare has increased and periods in education lengthen. This is on top of a very early start for schooling, with most children starting primary school between four and five years old, before the compulsory school age of five. Supported by an official entitlement, nearly all three- and four-year-olds now receive early childhood education, albeit the entitlement is part-time, 15 hours per week. In 2006, 71 per cent of children under three years attended some form of 'childcare', but less than half (33%) were in formal provision, the remainder attending 'informal' provision, a category including private family day carers, nannies, relatives and friends. Moreover, most of this group went on a part-time basis, only 13 per cent of the age group attending 30 hours a week or more (many in the 'formal' group would probably have been two-year-olds going a few hours a week to a playgroup) (Children in Scotland 2010).

Children are divided by gender. Girls in school do better than boys from a very early age and continue to do so through to GCSEs (an exam usually taken at 16 years of age) and beyond; in 2006–7, in England, around half of young women (51%) achieved two or more A level qualifications (an exam usually taken at around 18 years of age) or equivalent compared with two fifths of young men (40%). Boys are excluded from school much more often than girls. In 2006–7, of the total of 8680 permanent exclusions of pupils from primary, secondary and special schools in England, 6850 were boys, and three quarters of the fixed-term exclusions were boys, usually due to 'persistent disruptive behaviour' or fighting with another pupil. Taken together, these figures suggest that there is a systematic gender bias in the teaching, learning and assessment, and management, of school children. By the time they finish school at age 16, as borne out in the UNICEF research on well-being (2008), two thirds of students have experienced bullying – including name-calling, social exclusion, extortion, being threatened or being hit – within the previous three years.

In 2007–8, nearly 90,000 young people aged 10–17 entered the criminal justice system for the first time. Although 7 per cent fewer than the previous year, almost all (94%) of them were boys. Among young people found guilty of an offence, most commonly theft or violence against a person, boys aged 15–17 were held responsible for two thirds of them. Of those children who are killed in the UK, two thirds are male. Such an extreme gender divide suggests a gendered approach to the way societal structures operate that is affecting the experiences of boys and girls in different ways (National Statistical Office 2010).

Childhood in the UK is also marked by widespread deprivation and considerable inequality. Income inequality has increased substantially in the last four decades, the Gini coefficient (a measure of inequality in disposable income) rising from 27 in 1977 to 34 in 2007/8, above the EU average of 31 and placing the UK in 20th position among the 27 member states. There are also inequalities in household wealth, which, having fallen substantially during most of the 20th century, began to grow again from the late 1980s. Levels of child poverty are high by EU standards and are beginning to creep up again after substantial falls; the proportion of children living in low income households fell from 27 per cent in 1990–1 to 21 per cent in 2004–5, but stood at 23 per cent in 2007–8 (Maplethorpe *et al.* 2010). The other end of this spectrum is a small minority of children – about 7 per cent – who go to private schools, yet who, in adulthood, are greatly over-represented in high-earning employment and positions of power, the most glaring example being the current government, where 60 per cent of ministers were privately educated (Sutton Trust 2010).

This unequal society structures the lives of children and young people (Wilkinson and Pickett 2009), affecting well-being. On a multidimensional child well-being index covering a range of material and subjective indicators, the UK ranks 24th overall out of 29 European countries (Child Poverty Action Group 2009).

Although pedagogues can be found working in many settings, the chapters in this book concentrate mainly on two types: early childhood education and care (typically nurseries, kindergartens and age-integrated centres) and residential care for children and young people. This latter area has been, as already noted, a subject of grave and sustained concern in England. The reasons become clear when the situation of children in care is compared with that of all children.

Around 61,000 children and young people in England were in local authority care at the 2009 census date (Department for Children, Schools and Families 2009), although because many children enter and leave care placements rapidly, this is fewer than the number in care for some period during the course of a year (Boddy *et al.* 2009). The (census) figure represents about half of 1 per cent of all those under 18 years of age, which is low compared to other countries. In 2009, 60 per cent of young people in care in England were looked after under a compulsory care order, and one third were there with the voluntary agreement of their parents. The main reason for going into care was abuse or neglect (61%), followed by family illness or disability, acute stress or dysfunction (24%). In addition, some 3700 young people, mostly boys, were in care because they had arrived in England as unaccompanied asylum seekers and had no family to look after them (Department for Children, Schools and Families 2009).

Nearly three quarters of children and young people in care in 2009 were looked after by foster carers in domestic premises, while 14 per cent were in residential care homes of various kinds and around 7 per cent were living with their parents under supervision. Eleven per cent of young people had had three or more placements in this year, while around two thirds had lived in the same placement for the preceding two years (Department for Children, Schools and Families 2009). Initial studies suggest that although legal frameworks differ, young people in care in other European nations are likely to be there for the same reasons as in England, but to have a more stable experience of care, with fewer changes of placement (Cameron *et al.* 2011).

The childhoods of this group of children and young people are very different to the generality of children, and not only because of not living with parents. They are likely to come from highly socially and materially disadvantaged backgrounds (Bebbington and Miles 1989) with little or no educational support (Cameron *et al.* 2011). They are much less likely to gain educational qualifications than their contemporaries not in care: about 14 per cent of children who have been in care for at least 12 months obtain five 'good' GCSE passes compared with 65 per cent of all school children (Department for Children, Schools and Families 2009). Although statistics from other countries are difficult to obtain, it would appear that a higher proportion of young people in care in some Continental European countries leave school with the equivalent of GCSEs (Cameron, Hollingworth and Jackson 2011). Assessing how many young people in care attain qualifications at the age of 18 is difficult. According to English government statistics, about 26 per cent of young people aged 19 who were in care at the age of 16 are in education, but a recent survey of local authorities found that 44 per cent of young people known to local authority leaving care teams were in education and 9 per cent were attending universities (Casas and Montserrat Boada 2010). This represents a considerable improvement on participation rates in the past: earlier estimates were that 1 per cent of young people in care were attending university (Jackson, Ayaji and Quigley 2005). In Sweden about 13 per cent of young people from public care go on to tertiary education (Höjer and Johansson 2010) but rates elsewhere are lower.

As well as leaving care with few educational qualifications, young people in residential care are particularly likely to have mental health problems (Meltzer *et al.* 2003), to be unemployed, and to be over-represented in virtually every indicator of disadvantage when adults (Petrie 2007). Last but not least, young people from a public care background leave care earlier, most usually at the age of 18, than other young people leave home, usually at around 24 years, and this is also the case in other countries (Cameron, Hollingworth and Jackson 2011). The picture overall is truly a sorry one, showing a group of highly vulnerable young people facing disproportionate disadvantage and problems before, during and after being in care.

The intention of this book

This book was prompted by two developments. First, in 2010 the Institute of Education of the University of London began an MA in 'Social Pedagogy: working with children and families', the first of its kind in the country. Developing the MA, and during earlier research, we realised that there were very few English language texts that explored, in detail, aspects of social pedagogy in relation to professional care and education practice. There was a gap for students wishing to enrich their understanding of social pedagogy without recourse to the original language sources. But we hope the book will appeal not only to students and not only to UK readers, but to anyone in the Anglophone world concerned with working with children and young people – in policy or practice, teaching or research – and wanting to understand better an important approach that has much to offer, not only to thinking about the situation as it is today but also to how working with children and young people might develop in the future.

Which leads us to the second development. It seems to us that working with children and young people has reached a point where the nature of that task and the workforce who does it are in need of rethinking and, following that, restructuring. Certainly in the UK, the legacy of decades of piecemeal and ad hoc developments have wrought an unsatisfactory legacy: a fragmented and hierarchical workforce, many with low levels of qualification and poor pay, and many treated as essentially technicians whose task it is to follow prescriptive procedures to produce predetermined outcomes. This simply will not do if the need is for more holistic, more integrated and more reflective ways of working, comfortable with complexity and context and welcoming diversity and the unexpected. The selection of chapters for this book does not claim to exhaust all the topics of social pedagogy, but they do provide a valuable source of information and understanding about one option for the future children's and young persons' (and perhaps, too, adults') workforce. It sets out a stall for one future direction of workforce development.

Chapter 2, written by Gabriel Eichstellar and Sylvia Holthoff, the founders of the training agency ThemPra, and themselves social pedagogues trained in Germany, provides an introduction to the conceptual foundations of social pedagogy and to some of the key thinkers who have shaped the development of social pedagogy both practically and theoretically.

In Chapter 3, Michel Vandenbroeck, Filip Coussée, Lieve Bradt and Rudi Roose from Ghent University in Belgium use the issue of diversity and the field of early childhood education to consider the relationship between the practice of social pedagogy and its social and political context. Using the metaphor of 'social pedagogical embarrassment', they argue that questions such as how to respect diversity and yet at the same time safeguard social cohesion have long been in the hearts and minds of social pedagogues.

The next four chapters look at various aspects of two key features of social pedagogy: communication and relationships. In Chapter 4, Pat Petrie from the Thomas Coram Research Unit looks at interpersonal communication in one possibility for social pedagogy: a democratic and emancipatory social pedagogy – one possibility because, as several chapters make clear, social pedagogy can be inscribed with a wide variety of political and cultural values, including some that lead to authoritarian and oppressive purposes and practices. In Chapter 5, Inge Bryderup and Anna Kathrine Frørup, from the University of Aarhus in Denmark, also highlight varieties of social pedagogical practice and, focusing on work in residential care for children and young people, assess their value in acquiring the competencies that are needed in modern life. In Chapter 6, Janet Boddy from the Thomas Coram Research Unit discusses the potential of social pedagogy for supplying the supportive relationships that are so important in working with children and young people, and especially those in 'public care'. This is followed by a chapter on an important aspect of relationships: conflict. Stefan Kleipoedszus, also from the Thomas Coram Research Unit and himself a qualified pedagogue, argues that conflicts can play an important part in individual growth and that the pedagogue should, therefore, not avoid them (as so often happens in practice) but rather see and be able to work with them as an opportunity.

Chapter 8 is by Jytte Juul Jensen, from VIA University College in Denmark, and reports on some unique research that provides insight into how Danish pedagogues understand their work, in this case in early childhood services, and how they distinguish it from working with young children in countries that do not adopt a social pedagogical approach, including England.

Chapters 9 and 10, by Peter Moss and Michael Fielding, both from the Institute of Education, University of London, explore the relationship between social pedagogy and school-based education. But both focus their attention on particular experiences of such education: the early childhood education in Reggio Emilia in Northern Italy in Chapter 9 and radical democratic education in Chapter 10. These chapters not only open the question of the relationship between social pedagogy and school-based education, but also point to the rich possibilities for dialogue between approaches and traditions that seem to share a commitment to education in its broadest sense.

This theme of future possibilities is continued in the final chapter, by the two of us, on a future direction that social pedagogy might take:

as a main player in work with children and young people, and also perhaps adults. This raises a number of issues, including the relationship between social pedagogic education and school education, and between pedagogues and teachers, and the likelihood of the Anglophone world adopting a social pedagogic approach, or, put another way, what obstacles exist to adoption.

References

Bebbington, A. and Miles, J. (1989) 'The background of children who enter local authority care.' *British Journal of Social Work 19*, 1, 349–368.

Bengtsson, E.E., Chamberlain, C., Crimmens, D. and Stanley, J. (2008) *Introducing Social Pedagogy into Residential Child Care in England.* Available at www.ncb.org.uk/ncercc/ncercc%20practice%20documents/introducing_sp_into_rcc_in_England_feb08.pdf, accessed on 30 March 2011.

Boddy, J. and Statham, J. (2009) *European Perspectives on Social Work: Models of Education and Professional Roles, A Briefing Paper.* Available at http://eprints.ioe.ac.uk/717/1/European_Social_Work_Briefing_Paper_final_version_for_print.pdf, accessed on 1 November 2010.

Boddy, J., Statham, J., McQuail, S., Petrie, P. and Owen, C. (2009) *Working at the 'Edges' of Care? European Models of Support for Young People and Families.* London: Department for Children, Schools and Families.

Bon, C. (2009) 'Social Pedagogy in France.' In J. Kornbeck and N. Jensen Rasmussen (eds) *The Diversity of Social Pedagogy in Europe.* Bremen: Europäischer Hochschulverlag.

Boyce, N. (2010) *Social Pedagogy in Essex.* Available at www.childrenwebmag.com/articles/social-pedagogy/social-pedagogy-in-essex, accessed on 1 November 2010.

Cameron, C. (2007) *New Ways of Educating: Pedagogy and Children's Services.* London: Thomas Coram Research Unit, Institute of Education, University of London.

Cameron, C. and Moss, P. (2007) *Care Work in Europe: Current Understandings and Future Directions.* London: Routledge.

Cameron, C. and Petrie, P. (2009) 'Social pedagogy and its prospects in England's children's services.' *European Journal of Social Education 16/17*, 49–61.

Cameron, C., Hollingworth, K. and Jackson, S. (2011) *Young People from a Public Care Background: Secondary Analysis of National Statistics on Educational Participation.* Available at http://tcru.ioe.ac.uk/yippee/Portals/1/YiPPEE_WP3_COMPARATIVE_FINAL.pdf, accessed on 30 March 2011.

Cameron, C., Jackson, S., Haurari, H. and Hollingworth, K. (2011) *Young People from a Public Care Background: Pathways to Further and Higher Education in England. A Case Study.* Available at http://tcru.ioe.ac.uk/yippee/Portals/1/WP5report%20UKFINAL%2025.01.11.pdf, accessed on 30 March 2011.

Cameron, C., Jasper, A., Kleipoedszus, S., Petrie, P. and Wigfall, V. (2010) *Implementing the DCSF Pilot Programme: The Work of the First Year.* Social Pedagogy Briefing Paper II, Thomas Coram Research Unit, Institute of Education, University of London.

Cameron, C., McQuail, S. and Petrie, P. (2007) *Implementing the Social Pedagogic Approach for Workforce Training and Education in England: A Preliminary Study.* Available at ioe. ac.uk/study/departments/tcru/4804.html, accessed on 6 February 2011.

Cameron, C., Moss, P., Owen, C., Petrie, P., Potts, P., Simon, A. and Wigfall, V. (2008) *Working Together in Extended Schools and Children's Centres: A Study of Inter-Professional Activity in England and Sweden. A Report of Work Undertaken.* Unpublished report, Thomas Coram Research Unit, Institute of Education, University of London.

Casas, F. and Montserrat Boada, C. (2010) *Young People from a Public Care Background: Establishing a Baseline of Attainment and Progression beyond Compulsory Schooling in Five EU Countries.* Available at http://tcru.ioe.ac.uk/yippee/Portals/1/YiPPEE%20 WP34%20FINAL%2026%2003%20(3).pdf, accessed on 30 March 2011.

Casas, F., Montserrat, C. and Malo, S. (forthcoming) *The Case Study Report for Spain.* Unpublished report for the YiPPEE Project.

Child Poverty Action Group (2009) *Child Wellbeing and Child Poverty: Where the UK Stands in the European Table.* London: Child Poverty Action Group. Available at www. cpag.org.uk/info/ChildWellbeingandChildPoverty.pdf, accessed on 20 March 2011.

Children in Scotland (2008) *Working It Out: Developing the Children's Sector Workforce.* Edinburgh: Children in Scotland.

Children in Scotland (2010) *Working for Inclusion: An Overview of European Union Early Years Services and Their Workforce.* Available at www.childreninscotland.org.uk/wfi/ wfi5.htm, accessed on 1 November 2011.

Cousée, F., Bradt, L., Roose, R. and Bouverne-De Bie, M. (2010) 'The emerging social pedagogical paradigm in UK child and youth care: Deus ex machina or walking the beaten path?' *British Journal of Social Work 40,* 3, 789–805.

Danish Ministry of Education (2010) *Bachelor in Social Education.* Available at www. eng.uvm.dk/Uddannelse/Higher%20Education/Bachelor%20in%20Social%20 Education.aspx, accessed on 1 November 2010.

Department for Children, Schools and Families (2009) *Children Looked After in England (Including Adoption and Care Leavers) Year Ending 31 March 2009,* Statistical First Release SFR 25/2009. Available at www.education.gov.uk/rsgateway/DB/SFR/ s000878/index.shtml, accessed on 1 November 2010.

Department for Education and Skills (2007) *Care Matters: Time for Change,* cmd 7137. London: TSO.

Fullana, J. (2008) personal communication.

Hämäläinen, J. (2003) 'The concept of social pedagogy in the field of social work.' *Journal of Social Work 31,* 1, 69–80.

HM Government (2004) *Every Child Matters: Change for Children.* London: Department for Education and Skills. Available at www.infed.org/archives/gov_uk/every_ child_matters.htm, accessed on 1 November 2010.

HM Government (2005) *Children's Workforce Strategy: A Strategy to Build a World-Class Workforce for Children and Young People*. London: Department for Children, Schools and Families.

Höjer, I. and Johansson, H. (2010) *A Long and Winding Road, The Swedish National Report of Work Package 9.*

Jackson, S., Ayaji, S. and Quigley, M. (2005) *Going to University from Care*. London: Institute of Education, University of London.

Jensen, J. and Hansen, H. (2002) *Mapping of Care Services and the Care Workforce: Danish National Report*. Available at http://144.82.31.4/reports/Denmark.pdf, accessed on 1 November 2010.

Korintus, M. (2001) *Mapping Care Services and the Care Workforce*. National report, Hungary. Available at http://144.82.31.4/reports/Hungary.pdf, accessed on 30 March 2011.

Kornbeck, J. (2009) '"Important but Widely Misunderstood": The Problem of Defining Social Pedagogy in Europe.' In J. Kornbeck and N. Jensen (eds) *The Diversity of Social Pedagogy in Europe*. Bremen: Europäischer Hochschulverlag.

Kornbeck, J. and Jensen, N. (eds) (2009) *The Diversity of Social Pedagogy in Europe*. Bremen: Europäischer Hochschulverlag.

Lorenz, W. (2008) 'Paradigm and politics: Understanding methods paradigms in an historical context: The case of social pedagogy.' *British Journal of Social Work 38*, 4, 625–644.

Maplethorpe, N., Chanfreau, J., Philo, D. and Tait, C. (2010) *Families with Children in Britain: Findings from the 2008 Families and Children Study (FACS)*. London: Department for Work and Pensions. Available at http://research.dwp.gov.uk/asd/asd5/rports2009-2010/rrep656.pdf, accessed on 1 November 2010.

Meltzer, H., Gatward, R., Corbin, T., Goodman, R. and Ford, T. (2003) *The Mental Health of Young People Looked After by Local Authorities in England*. Available at www.statistics.gov.uk/downloads/theme_health/ChildrensMentalHlth.pdf, accessed on 1 November 2010.

Milligan, I. (2009) *Introducing Social Pedagogy into Scottish Residential Child Care: An Evaluation of the Sycamore Services Social Pedagogy Training Programme*. Available at www.sircc.org.uk/sites/default/files/Social_Pedagogy_Final.pdf, accessed on 1 November 2010.

Monteux, A. (2006) 'History and Philosophy.' In R. Jackson (ed.) *Holistic Special Education: Camphill Principles and Practice*. Edinburgh: Floris Books.

NHS Information Centre (2009) *Personal Social Services Expenditure and Unit Costs England, 2007–08*. Available at www.ic.nhs.uk/webfiles/publications/PSSEX10708/Personal%20Social%20Services%20Expenditure%20and%20Units%20Cost%2C%20England%202007-08_1.1.pdf, accessed on 1 November 2010.

National Statistical Office (2010) *Social Trends 2010*. Available at www.statistics.gov.uk/downloads/theme_social/Social-Trends40/ST40_2010_FINAL.pdf, accessed on 1 November 2010.

Oberhuemer, P., Schreyer, I. and Neuman, M. (2010) *Professionals in Early Childhood Education and Care Systems: European Profiles and Perspectives*. Farmington Hills, MI: Barbara Budrich Publishers.

With this chapter we aim to describe the most central of those notions and philosophies that could be portrayed as the conceptual foundations of social pedagogy, referring to key thinkers who have shaped the development of social pedagogy both practically and theoretically. Their ideas are presented within a conceptual framework that we have termed the 'Diamond Model' (Holthoff and Eichsteller 2009) to emphasise the idea of human beings as full of potential and possibilities, as intrinsically precious and valuable – a notion that unites the various concepts of different thinkers. Within this framework we explore four areas that illustrate the conceptual foundations of social pedagogy as concerned with individual and collective well-being, learning, relationships and empowerment. By introducing perspectives from different key thinkers about these areas of the Diamond Model, we aim to bring social pedagogy to life in a way that is relevant both at a theoretical and practical level. Although the groundbreaking work and innovative ideas of many people have contributed to the evolution of social pedagogy, the scope and structure of this chapter make it impossible to do justice to them and the importance of their ideas. However, we hope that this chapter might raise readers' interest in exploring further the origins of social pedagogy.

Our perspective in reconstructing the cultural foundations of social pedagogy is led by our experiences in relating social pedagogy to practice and traditions in the UK's children's workforce and by our notion that social pedagogy is therefore socially constructed: it emerges through dialogue about theory and practice, transcending national boundaries to the extent that inspiring ideas can be influential across different cultures. We have taken a more pedagogical/educational perspective that leaves many other perspectives un(der)explored – the historical development of the welfare state system, for instance, which has had an impact on how social pedagogy has progressed and is insightfully discussed by Lorenz (2008); or the social work tradition, which has undoubtedly been relevant for the evolution of contemporary understandings of social pedagogy in Germany and beyond. More accurately, our perspective can be described as one of many possible German perspectives on social pedagogy, and while many of the illustrated concepts are of German origin, we have aimed to introduce the reader also to others that have arguably contributed to German social pedagogy.

Cultural foundations of social pedagogy

In Germany, social pedagogy has emerged as an academic science in which theory and practice have developed in a dynamic and reflexive way. Due to this relationship, 'in which theoretical discourses and models for practice develop in mutual reference, without one simply being derived from the other' (Grunwald and Thiersch 2009, p.131), social pedagogy can be described as an action-orientated social science (*Handlungswissenschaft*): concerned with practical or social issues while referring to theoretic knowledge in a given discipline (Staub-Bernasconi 2007b). As social issues cannot be explained, let alone solved, based on just one discipline, an action-orientated science must be interdisciplinary or transdisciplinary. Social pedagogy is, therefore, often theoretically located within the educational sciences, albeit an educational science that is guided by social sciences and is conceptualised using society-based and action-orientated theory (Thiersch and Rauschenbach 1984). With roots in various areas of a range of disciplines, such as social sciences, education, psychology, but also macro-economics, theology and philosophy (Böhnisch, Schröer and Thiersch 2005), the use of theories thus adds more detail and perspectives to social pedagogic practice in context. And as an action-orientated science aiming to cause change and to have a positive impact on individuals and society, it is important that social pedagogy is value-based and that these values are constantly and critically reflected upon, given that values are specific to culture and time.

In order to simplify the complex processes through which social pedagogy has emerged, we suggest that three significant developments reflecting cultural values have been particularly influential: cultural concepts of children, societal notions about the nature of the relationship between the individual and society, and the emergence of a social welfare state. Throughout history, different cultures have found particular answers to the philosophical questions surrounding each of these developments and have constructed particular 'truths' around them. Ariès (1962) points out that childhood and notions about children are socially constructed (see also James and Prout 1997). The same could be said of notions around the relationship between individuals and the collective: the concepts of human nature found in Thomas Hobbes's *homo homini lupus est* (man is a wolf to man) and Immanuel Kant's *categorical imperative* (that reason commands us to treat others with respect as only then we can expect to be treated respectfully) could not be more different in their implications about human interaction. Different types of welfare state regimes and their varying commitment to tackling social issues are similarly constructed (Esping-Andersen 1991; Giddens 1998).

As a consequence, social pedagogy can be referred to as a 'function of society' (Mollenhauer 1964, p.21), which can only be fully understood within its historical and cultural context. 'Accordingly, anything which may be stated about social pedagogy may be meaningfully stated only in relation to this society', Mollenhauer (1964, p.19) notes, as social pedagogy has evolved in each place as an answer to specific social problems and conceptualisations. But despite the ensuing diversity of social pedagogy across different countries (Kornbeck and Rosendahl Jensen 2009), there are also shared conceptual foundations, a core of values and principles that epitomise social pedagogy and become evident in the notion of *Haltung*.

Developing a positive concept of children and the notion of *Haltung*

A fundamental feature of social pedagogy is how children, and adults too, are conceptualised. The concept of the competent child can already be found in one of its most important ancestors, the French social philosopher Jean-Jacques Rousseau (1712–1778). At a time when children were thought of as adults-to-be, Rousseau's focus on the present and on bringing children up in harmony with nature to preserve their inherent goodness laid the foundations for (social) pedagogy. He argued that learning needed to start from where the child was at, 'that the momentum for learning was provided by the growth of the person (nature) – and that what the [pedagogue] needed to do was to facilitate opportunities for learning' (Doyle and Smith 1997).

Rousseau's radically different notion of children, which infused his pedagogic philosophy, inspired the ideas of many educationalists to come and demonstrated early on that what is most fundamental to pedagogic practice is *Haltung*, which roughly translates as attitude, mindset, ethos. *Haltung* is based on our values, our philosophy, our notions about morality and our concept of mankind. All of these affect how we conceptualise the people we interact with, which in turn affects how we behave towards them and colours their behaviour towards us. In social pedagogy, *Haltung* expresses an emotional connectedness to other people and a profound respect for their human dignity. The Swiss pedagogue Johann Heinrich Pestalozzi (1746–1827) stated: 'I seek education towards humanity, and this only emanates through love' (Pestalozzi 1964, p.226). The pedagogic task requires a congruent *Haltung* that reinforces this aim, brings it to life and transcends all pedagogic practices.

A prime example of a social pedagogic concept of children is provided by Loris Malaguzzi, one of the founders of the municipal early childhood centres in Reggio Emilia in Italy (further discussed in Chapter 9). His pedagogic philosophy for the early years conceptualises children as 'rich', as competent and active agents, arguing that 'the child has a hundred languages, a hundred hands, a hundred thoughts, a hundred ways of thinking, of playing, of speaking' (Malaguzzi, cited in Edwards, Gandini and Forman 1998, p.3). It is this valuing of children in particular and human beings in general that is characteristic of and fundamental for social pedagogy both in theory and practice.

Another important, related concept, that human beings are experts in their own lives, is theoretically underpinned by a strong hermeneutic tradition, which gained prominence in German social pedagogy during the first half of the 20th century through the works of Herman Nohl (1879–1960) who contributed to a more humanistic science orientation of social pedagogy. As the science of interpretation, hermeneutics follows the constructivist view that people construct their own reality based on their experiences and perceptions of the world around them. Consequently, social pedagogy can only understand individuals' lives and problems through their eyes and in their social context, by understanding how individuals interact with their social environment. In this sense, hermeneutic pedagogy acknowledges that experience is always subjective, and therefore that social problems have a strong subjective element that is important for finding appropriate solutions.

The conceptually connected *Lebensweltorientierung*, which translates as life-world orientation, has, since the 1970s, gained centrality in German social pedagogy through the work of Hans Thiersch. *Lebensweltorientierung* is conceptually based on critical-hermeneutic pedagogy and the social constructionist tradition (Berger and Luckmann 1966), which highlight how processes of interaction between people form subjectivity, thinking patterns and the structures of people's everyday life (Grunwald and Thiersch 2009). It starts from the premise that social pedagogic practice can only be successful where it meets individuals in their everyday reality, focusing on their 'direct experiences, their living contexts, their life skills and the strength of their self-responsibility' (Grunwald and Thiersch 2009, p.132). Taking the everyday life-world as a starting point for practice requires a *Haltung* underpinned by respect – unconditional appreciation of who the other person is – and by tact – to know when to respectfully challenge a person to leave their 'comfort zone' and enter their 'learning zone'.

> Knowing when to push, when to let go, what to listen to, and what to ignore – all these skills are based on the profound respect for human dignity and working to restore a sense of who they are and what they want to be. (Kim Berg, cited in Short 1998, p.9)

At a societal level, the concept of life-world also demonstrates social pedagogy's commitment towards social justice by aiming to improve living conditions and social circumstances, so that people have the skills and opportunities for social participation (Grunwald and Thiersch 2009). Social pedagogic *Haltung* does not, therefore, just refer to an attitude towards individuals but provides the context for social pedagogy's aims and purposes at the level of the community and society. It requires commitment to supporting the development of individuals and society in the four areas outlined by the Diamond Model (see Figure 2.1).

WELL-BEING & HAPPINESS

EMPOWERMENT   **POSITIVE EXPERIENCES**   **RELATIONSHIPS**

HOLISTIC LEARNING

Figure 2.1 The Diamond Model of social pedagogy

In our view, the Diamond Model provides a simplified framework that serves to outline the conceptual foundations of social pedagogy, their relevance and interconnectedness. It suggests four cardinal points serving like a compass in navigating through the 'garden': well-being, learning, relationships and empowerment. At its core lies the social pedagogic aspiration to provide people with experiences that have a long-term positive impact on their lives, leading to a 'successful everyday' (Grunwald and Thiersch 2009, p.137). All of these overarching aims apply both to pedagogic practice at an individual level and to social pedagogy at a societal level. We have termed this the Diamond Model in order to highlight the fundamental notion underpinning social pedagogy, that human beings are intrinsically rich, full of potential, abilities, knowledge and resources. And whether they are children, parents or other members of the community, they all deserve to be respected and valued as human beings.

Well-being: A social pedagogic perspective

Social pedagogy is essentially concerned with enhancing individual and collective well-being and human dignity. As the overarching aim, the notion of well-being suggests a positive conceptualisation of the social pedagogic task, in stark contrast to the more pathological deficit-based model that has spread across UK social work in recent decades (Smith and Whyte 2007). Given that well-being has many facets – ranging from physical well-being through mental, spiritual and emotional well-being to social well-being – the interdisciplinary aspect of social pedagogy ensures a multidimensional, holistic understanding of well-being from a medical, psychological, sociological, theological and philosophical perspective.

In the absence of an agreed definition, Ryan and Deci (2001, p.143) note that well-being 'consists of more than just happiness. It lies instead in the actualization of human potentials.' The uniqueness of people's potential implies that well-being is subjective, that it can mean different things to different individuals. Following Seligman and Csikszentmihalyi (2000), the founders of positive psychology, well-being could be seen longitudinally, comprising satisfaction about the past, happiness in the present and optimism about the future. As such, well-being requires a process-orientated and sustainable approach from social pedagogues through which the individual gains a thorough understanding of his or her self, can construct a positive self-concept and consequently find ways of gaining a long-lasting sense of well-being.

At a collective level, social pedagogy has been concerned with creating societal well-being from its earliest development by Paul Natorp (1854–1924). Living at a time when industrialisation was leading to huge social changes and new inequalities, he argued for the establishment of social pedagogy as a decidedly pedagogical answer to the prevalent social issues of that time, caused by the morally and socially devastating consequences of the rule of capital over the poor working class (Niemeyer 2005). Natorp was influenced by Pestalozzi's concepts on community education, outlined in the Swiss pedagogue's 1819 popular novel *Lienhard and Gertrud*. In this he described an oppressed village community, morally and economically impoverished as a consequence of the corruption and greed of the squire, and how, through restructuring and a series of socio-economic and pedagogic interventions, the inhabitants are gradually enabled to live in justice, realise their intrinsic potential and live their lives as their own creation (Thiersch 1996). Pestalozzi's views on educating for humanity and on improving societal conditions reinforced Natorp's perception that 'all pedagogy should be social, that is, that in the philosophy of education the interaction of educational processes and society must be taken into consideration' (Hämäläinen 2003, p.73). Hence Natorp proposed a *social* pedagogy, which aims to encourage a strong sense of community, educates both children and adults to ensure positive relations between the individual and society, and fights to close the gap between rich and poor. All of these aims are significant for societal well-being and people's sense of responsibility for each other.

Initiating holistic learning opportunities

A positive concept of children clearly influences a social pedagogic understanding of education – both formal and informal – by demonstrating that children are active and competent learners rather than empty vessels to be filled. Most notably, the Czech philosopher John Amos Comenius (1592–1670) – who lived at a time when it was thought that children should be formed as a sculptor would mould a lump of clay – described the role of a pedagogue as comparable to a gardener who provides the best possible environment for growth:

> The proper education of the young does not consist in stuffing their heads with a mass of words, sentences, and ideas dragged together out of various authors, but in opening up their understanding to the outer world, so that a living stream may flow from their own minds, just as leaves, flowers, and fruit spring from the bud on a tree. (Comenius 1896, p.147)

Similar ideas about learning can be found with Pestalozzi, who emphasised that education needs to be holistic, addressing 'head, heart, and hands' in harmonious unity: 'Nature forms the child as an indivisible whole, as a vital organic unity with many-sided moral, mental, and physical capacities… Each of these capacities is developed through and by means of the others' (cited in Heafford 1967, p.47). To develop children's mental capacities (head), he stressed, education must not impose knowledge but form children's capacity to think for themselves and arouse their curiosity of the world around them. The moral capacities are fundamental to Pestalozzi as the heart provides a sense of direction, 'of the inner dignity of our nature, and of the pure, higher, godly being, which lies within us. This sense is not developed by the power of our mind in thought, but is developed by the power of our heart in love' (Pestalozzi, cited in Heafford 1967, p.61). Pestalozzi also highlighted the relevance of the hands – or more exactly the whole body – as grasping the world leads to understanding it; in that sense, 'physical experiences give rise to mental and spiritual ones' (Heafford 1967, p.67). As a result, pedagogic practice must keep head, heart and hands in balance.

Pestalozzi's method stresses that, in order to be holistic, learning opportunities should be created based on 'close observation of children and on deep insight into the way a child's mind works and develops' (Heafford 1967, p.46). Reflective practice is central to his doctrine of *Anschauung*, direct observation. Through observation, the pedagogue can better support children in their unique natural development by understanding the potential of the individual child which is implemented by nature, in the same way as 'a little seed…contains the design of a tree' (Pestalozzi, cited in Smith 2005). In a description reminiscent of Comenius's metaphor, Pestalozzi attributes to the pedagogue the role of taking care 'that no untoward influence shall disturb nature's march of developments' (Pestalozzi, cited in Smith 2005).

Pestalozzi's person-centred model strongly resonated with the educational thinkers of the New Education movement, which spread across and beyond Europe in the late 19th century and included pedagogues like Maria Montessori, Kurt Hahn, Rudolf Steiner, Janusz Korczak and John Dewey, who developed their own pedagogic framework and applied it in various contexts. The New Education movement also outlined its ambition to use pedagogy for social change by stating two fundamental points: 'First, in all education the personality of the child is an essential concern; second, education must make for human betterment, that is for a New Era' (Boyd and Rawson 1965, p.viii).

Within the social pedagogic tradition, therefore, education has two aspects, person-centred and socio-political: it provides opportunities for personal development towards independence, but also has a socialising function in reinforcing social solidarity and interdependence. The French sociologist Émile Durkheim highlighted the latter aspect, arguing that society depends on a certain degree of homogeneity among its members in their culture and values, but, on the other hand, society requires diversity in order to progress. In this process Durkheim considered education vital for society as it is 'the means by which society continuously recreates the conditions for its existence' (Durkheim 1922, cited in Reyer 2002, p.181), making people feel part of society and training them to fulfil particular roles.

Social pedagogy works within these opposing poles of being person-centred and being community-centred in order to mediate between the individual and society. This requires a critical reflective position to keep the right balance. The experiences of an exclusive focus on collective education during the Third Reich in Germany, with its Hitler youth groups that 'educated' the young generation to contribute to the Nazis' *Volksgemeinschaft* (people's community), demonstrate the potential dangers of a depoliticised and uncritical pedagogy (a theme developed further in the next chapter).

In post-war Germany and through the contributions of Klaus Mollenhauer (1928–1998), social pedagogy became more critical and strove for more autonomy. Mollenhauer (1964) argued that social pedagogy should aim to educate children to be self-responsible, critical and self-enlightened in order to be able to challenge what they were taught, as well as educate them to take responsibility within their community, so that it would never again be possible for a totalitarian regime to take control. Society, he argued further, had to be dynamic and democratic, and for this purpose the pedagogic task was a dialectic mix of socialisation and liberalisation – both conservatively preserving 'culturally unquestioned self-evident truths [and providing] the means for social change or social progress' (Mollenhauer 1964, p.28).

Finding a way to balance society's demands with the individual's own idea of what constitutes well-being becomes a key challenge in creating learning opportunities.

Relationship: The authentic pedagogue

Social pedagogy is brought to life through the relationship between the professional and the subject. Their relationship is defined through the task of social pedagogic action within a given setting, which gives purpose to their relationship (*pädagogischer Bezug*; see Badry and Knapp

2003). Herman Nohl (1970) aimed to capture the nature of the pedagogic relationship by describing it as the basis of education. He identified three characteristics: an emotional component of strong affection towards the child, the pedagogue as being more mature in her development compared to the child, and a focus on the 'self' of the child rather than on external aims (Lockenvitz undated). In Nohl's view, the relationship is underpinned by a particular *Haltung* that includes an emotional connection, with the child at the heart in a double sense. What makes the relationship professional in social pedagogic terms is that the professional uses her personality and is authentic, but understands that her personal life experience should only be introduced to the relationship where it would enhance or enlighten the child's own experience – otherwise this should be kept private. It can be further argued that such a social pedagogic relationship is authoritative and thus needs to strike a balance between being affectionate and being firm in establishing boundaries in order for the child to feel secure and learn to act responsibly (see Baumrind 1991).

The relevance of strong supportive relationships for learning is described by the Soviet psychologist Lev Vygotsky (1896–1934). His concept of a Zone of Proximal Development (Vygotsky 1978) depicts learning as a socially mediated process that takes place first between people (interpsychological) and then within a person (intra-psychological). Defined as 'the distance between the actual developmental level as determined by independent problem solving and the level of potential development as determined through problem solving under adult guidance or in collaboration with more capable peers' (Vygotsky 1978, p.86), the Zone of Proximal Development highlights the importance of forming valuing relationships that enhance growth. Vygotsky's concept can be related not only to formal educational contexts but also to supporting a person in developing social skills and thus being able to form positive and strong relationships with other people.

Central to social pedagogic relationships is the development of trust between the social pedagogue and the child. As trust can only be nurtured gradually and carefully, building strong relationships takes time and is a joint process, requiring both parties to trust the other person and to be trusted by him or her. Placing trust in children, in their competence and responsibility, can be an empowering experience for them, not only strengthening the relationship but also their self-confidence. Hence many of the key pedagogic philosophers – for instance, Friedrich Fröbel, the founder of the *kindergarten* movement, and Maria Montessori, who developed a pre-school and school method designed to stimulate all senses and children's 'absorbent mind' – emphasised the importance of having confidence and trust in children's capabilities from a very early age, thus supporting self-directed learning within a social context.

As part of building relationships to support children in their holistic learning and well-being, social pedagogues must recognise and focus on the social aspects of childhood, seeing children as part of a group, not just as individuals. This aspect is crucial as it defines social pedagogic practice as essentially relationship-centred and social pedagogic settings as providing opportunities for children to practise building relationships. Malaguzzi (1993, p.56) views these settings as 'an integral living organism, a place of shared lives and relationships among many adults and very many children'.

The above demonstrates the centrality of relationships and their role in enhancing well-being, learning and growth. The following discussion of empowerment has to be understood in this context: the concept is ultimately about living together in a constructive way that builds on our equal value and inner 'richness' and upholds our own and others' human dignity. Relationships are an end in themselves, not merely a means to an end. They form the framework for empowering approaches towards children's rights, lifespace, participation and life-world.

Nurturing individual and social empowerment

In our social pedagogic understanding of the concept, empowerment highlights children's human rights, their active involvement in decisions that affect them, and the emancipation of human beings at an individual and collective level. The relevance of empowerment as complementary to relationships suggests that two key elements are dialectically connected in social pedagogy: independence and interdependence. In the words of Johann Wolfgang von Goethe, 'children need two things from their parents: roots and wings'. The role for empowerment in the social pedagogic relationship is, therefore, to ensure that it is a relationship amongst equal human beings where power is used not as a form of control but as responsibility, a relationship that leads to less dependence on the social pedagogue and facilitates a person's increasing ability to access resources themselves (*Ressourcenerschließung*).

In this understanding, empowerment aims to positively affect a person's 'sense of coherence', which Antonovsky (1979, p.184) defines as:

a global orientation that expresses the extent to which one has
a pervasive, enduring though dynamic feeling of confidence
that one's internal and external environments are predictable
and that there is a high probability that things will work out
as well as can reasonably be expected.

This sense is developed through the feeling of being able to make sense
of and influence our circumstances, of life appearing comprehensible,
manageable and meaningful. Rather than feeling lost in an uncontrollable
current of events, a strong sense of coherence facilitates a feeling of
security and, according to Antonovsky (1979), is fundamental to well-
being and health. In this sense, empowerment is closely related to well-
being in a holistic way.

Empowerment relies on people's active engagement, for which social
pedagogues can provide opportunities that enable people to empower
themselves. This requires a perspective that goes beyond a focus on
meeting their needs by exploring how they can be supported in ways
that strengthen their resilience and enable them to cope with life
situations, thus being resourceful in meeting their own needs. Böhnisch
(2002, p.125) has termed this *Lebensbewältigung*, which he defines as 'the
yearning of an individual to remain or become able to act in open life
situations' – situations in which options of how to act are open-ended
rather than predefined or limited and, therefore, require the individual
to navigate responsibly through unchartered territory, with no paths that
can just be followed. He considers empowerment the leading principle of
social pedagogic practice throughout the life stages, but emphasises that
it needs to be connected to the creation of social milieux (*Milieubildung*),
which ensure integration into and socio-structural support from within
the community (Böhnisch 2008). In this understanding, empowerment
aims to enable people to create social networks that connect them to
others and offer them the support they need (Keupp 1996). This gives
them a sense of identity and belonging, of knowing where and how
to access resources in order to overcome potential difficulties and to
grow within their Zone of Proximal Development. Thus empowerment
processes within social pedagogic practice can achieve long-term and
sustainable improvements in all areas of the Diamond Model.

In order to provide empowering conditions, it is fundamental for
social pedagogues to respect human rights and, in particular, children's
rights. The development of children's rights in a social pedagogic
understanding is illustrated in the work of the Polish-Jewish doctor and

pedagogue Janusz Korczak (1878–1942), an early and vigorous advocate for children's rights (Eichsteller 2009). Korczak's notion of children's rights was underpinned by considering the child as a human *being* rather than a human *becoming* (Qvortrup 2005) and, therefore, 'as a separate being with the inalienable right to grow into the person s/he was meant to be' (Freeman 1996, p.31). In Korczak's understanding, as this makes clear, human nature determines children's human rights.

By conceptualising children as right-owners, Korczak aimed to ensure that children were not reliant on adults' humanistic attitude and charitable actions but could be certain to have clear, enforceable rights (Ungermann 2006). Consequently, the two orphanages, Dom Sierot and Nasz Dom, which Korczak set up in Warsaw, were run with the highest regard for children's rights, as a Children's Republic. General decisions about running the home were made by the Children's Parliament, a group of 20 young residents elected by the children that formed the legislative power. Judicial power was exercised by the Children's Court, which consisted of five child judges elected weekly to adjudicate conflicts and to ensure that the children's rights were respected, but also that children learned to forgive each other. In front of the Children's Court, everyone had the same rights, including adults, and Korczak himself was sued five times and four times acquitted (Lifton 1988). All of these events of the everyday were captured in the Children's Newspaper, which was written by the children and chronicled life at the orphanage, giving children an opportunity to voice their views and concerns and hold on to their memories in a way that connected them to each other and to the staff. Evidently, relationships were fundamental to how Korczak understood and practised children's rights, not to support individualism but to strengthen a respectful culture of togetherness.

In 1919, he published *The Child in the Family*, in which he called for 'a Magna Charta Libertatis concerning the Rights of the Child' (Korczak 1999, p.45). At around the same time, children's rights attracted international attention and were increasingly part of the pedagogic concepts of other thinkers within the New Education movement, such as Maria Montessori and Ellen Key. Their awareness of children's intellectual potential and competence prompted them to advocate children's rights as they saw that, without rights, children were at the mercy of adults. Much emphasis in their understanding of children's rights is placed on the right to be treated with respect, for children's opinions to be valued and for adults to provide them with a good upbringing.

This conceptualisation of children's rights went much further than the Declaration on the Rights of the Child drafted by Eglantyne Jebb, the founder of the Save the Children International Union, and adopted by the League of Nations in 1924 (Alston and Tobin 2005). Korczak (cited in Veerman 1987, p.7) criticised 'the tone of this Declaration [as] only an appeal for good will, a request for more understanding'. His rights gave children the security of not having to rely on adults' philanthropy and of having their dignity acknowledged, which is the original meaning of the Polish term *szacunek* that he uses for 'respect'. Freeman (2006, p.89) highlights the significance of respect for rights: 'to accord rights is to respect dignity: to deny rights is to cast doubt on humanity and on integrity'.

As a profession, social pedagogy is, therefore, strongly based on promoting and enhancing children's rights and, more widely, human rights (see Staub-Bernasconi 2007a). In particular, the right to meaningful participation in decisions affecting people's lives is a cornerstone that enables people to empower themselves by gaining more ownership and feeling respected. Meaningful participation in a social pedagogic relationship is always a social and inclusive process, about engaging in dialogue as equal human beings exploring different perspectives. This is exemplified in the work of Paulo Freire (1921–1997), the Brazilian community educator who developed a *Pedagogy of the Oppressed* (1972). His empowering practice around conveying literacy skills to the illiterate poor was founded on enabling disadvantaged groups within society to participate meaningfully in democracy (at that time only literate Brazilians were allowed to vote). His pedagogy emphasised dialogue, which 'wasn't just about deepening understanding – but was part of making a difference in the world' (Smith 1997), and was also concerned with *conscientisation*, the process of 'developing consciousness, but consciousness that is understood to have the power to transform reality' (Taylor 1993, p.52). His aims were revolutionary: social justice through providing the disadvantaged with the means to democratic engagement and a sense of well-being by feeling empowered.

Constructing the social: Concluding thoughts

As the individual and social dimensions of well-being, learning, relationship building and empowerment suggest, social pedagogy relies on providing people with experiences that strengthen them within these dimensions, wherein they can gain a sense of being competent agents and can encounter a respectful social environment. While not all these experiences will be happy, they can be reflected on together with the individual and thus reframed as experiences that further people's development and contain important learning. In other words, they can lead to a more 'successful everyday' (Grunwald and Thiersch 2009, p.137). Through the positive experience of succeeding in their everyday life, people can develop a self-concept of being resourceful and resilient, thus feeling empowered to take over more responsibility for themselves and others.

Yet, social pedagogy aims not only to support the individual in constructing his or her own life successfully. It also contributes to constructing the social. Thiersch (2002) suggests that constructing the social consists of a descriptive and a morally orientated category, raising fundamental questions about social justice by describing and analysing inequalities and aiming for social change by pursuing value-based concepts leading towards more solidarity, justice, equality, respect, fairness, tolerance. To influence, directly and indirectly, people's social interactions, their milieu and the public realm through ongoing constructive dialogue and engagement is a hugely important task that comes with great responsibilities. It requires social pedagogues to be constantly reflective, especially about how their own personality and value system influence their professional work. They need to strike a careful balance between knowing when to be persistent and when to withdraw. Therefore, their reflections must draw on both their own experience and their understanding of theory (Petrie *et al.* 2006). This allows them to contribute in a responsible, inclusive, thoughtful and meaningful manner to the social and political sphere, advocating for the disempowered while enabling them to empower themselves.

As we have tried to convey, social pedagogy works with fluidity, within dynamic processes as all areas of the Diamond Model are continuously developing and, therefore, require ongoing care. Given the dynamic and responsive character of social pedagogic practice, it requires an equally fluent – and interdisciplinary – theory base. What provides consistency and stability within these complex dynamics, what serves as the key to understanding social pedagogy, and what unites its theory with its practice is a social pedagogic *Haltung*. It determines how we meet other people, how we engage with them, and ultimately how much we can touch their lives in a positive and profound way. The most fundamental resource available to the professional is, therefore, the person within.

In searching for conditions that are conducive to human growth, cultural differences and practical responses to social issues have interwoven into different social pedagogic traditions across Europe. Some key thinkers were influential beyond their national borders, yet their thinking may have had limited resonance and impact within a given society. Often ahead of their time, their work is worth revisiting now; they can enable us today to work socially pedagogically and to make sense of our actions as part of a socially pedagogic tradition of constructing the social and nurturing growth in the 'thriving garden' we alluded to in our introductory metaphor.

Even though it is impossible to fully understand the complexities of human growth and social interactions, social pedagogues consider it important to trust, and be confident in, the processes they can initiate together with individuals and groups to enhance their well-being, provide learning opportunities, develop relationships and enable them to empower themselves. Such positive experiences will bear fruit if we help create and sustain nurturing conditions in which individuals and communities enjoy trust and responsibility – and, importantly, are educated towards being socially pedagogic in their interactions with each other.

References

Alston, P. and Tobin, J. (2005) *Laying the Foundations for Children's Rights.* Florence: UNICEF.

Antonovksy, A. (1979) *Health, Stress and Coping.* San Francisco, CA: Jossey-Bass.

Ariès, P. (1962) *Centuries of Childhood: A Social History of Family Life.* New York: Vintage Books.

Badry, E. and Knapp, R. (2003) 'Grundlagen und Grundfragen des Pädagogischen.' In E. Badry, M. Buchka and R. Knapp (eds) *Pädagogik – Grundlagen und Sozialpädagogische Arbeitsfelder.* Munich: Luchterhand.

Baumrind, D. (1991) 'The influence of parenting style on adolescent competence and substance use.' *Journal of Early Adolescence 11,* 1, 56–95.

Berger, P.L. and Luckmann, T. (1966) *The Social Construction of Reality.* Garden City: Anchor.

Böhnisch, L. (2002) 'Zum Verhältnis von Bildung und Bewältigung am Beispiel der Jugendberufshilfe in Ostdeutschland.' In R. Münchmeier, H.U. Otto and U. Rabe-Kleberg (eds) *Bildung und Lebenskompetenz. Kinder- und Jugendhilfe vor neuen Aufgaben.* Opladen: Leske & Budrich.

Böhnisch, L. (2008) *Sozialpädagogik der Lebensalter: eine Einführung (5th ed.).* Weinheim: Juventa Verlag.

Böhnisch, L., Schröer, W. and Thiersch, H. (2005) *Sozialpädagogisches Denken. Wege einer Neubestimmung*. Weinheim: Juventa.

Boyd, W. and Rawson, W. (1965) *The Story of the New Education*. London: Heinemann.

Comenius, J.A. (1896) *The Great Didactic*. London: Adam & Charles Black. (original work published 1649).

Doyle, M.E. and Smith, M.K. (1997) 'Jean-Jacques Rousseau on Nature, Wholeness and Education.' *Infed – the Encyclopaedia of Informal Education*. Available at www.infed. org/thinkers/et-rous.htm, accessed on 20 February 2009.

Durkheim, E. (1979) 'Pédagogie et Sociologie'. In W.S.F. Pickering (ed.) *Durkheim: Essays on Morals and Education*. London: Routledge & Kegan Paul. (Original work published 1922.)

Edwards, C., Gandini, L. and Forman, G. (1998) *The Hundred Languages of Children: The Reggio Emilia Approach – Advanced Reflections (2nd ed.)*. Westport: Ablex.

Eichsteller, G. (2009) 'Janusz Korczak – His legacy and its relevance for children's rights today.' *International Journal of Children's Rights 17*, 2, 377–391.

Esping-Andersen, G. (1991) *The Three Worlds of Welfare Capitalism*. Princeton, NJ: Princeton University Press.

Freeman, M. (1996) 'Children's Education: A Test Case for Best Interests and Autonomy.' In R. Davie and D. Galloway (eds) *Listening to Children in Education*. London: David Fulton Publishers.

Freeman, M. (2006) 'What's right with children's rights.' *International Journal of Law in Context 2*, 1, 89–98.

Freire, P. (1972) *Pedagogy of the Oppressed*. Harmondsworth: Penguin.

Giddens, A. (1998) *The Third Way: The Renewal of Social Democracy*. Cambridge: Polity.

Grunwald, K. and Thiersch, H. (2009) 'The concept of the lifeworld orientation for social work and social care.' *Journal of Social Work Practice 23*, 2, 131–146.

Hämäläinen, J. (2003) 'The concept of social pedagogy in the field of social work.' *Journal of Social Work 3*, 1, 69–80.

Heafford, M. (1967) *Pestalozzi*. Bungay: The Chaucer Press.

Holthoff, S. and Eichsteller, G. (2009) 'Social pedagogy in practice.' *Every Child Journal 1*, 1, 58–63.

James, A. and Prout, A. (eds) (1997) *Constructing and Reconstructing Childhood*. London: Falmer.

Keupp, H. (1996) 'Empowerment.' In D. Kreft and I. Mielenz (eds) *Wörterbuch Soziale Arbeit*. Weinheim: Juventa.

Korczak, J. (1999) *Sämtliche Werke, Vol. 4* (ed. F. Beiner and E. Dauzenroth). Gütersloh: Gütersloher Verlagshaus. (Original work published 1919.)

Kornbeck, J. and Rosendahl Jensen, N. (2009) *The Diversity of Social Pedagogy in Europe*. Bremen: Europäischer Hochschulverlag.

Lockenvitz, T. (undated) *Der Pädagogische Bezug bei Herman Nohl*. Available at http://149.222.20.63/fileadmin/data/sug/pdf-Dokument/Lockenvitz/bezug_ nohl_paedagogischer_bezug.pdf, accessed on 5 March 2010.

Lifton, B.J. (1988) *The King of Children: A Biography of Janusz Korczak*. London: Chatto & Windus.

Lorenz, W. (2008) 'Paradigms and politics: Understanding methods paradigms in an historical context: The case of social pedagogy.' *The British Journal of Social Work 38*, 4, 625–644.

Malaguzzi, L. (1993) 'For an education based on relationships.' *Young Children 11*, 9–13.

Malaguzzi, L. (1998) 'History, Ideas, and Basic Philosophy: An Interview with Lella Gandini.' In C. Edwards, L. Gandini and G. Forman (eds) *The Hundred Languages of Children: The Reggio Emilia Approach – Advanced Reflections (2nd ed.)*. Westport: Ablex.

Mollenhauer, K. (1964) *Einführung in die Sozialpädagogik*. Weinheim: Beltz Verlag.

Niemeyer, C. (2005) *Klassiker der Sozialpädagogik: Einführung in die Theoriegeschichte einer Wissenschaft (2nd ed.)*. Weinheim: Juventa Verlag.

Nohl, H. (1970) *Die pädagogische Bewegung in Deutschland und ihre Theorie (7th ed.)*. Frankfurt am Main: SchulteBulmke. (Original work published 1935.)

Pestalozzi, J.H. (1964) *Schriften aus den Jahren 1808–1809* (ed. E. Dejung and H. Schönebaum). Zürich. (Original work published 1808–1809.) De Gruyter Verlag

Pestalozzi, J.H. (1999) *Lienhard und Gertrud*. Bad Heilbrunn: Verlag Julius Klinkhardt. (Original work published 1819.)

Petrie, P., Boddy, J., Cameron, C., Wigfall, V. and Simon, A. (2006) *Working with Children in Care: European Perspectives*. Maidenhead: Open University Press.

Qvortrup, J. (2005) 'Varieties of Childhood.' In J. Qvortrup (ed.) *Studies in Modern Childhood*. Basingstoke: Palgrave Macmillan.

Reyer, J. (2002) *Kleine Geschichte der Sozialpädagogik. Individuum und Gemeinschaft in der Pädagogik der Moderne*. Schondorg: Schneider Verlag.

Rousseau, J.J. (1993) *Emile, or on Education*. London: Phoenix/Everyman. (Original work published 1762.)

Ryan, R.M. and Deci, E.L. (2001) 'On happiness and human potentials: A review of research on hedonic and eudaimonic well-being.' *Annual Review of Psychology 52*, 141–166.

Seligman, M. and Csikszentmihalyi, M. (2000) 'Positive psychology: An introduction.' *American Psychologist 55*, 1, 5–14.

Short, D. (1998) *An Interview with Steve de Shazer and Insoo Kim Berg*. Available at www.solution-focused.nl/documenten/interviewInsooenSteve.doc, accessed on 18 March 2010.

Smith, M. and Whyte, B. (2007) 'Social education and social pedagogy: Reclaiming a Scottish tradition in social work.' *European Journal of Social Work 11*, 1, 15–28.

Smith, M.K. (1997) 'Paulo Freire.' *Infed – the Encyclopaedia of Informal Education*. Available at www.infed.org/thinkers/et-freir.htm, accessed on 4 March 2010.

Smith, M.K. (2005) 'Johann Heinrich Pestalozzi.' *Infed – the Encyclopaedia of Informal Education*. Available at www.infed.org/thinkers/et-pest.htm, accessed on 20 February 2009.

Staub-Bernasconi, S. (2007a) 'Soziale Arbeit als Dienstleistung oder Menschenrechtsprofession?' In A. Lob-Hüdepohl (ed.) *Ethik Sozialer Arbeit: Eine Einführung*. Paderborn: Verlag Ferdinand Schöningh.

Staub-Bernasconi, S. (2007b) *Soziale Arbeit als Handungswissenschaft*. Bern: Haupt Verlag.

Taylor, P. (1993) *The Texts of Paulo Freire*. Buckingham: Open University Press.

Thiersch, H. (1996) 'Sozialarbeitswissenschaft: Neue Herausforderung oder Altbekanntes?' In R. Merten, P. Sommerfeld and T. Koditek (eds) *Sozialarbeitswissenschaft: Kontroversen und Perspektiven*. Neuwied: Luchterhand.

Thiersch, H. (2002) *Positionsbestimmungen der Sozialen Arbeit*. Weinheim: Juventa.

Thiersch, H. and Rauschenbach, T. (1984) 'Sozialarbeit/Sozialpädagogik: Theorie und Entwicklung.' In H. Eyferth, H.-U. Otto and H. Thiersch (eds) *Handbuch zur Sozialarbeit/Sozialpädagogik*. Neuwied: Luchterhand.

Ungermann, S. (2006) *Die Pädagogik Janusz Korczaks: Theoretische Grundlegung und Praktische Verwirklichung 1896–1942*. Gütersloh: Gütersloher Verlagshaus.

Veerman, P.E. (1987) 'Janusz Korczak and the rights of the child.' *Concern 62*, 1, 7–9.

Vygotsky, L. (1978) *Mind and Society*. Cambridge, MA: Harvard University Press.

CHAPTER 3

Diversity in Early Childhood Education: A Matter of Social Pedagogical Embarrassment

MICHEL VANDENBROECK, FILIP COUSSÉE,
LIEVE BRADT AND RUDI ROOSE

Working the tension between diversity and cohesion

In this chapter, we explore a possible interpretation of what social pedagogy may mean, when considering issues of diversity in early childhood education. In our view, a social pedagogical perspective deliberately connects pedagogical practices to underlying social and political assumptions and objectives. A social pedagogical perspective throws light on the way social and political problems are transformed into pedagogical questions. This is particularly the case when discussing issues of diversity. Indeed, questions such as how to respect diversity and yet at the same time safeguard social cohesion have long been in the hearts and minds of social pedagogues.

We explain this by using the metaphor of 'social pedagogical embarrassment'. The German-Dutch social pedagogue Carl Mennicke (1887–1959) coined this term to express how concerns about social cohesion, especially in times of crisis, impel policymakers and pedagogues to call for a renewed social pedagogical strategy. Society is embarrassed (discomfited) because the social consensus that lays down how to handle the tension between tolerance for diversity and concerns for equity comes under great pressure. Educators from all different fields are called on to close this social pedagogical gap. This means that pedagogues are given a huge social responsibility.

But it also draws our attention to the tentative and fragile steps that pedagogues have to take to position themselves in the tensions created by attempts to deal with both diversity and social cohesion. By tracing the history of how the issue of diversity has been considered in early childhood education (ECE), we certainly do not wish to resolve these tensions and the embarrassment they create. On the contrary, we believe it is more useful to give these tensions a more prominent place in our policies and practices.

An introduction to social pedagogical embarrassment

In this chapter we wish to discuss a possible social pedagogical perspective on the issue of diversity in ECE. Before we do so, it is necessary to clarify what we mean by a social pedagogical perspective. As argued elsewhere (Vandenbroeck, Coussée and Bradt 2010), we do not consider social pedagogy as a solution to (social or pedagogical) problems. Reducing social pedagogy to a method could turn it into a useful instrument to control social problems by adjusting children (and their parents) to the prevailing consensus on how to behave as good citizens, albeit in more empathic and humane ways than through mere repression, behavioural therapy or charity. From a social pedagogical perspective, the issue at stake is not merely to find the best solutions to a given social problem, but rather – before thinking about solutions – to continually re-examine in participatory ways what the problem might be and whether our pedagogical practices question or confirm prevailing understandings of the problem.

A social pedagogical perspective deliberately connects pedagogical practices to underlying social and political assumptions and objectives. So while social pedagogy has its roots in ideas on holistic education, child-centredness and life-world orientation, these core ideas have always been underpinned by very different assumptions and aims, leading to very different interpretations. Throughout history one can identify both conservative and restorative forms of social pedagogy, and ideas that were developed starting from progressive or radical perspectives on the question of how pedagogical practice should shape and reflect the relationship between the individual and society. Consequently, we have to make the underlying assumptions of our pedagogical practices and policy much more explicit.

These underlying assumptions may be seen as natural or self-evident, but they are in fact historical and cultural constructions, reflecting dominant ideas on education and the shaping of society (Barthes 1957). If we leave out this historical and political analysis, it becomes very difficult to discuss the broader social functions of education. Perhaps that is why discussions on social pedagogy so often stick to methodological questions focusing on 'how to do things right'. Yet, we may tend to forget to ask 'Are we doing right things?'

A social pedagogical framework shifts our attention from a better organisation of ECE, or pedagogical practices in general, to the relationship between pedagogical practices and views on social cohesion and the desired social order. Throughout history, this relationship has received renewed attention in each period of drastic societal transformation. In such times of uncertainty, a kind of social pedagogical 'embarrassment' crops up (Mennicke 1937). The key question thrown up by this social pedagogical embarrassment is 'How is it possible to prevent social disintegration and preserve social cohesion without eliminating diversity?' While profound tensions (e.g. the fundamental tension between individual liberty and social equality) are inherent to this question, we can observe an ongoing tendency to resolve (or rather neglect) these tensions in two ways.

One way of doing this is by distancing the social from the pedagogical, by shaping pedagogical practices in isolation from the social context. In this case, pedagogues act as if pedagogical quality is disconnected from social political objectives. What remains is a 'desocialised' plea for a holistic child-centred approach (Mollenhauer 1965). Even though such an approach is important, it impoverishes the discussion on the social functions of education (including discussions on the inherent tensions between emancipation and control).

A second way is by removing the pedagogical from the social. Pedagogy is not seen as instrumental to social change, rather the opposite. What remains, then, is a political plea for a more just and democratic society. Again, there is nothing wrong with such a plea, but this 'depedagogisation' leaves educators and social workers empty-handed in their commitment in real-life situations.

In our view, a social pedagogical perspective on diversity needs to strive continuously to connect the social and the pedagogical by resocialising pedagogical practices and repedagogising social practices. This response enables practitioners to connect micro and macro politics and to reflect in a constructive way on their practice and its function in shaping the relationship between the individual and society. This implies the discussion not only on how to do things right but also on doing the right things, acknowledging at the same time, however, that consensus on the latter is not possible (Mouffe 2005; Sen 2009). This is not to say that such consensus is completely rejected, as some guidelines are necessary in order to act as social pedagogues. It is, however, to say that we need to keep in mind that consensus in pedagogical matters is always fragile, temporary and open for discussion. In this way, social pedagogical practices can be considered as platforms to enable this discussion and to strengthen the voice of the voiceless (Freire 1970).

A social pedagogical perspective on diversity in early childhood education

The issue at stake here – diversity in early childhood education – is a topical issue to examine what a social pedagogical perspective might mean. First, because ECE has from its very origins been constructed as a place where societal interests (labour policies, combating poverty, civilisation of the masses) intersect with the intimacy of the daily lives of mothers, fathers and children (Vandenbroeck 2006). ECE facilitates the negotiation between the individual aspirations of children and families and societal expectations. It is a sphere in which the relationship between individual and society is constantly questioned and constructed.

Second, because the issue of diversity is inextricably linked with discussions on social cohesion that are core to social pedagogy (Dollinger 2006). The discussion on social cohesion and how it relates to education is as old as pedagogy. It was discussed by Plato and Aristotle (Hämäläinen 1989) as well as by Luis Vives in the 16th century (Notten 2002). Today, ECE is expected to respect diversity and difference and at the same time strive for equality and cohesion. As a pedagogical practice, it cannot disconnect itself from its social context, from the ideas that underpin its existence and, more specifically, from the construction of a democratic welfare state and prevailing ideas of active citizenship.

Initiatives that do attempt to disconnect themselves from these questions may be child-centred, but they fail to question their significance for society. Pedagogical initiatives may 'disembarrass' themselves by neglecting the tensions that go together with their mandate and position in the social field. But in doing so they risk their identity being increasingly defined externally, in terms of labour market needs, early detection, remedial opportunities and so on (Vandenbroeck et al. 2010).

In the next part, we will take a closer look on what Mennicke (1937) has described as social pedagogical embarrassment, adopting a historical perspective on the tensions between social cohesion and diversity. Next, we will give a brief account of what is known today about *doing things right*, from a merely pedagogical perspective, with respect to diversity in ECE. This will be followed by a reflection on *doing the right things*, in a modest attempt to introduce an example of what a social pedagogical perspective on this issue might mean today.

Diversity in ECE: An old story, but not the same old story

The issue of social cohesion became very salient in the late 19th and early 20th century, as a result of industrialisation. The proletarianisation and impoverishment of large parts of the new urban population threatened the integrity of the recently formed nation states and their very social order – a liberal social order in which the state was supposed not to intervene in private matters (Dollinger 2007). Social uproar (and the use of strikes as a political instrument), high child mortality and the formation of working-class movements led to a growing focus on the care of the youngest, the education of youth and the civilisation of adults (Donzelot 1977). It is in this historical context that the first day care centres were established all over Western Europe, alongside infant consultation schemes, offering advice to mothers about infant care (Vandenbroeck 2006).

Some protagonists may have viewed these new services as beneficial to working-class women from the point of view of their emancipation (Plasky 1910). But the dominant view was that the care of young children called for civilising their ignorant and irresponsible parents (Velghe 1919). Childcare, organised by the bourgeoisie, would eventually 'show the poor that authority, seconded by the rich, looks after their children with maternal attention and the holy bell tells the poor (person) that one thinks of him, as it announces to the rich (person) that he has to give [to charity]' (Marbeau 1845, pp.90–91).[1] Space precludes elaborating here on the specific techniques used to civilise the poor. Elsewhere, we have explained in more detail how the dominant discourse was that the leading bourgeoisie established its own norms on what a family should be as universally applicable (Vandenbroeck 2003).

---

1 Quand tout est prêt, une seconde réunion des fondateurs vote les statuts, le règlement, et fixe le jour d'ouverture de la Crèche. Les pauvres mères attendent ce jour comme le Messie. Une cérémonie touchante fait voir aux indigents que l'autorité, secondée par les riches, veille sur leurs enfants avec une sollicitude maternelle, et la cloche sainte annonce au pauvre qu'on pense à lui, annonce au riche qu'il faut donner...

The emergence of the potentially dangerous working class occurred in the context of new and therefore politically fragile nation states, which developed policies geared towards the creation of a sense of unity in the hearts and minds of their inhabitants. These inhabitants were supposed to be internally homogeneous, speaking one language, adhering to one culture and sharing one history consisting of selected victories and forgotten defeats, to establish an imagined community (Anderson 1991). 'Culture' was used to foster unity, neutralising local and linguistic variations and direct, unmediated contact between individuals and the state was considered to be promoting equality. Citizens – free of any affiliation to ethnic, religious or other groups – were believed to be entitled to political equality (Mendus 1989).

In short, where diversity was acknowledged, it was in order to frame specific populations that needed to be civilised, in a context of denial of ethnic and cultural diversity. The most powerful machinery created to achieve this civilising process was massive educational regulations (Gellner 1997; Smith 2001). Civilisation in this case can be understood as 'making the other into the same', reinforced by the colonial history of 'Othering the Other' that constructed the 'primitive' and 'tribal' Other into a mirror of the 'educated' Self (Said 1978; Smith 2001). The tensions that Mennicke formulated as social pedagogical embarrassment – unity in diversity – were dismissed because the focus was on social integration that took neither diversity nor social inequality into account.

Desocialising the pedagogical

Things changed considerably after the Second World War. In a period of booming economies, it was believed that the rapidly growing welfare state would eradicate poverty and bring about equality and happiness for all. As a consequence, there was no need for social pedagogical work. Furthermore, the historical lessons of the atrocities perpetrated by Nazi Germany led to a growing awareness of how social pedagogical ideas and methods can be instrumental to radical solutions to escape the tensions between equity and diversity, namely by eliminating diversity. The idea that social problems need to be tackled by pedagogy remained, but social cohesion was explicitly considered as the result of an adequate individual education. The explicit link between pedagogy and the design of the state disappeared to the benefit of more introspective approaches, reinforcing the belief that pedagogical aims and principles can be determined 'vom Kinde aus' (*from the child itself*), irrespective of social contexts (Mollenhauer

1983). This led to methodical and technical (didactic) reflections, on the 'social education' of individuals rather than to reflections on the societal outcomes of education. In the field of diversity, the growing introspective sciences (e.g. orthopedagogy and other applied psychologies) were concerned with studying the emergence of prejudice in the developing human, in the aftermath of the holocaust (Aboud 1988).

It was only with the economic crisis of the 1970s that the issues of inequality and diversity and, therefore, the forgotten link between the pedagogical and the social came back on the agenda. As Giesecke (1985) claimed, we forgot that every pedagogical act also comprises political and social elements. Especially in liberal-oriented welfare states (Esping-Andersen 2001), it became difficult to resocialise the pedagogical. When an influential politician (Margaret Thatcher, UK Prime Minister in the 1980s) could assert that 'There is no such thing as society. There are individual men and women, and there are families', this left little space for *social* pedagogical discussions. Great confidence in the invisible hand of the market in the liberal welfare state – though traditionally social democratic welfare states also followed this global neoliberal trend – led not only to few investments (or even to disinvestments) in welfare, but also to growing investments in control and the judicial apparatus (Wacquant 2002).

However, in the 1990s it could no longer be denied that the invisible hand had led to growing poverty and less equality, and this insight paved the way for a renewal of the politics of the Third Way (Giddens 1998). As the political horizon changed, so the societal project was naturalised (Barthes 1957) and thus became indisputable. In all affluent countries and beyond, welfare and social work in general and education (and ECE) in particular are now back on the political agenda (Lorenz 2001). But today they are seen and rationalised as investments that will pay off in later life.

From mono- to multiculturalism

Alongside these developments, from the 1970s onwards, the homogenising policies of nation states have been seriously challenged, due to civil right movements (e.g. black power, women's liberation), decolonisation, and the massive import of cheap labour forces from the south into Western Europe during the booming 1950s and 1960s as the new slaves. Public discussion about the possible forced return of this migrant workforce to their 'home countries' emerged in the period of economic crisis and growing unemployment in the primary and secondary sectors where they were employed. Interestingly, the discussions on the 'integration' of these ethnic minority workers occurred at the time when they *were* actually integrating – that is, at the time when they had their families coming over and the downward social mobility of the majority workers in the post-Fordist countries encountered the still upward social mobility of ethnic minority workers.

It is in this context that in education the homogenising approach was left and a new *multicultural* approach was embraced, building on the notion of culture and cultural identity, in line with the introspective (depoliticised) approach described earlier. Progressive educationalists studied the cultural beliefs and habits of ethnic minorities and advocated passionately for educators to take into account these fundamental cultural differences (Derman-Sparks and ABC Task Force 1989; Vedder, Bouwer and Pels 1996). The anti-bias and anti-racist approaches of the 1990s were partly founded on the developmental psychology research on the emergence of prejudice and partly on the civil rights movements, elaborating on the concept of distinct racial, ethnic and cultural identities. This approach has been a major contribution to ECE, as it tried to reconnect practical methodical advice to broader political discussions; and, in so doing, it attempted to let the pedagogical embarrassment (how to preserve social cohesion without eliminating diversity) re-emerge.

Doing things right

Despite their merits, the anti-bias and anti-racist pedagogies in ECE have been seriously challenged, both on conceptual and political grounds. From a conceptual point of view, it has been argued that there is little evidence that prejudices that emerge at an early age evolve into discriminatory behaviour at a later age. The linear developmental approach has been seriously criticised by post-foundational scholars and by the new sociology of childhood for being too adult-oriented, gendered and – indeed – euro-centric (Burman 1994; James, Jenks and Prout 1998; Vandenbroeck *et al.* 2010).

The victimisation of the ethnic minority child, constructed as a weak, passive object, acquiring its cultural identity from his or her parents (his or her 'roots'), leads to a remarkable political paradox. It is indeed striking to see how this concept of cultural identity resembles the monolithic and essentialist concept of culture advocated by the politics of the far right that emerged in the 1990s, where the old discourse on 'race' was replaced by a similar discourse on 'culture'. Children are, in this perspective, framed according to their history and associated with their 'different origins', rather than protagonists with agency in the present or co-constructors of their self-chosen future. Many scholars have argued that we do not belong to one culture, that our choices are no longer moulded by traditional roles (e.g. Beck 1997), and that this needs to be expressed by adhering to concepts such as hyphenated identities, multiple identities, or nomadic and hybrid identities (Vandenbroeck *et al.* 2009).

This is not to say that the anti-bias and anti-racist pedagogies need to be dismissed. On the contrary, they taught us that (minority) children from a very early age onwards may be hurt in their identity, in who they are; that long before compulsory school age, they construct negative answers to existential questions such as 'Who am I?' and 'Is it OK to be who I am?' This is not so much a matter of racist or classist attitudes of educators, but rather of an abundance of micro-events, by which they learn that their language, their clothes, their food, their music are not as valuable as the dominant 'average' child's, or at least as the social construction of the desired culture, needs and behaviour of what is believed to be an average child.

High quality ECE can substantially contribute to bridging the educational gap between minority and majority children (Penn 2009; Sylva *et al.* 2004; UNICEF Innocenti Research Centre 2008). However, we also know that children do not thrive in an environment where there is no belonging, and thus low well-being and involvement (Laevers 1997). Consequently, any pedagogy of the early years will have to deal with methodical questions about how to bridge the gap between family cultures (in plural) and the culture of the early childhood centre. This will inevitably imply not only a holistic child-centred approach but also an (ecological) approach including parents and the local communities.

Over the last decades, there are many examples of enabling practices to be found, developed by inspired educators, often in connection with national and international networks such as the Western European DECET (Diversity in Early Childhood Education and Training) network (www.decet.org), the Central and Eastern European ISSA (International Step by Step Association) network (www.issa.nl), or the more global UNA network (www.unaglobal.org). They have documented a large variety of methods to build these bridges and to discuss diversity issues with children, parents and communities (including, for instance, family walls, persona dolls, activities that strengthen positive identities), as well as many training modules for educators who wish to deepen their insights and construct new practices in this field. As a consequence, we may say that there is a substantial knowledge as well as international consensus on what it is to do things right.

Doing the right things

From a social pedagogical perspective, a compelling question may be: Why? Why is this consensus emerging now? In what context is it emerging? And, eventually: Whom does it serve and whom does it exclude? In order to begin to answer these questions, we need to reconnect pedagogy with a critical analysis of the social context in which the pedagogical consensus emerges.

As said earlier, ECE is increasingly framed as an investment in later life. Many post-industrial nation states are confronted with a serious educational gap: children from poor and ethnic minority families do less well at school. The OECD Programme for International Student Assessment (PISA) has urged policy makers and the public to acknowledge this important inequality (see www.pisa.oecd.org). Moreover, international reports (e.g. Penn 2009; UNICEF Innocenti Research Centre 2008) as well as longitudinal studies (e.g. Sylva *et al.* 2004) concur in saying that ECE can at least buffer this inequality. It needs to be noted that the discussion on the educational gap is not new. Forty years ago, Bourdieu and Passeron (1970, 1977) explained in detail how the educational system reproduced social inequality. However, the discourse on what the problem is has changed considerably over the course of these four decades, coinciding with the rising consensus on respect for diversity.

The case of Flanders (Belgium) is particularly interesting to study the shift in discourse. The discussion here is not on access, as all children from two and a half years on can attend ECE for full days; moreover, all staff in the nursery schools are trained at bachelor's (degree) level. Poor families and families from minority ethnic groups living in Flanders receive home visits, when their child is about 30 months old, to explain the beneficial effects of ECE to the parents. Children with a home language other than the dominant one cannot enrol in the first year of (compulsory) primary school unless they have attended at least 220 days of ECE, meaning a de facto lowering of the compulsory school age for ethnic minority children (though not, it should be noted, for the children of expats or European civil servants attending special 'European', 'English' or 'Japanese' schools). The general belief is that ethnic minority and poor parents are not accustomed 'culturally' to ECE and need to be convinced of its merits. In France, since the Bénisti report for the Senate (Bénisti 2005) on the prevention of adolescent delinquency, a similar coercive policy is to be found towards parents who are non-French-speaking, requiring social workers to report these 'at risk' families to the local authorities (Vandenbroeck, Roets and Snoeck 2009).

In both cases, the focus is no longer on what is wrong with ECE or school, which might deter attendance, but on deficiencies in the families that are believed to be related to cultural diversity. In relation to this, a group of experts from different continents[2] studying examples of 'good practice' in many different countries concluded that ethnicity and culture cannot be studied in separation of class and poverty:

> Race and ethnicity become social and political issues when they are related to the poor and disenfranchised groups. Being rich is associated with being similar and not being rich is associated with being different, thus making 'difference' a reason for discrimination, albeit disguised in good intentions which make them politically correct. The linguistic turn in thinking about these issues in terms of culture, rather than class, urges us to critically examine the terms we use: ethnicity, diversity, intercultural, minority, language differences, and often culture itself apply when given poverty, but not otherwise. (Vandenbroeck *et al.* 2010, p.9)

This shift in discourse on what constitutes 'good practice' occurs in the context of neoliberal welfare states, in which social welfare in general and education in particular are seen as investments in future success and individuals are conceived as autonomous subjects, entrepreneurs of their own life, adhering to the ideology of free choice, but at the same time responsible and accountable for the effects of their personal choices. Despite the failures of the liberal market, considering the bank crisis of 2008–2010, and despite the critique that the concept of 'free' choice masks structural inequalities (Burman 1994), the concept of free choice and individual responsibility is hardly challenged, leaving little room to

---

2   The group was called the Learning Group on Programme Development in ECE, and is one of the six Learning Groups of UNA, a global learning initiative on children and ethnic diversity, coordinated by Paul Connolly (Queen's University, Belfast). The group was chaired by the first author together with Ileana Seda-Santana (Mexico) and included Zvi Bekerman (Israel), John Bennett (France), Karina Davis (Australia), Silvia Helena Koller (Brazil), Mugyeong Moon (Korea), Rita Swinnen (Belgium), Zorica Triki (Serbia) See www.unaglobal.org for more information.

discuss structural inequalities rather than personal choices, embedded in cultural traditions.

Discussion

ECE is a social, a pedagogical and a political practice that facilitates negotiation between the individual aspirations of children and families and societal expectations. Consequently, early childhood educators play, willy-nilly, a political role by confirming or questioning mainstream societal expectations, by fostering or lowering particular individual ambitions. As with all educational practices, ECE is a field that asks for a social pedagogical *perspective* rather than a method, a perspective that connects the social to the pedagogical. In this perspective, ECE wishes to respect diversity and difference, yet at the same time it strives for equity and social cohesion. This double aspiration has been and still is the source of ongoing tensions, framed as social pedagogical embarrassment. Let us not dis-embarrass ourselves by neglecting those tensions or by implying solutions.

It is the practitioner's job to practise. This inevitably entails contestable decisions. The social pedagogical perspective we have proposed in this chapter calls for keeping ensuing discussions open by questioning the perspectives that may be legitimating pedagogical actions. This means asking critical questions. Who says what (or who) constitutes the problem? Who was involved in this definition of the problem and who was excluded? And even more important: How do our actions influence the perspective on what the problem is supposed to be?

Consequently, this reflexive attitude is better served by disagreement than by consensus. By disagreement, we mean to seek deliberately for alternative voices and perspectives. One way of doing this is pedagogical documentation as a way of making practice visible, transparent and, therefore, subject to dialogue and contestation with children, parents and other stakeholders (Dahlberg and Moss 2005; Rinaldi, 2005) (discussed further in Chapter 9). Recent and ongoing cross-cultural studies have shown that educators as well as parents have strong (though not always explicit) ideas about the links between everyday educational practice and the organisation of society, but also that these ideas are far from consensual (see, for instance, Brougère, Guénif-Souilamas and Rayna 2008; Tobin, Hsueh and Karasawa 2009 or other forthcoming publications from the ongoing 'Children crossing borders' study). Obviously, this confrontation with different perspectives is challenging, but it offers at least possibilities of reflecting on what it might mean to do the right things.

Eventually, this dissensus may enable us to 'name the world again, in order to transform it' (Freire 1970) and, therefore, to destabilise the existing social order. Resocialising the pedagogical, as we advocate, is to confront social problems, instead of dismissing them by making them purely educational problems. Dismissing social problems is inevitably also dismissing the most vulnerable: those who cannot participate in the definition of the problems they are supposed to have.

Conclusion

In this chapter we have sketched a possible perspective on social pedagogy, related to the discussions on diversity in early childhood education. A historical hindsight reveals how educational and political matters are inextricably linked together. Early childhood education in contexts of diversity inevitably raises questions on living together in complex societies, on the nature of identities, on tolerance, on hospitality and, ultimately, on how to foster social cohesion without denying diversity. Educational debates on 'doing the things right' should, therefore, always coincide with social and political discussions about 'doing the right things'. This calls for ongoing debates with educators, parents and other stakeholders, not only on the solution to societal problems, but, in the first place, on different possible perspectives on what these problems may be.

References

Aboud, F. (1988) *Children and Prejudice*. Oxford: Blackwell.

Anderson, B. (1991) *Imagined Communities: Reflections on the Origins and Spread of Nationalism*. London: Verso.

Barthes, R. (1957) *Mythologies*. Paris: Editions de Seuil.

Beck, U. (1997) 'Democratisation of the family.' *Childhood 4*, 2, 151–168.

Bénisti, J.A. (2005) *Rapport de la Commission Prévention du Groupe d'étude Parlementaire sur la Sécurité Intérieure*. Paris: Assemblée Nationale.

Bourdieu, P. and Passeron, J.C. (1970) *Le Reproduction. Eléments pour une Théorie du Système d'Enseignement*. Paris: Editions de Minuit.

Bourdieu, P. and Passeron, J.C. (1977) *Reproduction in Education, Society and Culture*. London: Sage.

Brougère, G., Guénif-Souilamas, N. and Rayna, S. (2008) 'École maternelle (preschool) in France: a cross-cultural perspective.' *European Early Childhood Education Research Journal 16*, 3, 371–184.

Burman, E. (1994) *Deconstructing Developmental Psychology*. London: Routledge.

Dahlberg, G. and Moss, P. (2005) *Ethics and Politics in Early Childhood Education*. London: Routledge.

Derman-Sparks, L. and ABC Task Force (1989) *Anti-Bias Curriculum: Tools for Empowering Young Children*. Washington, DC: NAEYC.

Dollinger, B. (2006) *Die Pädagogik der Sozialen Frage. (Sozial-)Pädagogische Theorie vom Beginn des 19. Jahrhunderts bis zum ende der Weimarer Republik*. Wiesbaden: VS Verlag.

Dollinger, B. (2007) 'Der soziale Liberalismus und die Entstehung der Sozialpädagogik.' In B. Dollinger, C. Müller and W. Schröer (eds) *Die sozialpädagogische Erziehung des Bürgers. Entwürfe zur Konstitution der modernen Gesellschaft*. Wiesbaden: VS Verlag.

Donzelot, G. (1977) *La Police des Familles*. Paris: Les Editions de Minuit.

Esping-Andersen, G. (2001) 'Quel état-providence pour le XXIe siècle? Convergences et divergences des pays européens.' *Esprit 2*, 122–150.

Freire, P. (1970) *Pedagogy of the Oppressed*. New York: Herder and Herder.

Gellner, E. (1997) *Nationalism*. New York: New York University Press.

Giddens, A. (1998) *The Third Way: The Renewal of Social Democracy*. Cambridge: Polity Press.

Giesecke, H. (1985) *Das Ende der Erziehung. Neue Chancen für Familie und Schule*. Stuttgart: Klett-Cotta.

Hämäläinen, J. (1989) 'Social pedagogy as a meta-theory of social work education.' *International Social Work 32*, 2, 117–128.

James, A., Jenks, C. and Prout, A. (1998) *Theorizing Childhood*. Cambridge: Polity Press.

Laevers, F. (1997) 'Assessing the quality of childcare provision: "Involvement" as criterion.' *Researching Early Childhood 3*, 151–165.

Lorenz, W. (2001) 'Social work responses to "New Labour" in Continental European countries.' *British Journal of Social Work 31*, 595–609.

Marbeau, J.B.F. (1845) *Des Crèches. Ou Moyen de diminuer la Misère en augmentant la Population*. Paris: Comptoir des Imprimeurs-Unis.

Mendus, S. (1989) *Toleration and the Limits of Liberalism*. New York: Macmillan.

Mennicke, C. (1937) *Sociale Paedagogie. Grondslagen, vormen en middelen der gemeenschapsopvoeding*. Utrecht: Erven J. Bijleveld.

Mollenhauer, K. (1965) *Einführung in die Sozialpädagogik*. Weinheim: Juventa Verlag.

Mollenhauer, K. (1983) *Vergessene Zusammenhange*. Weinheim: Juventa Verlag.

Mouffe, C. (2005) *On the Political*. London: Routledge.

Notten, T. (2002) 'Ambition and ambivalence, or: Is there any system in andragology?' *Systems Research and Behavioural Science 19*, 3, 137–144.

Penn, H. (2009) *Early Childhood Education and Care: Key Lessons from Research for Policy Makers*. Brussels: Nesse.

Plasky, E. (1910) *La Crèche et sa Nécessité Sociale. Conférence donné le 5 février 1910 à l'Exposition d'Hygiène des Enfants du Premier Age*. Anvers: Buschman.

Rinaldi, C. (2005) *In Dialogue with Reggio Emilia: Listening, Researching and Learning*. London: Routledge.

Said, E. (1978) *Orientalism.* New York: Pantheon Books.

Sen, A. (2009) *The Idea of Justice.* New York: Allan Lane.

Smith, A.D. (2001) *Nationalism: Theory, Ideology, History.* Cambridge: Polity Press.

Sylva, K., Melhuish, E., Sammons, P., Siraj-Blatchford, I. and Taggart, B. (2004) *The Effective Provision of Preschool Education (EPPE) Project: Final Report.* London: DfES/Institute of Education, University of London.

Tobin, J., Hsueh, Y. and Karasawa, M. (2009) *Preschool in Three Cultures Revisited: China, Japan and the United States.* Chicago, IL: University of Chicago Press.

UNICEF Innocenti Research Centre (2008) *The Child Care Transition (Report Card 8).* Florence: UNICEF.

Vandenbroeck, M. (2003) 'From crèches to childcare: Constructions of motherhood and inclusion/exclusion in the history of Belgian infant care.' *Contemporary Issues in Early Childhood 4,* 3, 137–148.

Vandenbroeck, M. (2006) 'The persistent gap between education and care: A "history of the present" research on Belgian child care provision and policy.' *Paedagogica Historica. International Journal of the History of Education 42,* 3, 363–383.

Vandenbroeck, M., Boonaert, T., Van der Mespel, S. and De Brabandere, K. (2009) 'Dialogical spaces to reconceptualize parent support in the social investment state.' *Contemporary Issues in Early Childhood 10,* 1, 66–77.

Vandenbroeck, M., Coussée, F. and Bradt, L. (2010) 'The social and political construction of early childhood education.' *British Journal of Educational Studies 58,* 2, 139–54.

Vandenbroeck, M., Roets, G. and Snoeck, A. (2009) 'Mothers crossing borders: Immigrant mothers on reciprocity, hybridisation and love.' *European Early Childhood Education Research Journal 17,* 2, 203–216.

Vandenbroeck, M., Seda-Santana, I., Bekerman, Z., Bennett, J., Davis, K., Koller, S.H. *et al.* (2010) *Early Childhood Services in Contexts of Ethnic Divisions.* Belfast: UNA.

Vedder, P., Bouwer, E. and Pels, T. (1996) *Multicultural Child Care.* Clevedon, PA: Multilingual Matters.

Velghe, H. (1919) *La Protection de l'Enfance en Belgique. Son Passé, son Avenir.* Bruxelles: Goemaere.

Wacquant, L. (2002) *Punir les Pauvres. Le Nouveau Gouvernement de l'Insécurité Sociale.* Marseille: Agone.

CHAPTER 4

Interpersonal Communication: The Medium for Social Pedagogic Practice

Pat Petrie

Communication in a democratic and emancipatory social pedagogy

This chapter brings together two different sets of theory and practice: those of social pedagogy and those of interpersonal communication. Both apply to work with adults, young people and children, and both are deeply concerned with humans as social beings and ways of thinking about human beings that focus on the relationships between them. So how do they link? What has each to offer the other?

For the purposes of this chapter, I shall use 'children' to include all young people under the age of majority. I shall also refer mainly to work with children, although much will be equally applicable to working with adults. The professionals to be considered in the context of interpersonal communication are those who in much of Continental Europe would work in the field of social pedagogy – broadly speaking, policy and practice which addresses social issues by means of education in the broadest sense of that word, including services such as family support, youth work and, in some countries, early years education and care: I shall refer to them as 'professionals' covering all such work. The term social pedagogy, especially in relation to interpersonal communication, is discussed at greater length later in the chapter.

Many theoretical areas can contribute to an understanding of interpersonal communication, such as psychological theories of perception and motivation and sociological theories of culture and of status and power. In this chapter, I will concentrate primarily on interpersonal communication as it applies to professionals working with people in social pedagogic settings, but taking into account a wider social context. There have been different understandings and critiques of the social pedagogy used in particular societies at specific times. For example, Heinz Sünker and Hans-Uwe Otto (1997) drew attention to how, in the Third Reich, 'pedagogisation' extended to all areas of life, from the cradle to the grave. The intention was to gain complete control of the population by instilling common understandings and values based on racial 'purity' and the superiority of the Germanic peoples (see also Chapter 3 in this volume). The social pedagogic communication on which this chapter is based is informed by democratic and emancipatory values and practice.

Interpersonal communication skills

I want to start by looking briefly at interpersonal communication and the related field of interpersonal skills. Areas usually covered in work about interpersonal communication include non-verbal communication, paralinguistics, listening, asking questions, circumstances that interfere with effective communication, reflecting back, negotiating, dialogue, conflict, and communicating in groups. The term covers all the situations where people are (most usually) face to face. Interpersonal communication does not include communication to a mass audience through the media or communication systems such as transport.

Interpersonal communication takes place when a person is in the presence of one or more others. It is difficult *not* to communicate when in the presence of other people and this is frequently referred to in the interpersonal communication literature. For example, in a crowded train, strangers who, in common sense terms, appear not to be in communication with each other, are in fact letting others know, by the way they hold themselves and avoid eye contact, that they are not seeking interaction – this meaning is conveyed and exchanged.

Seeing interpersonal communication in this light allows us to realise that a child who does not wish to answer another person's question but remains silent is *not* not communicating nor is he or she communicating 'badly'. The child is conveying information, by silence and by body language, about his or her feelings and relationship with the other person. In this way, the child can be seen as providing feedback to the questioner and affecting her response. The questioner has a range of possible responses to the child's behaviour: she may repeat the question in a louder voice, express the question in a different way, or smile and adopt a more friendly attitude. This feedback can be received and responded to by the child in many different ways, such as relaxing the shoulders, smiling, answering the question, explaining what he or she doesn't understand or by hanging his or her head and remaining silent. Because communication is in a feedback system, the questioner will again be affected by the response, whatever it is, and react accordingly.

Interpersonal communication theory sees communication as a dynamic system between the parties to the communication. Each has an effect on the communication of the other. But while it may be, on occasion, helpful to see communication as analogous to a mechanical feedback system, this is rather an impersonal way of conceptualising an inherently personal and human activity.

Central to employment and people work

The centrality of personal communication in social life has often been commented on; communication 'represents the very essence of the human condition' (Hargie and Dickinson 2004, p.2). Clearly, being aware of how interpersonal communication functions is important for all who work face to face with others. Some people seem to be 'natural' communicators; they are aware of other people's reactions and how best to behave in different social situations. Such people have what has been called tacit knowledge: they may not be able to spell out what they're doing, or why, but they seem to communicate very well and be effective in achieving their own or their employer's wishes. Others appear to be less skilled communicators; they find it difficult to 'read' other people's communications and to respond to them effectively.

The word 'effectively' is important here. People may communicate in a powerful manner, speak clearly and make their feelings plain, and yet not communicate in a way that best serves their professional ends. Effective professional communication on the part of one of the parties to it, whether intuitively or consciously, is goal-directed. Research has shown that training in interpersonal skills can support successful communication: with training and practice, staff can learn to listen and respond, confront and negotiate effectively: that is, they communicate in such a way as to be most likely to achieve their professional purpose.

It might seem, therefore, that effective interpersonal skills, alongside appropriate professional knowledge, understanding and experience, is an essential professional component of areas such as family support, social work, youth work and early years care and education. While this may be true, I would argue that it is not a sufficient understanding, because it ignores other important aspects of 'people work'. Ideas drawn from social pedagogy can throw light on these, not least because social pedagogic theory brings into question the value base, indeed the political basis, of such work with such people. It leads us to consider that in professional communication there are issues at play that go deeper than whether the communication is effective or not. A more fundamental question is: to what purpose is communication effective?

Professionals in social work and youth work may be seen as serving two masters: if they are employed in the public sector they serve both the state – in that they deliver public policy – and the client group. For other professionals, a third sector organisation or a private employer, with their own policy agendas, is an interested and influential partner. Professionals also serve the children and adults with whom they work in that – ideally – they seek to include them, or include them more fully, in the advantages of social life. In my experience, many professionals speak of this aim in terms of 'That is why I came into the work'. At the same time, it is clear that public and private policy does not always serve the population, more particularly its disadvantaged members, well. Here I would like to point to two theorists from different traditions, whose work throws light on the processes involved in the relationships and communications of daily life, and how these themselves are embedded in and affected by the wider society.

Urie Bronfenbrenner, the developmental psychologist, describes how a child's development takes place through processes of progressively more complex interaction between the person and the immediate social environment (Bronfenbrenner and Morris 1998, p.996). (I would emphasise that humans continue to develop throughout their lives). In addition, he draws attention to the wider ecology of human development (Bronfenbrenner 1979). Human beings do not develop only as a result of their relationship with family members. Bronfenbrenner proposes a model in which, for the child, the most immediate component is the *microsystem* where he or she is with adults and other children, such as in the family, in friendship groups, at school, nursery or youth club. These are sites for relationships and the face-to-face communications that are the basis of relationships. As such, the microsystem is where professionals relate to others: children, adults and colleagues.

Bronfenbrenner identifies three other components in his model. He distinguishes the *mesosystem* or the *set* of the microsystems in which a person participates, such as the home, the school and the playground, and how these may, for better or worse, as far as the child is concerned, be in interaction. For example, the home and the school may not share the same understandings about bringing up children and it is likely that this mismatch will affect communications and, therefore, relationships between parents and teachers. The *exosystem* consists of those 'settings which do not involve the developing person as an active participant, but in which events occur that affect, or are affected by, what happened in that setting' (Bronfenbrenner 1979, p.237). For example, events at the parents' workplace may have consequences for parents' relationships and communications with their children.

Finally, in Bronfenbrenner's model, the *macrosystem* is the larger social and political background, which affects relationships and communications in the lower systems. In other words, for Bronfenbrenner cultural and political meanings inherent in the macro-level are mediated through communications between people at a more local level. So a concern for child protection on the part of government and a sensationalist press can both be factors present in the wider macrosystem which affect social workers and their relationships and communications with young people.

Bronfenbrenner allows us to understand that while interpersonal communication is a central human activity, which affects our lives in many ways, it is not merely a means of getting things done or of pleasant social interchange. It relates to how we understand ourselves and to our sense of identity. In fact, we have become the people we are partly as a result of our interchanges with others. This is not to deny a role for genetic inheritance, nor the influences of the social and economic context, but to say that the way in which individuals are affected by such factors is strongly influenced by the meanings and messages that have been, and continue to be, conveyed in their dealings with other people at the level of the microsystem.

Communication is about meaning making, a two-way process that coordinates actions, manages meanings, between people (cf. Barnett Pearce 2007). But communication not only manages meaning, it also produces social meanings. For example, children learn what it is to be a child in any society in large part from the way people speak, listen and respond to them. To take one example, if children's expressed wishes, and those of their friends and fellow pupils, are always ignored, then clearly children have a low standing in the society where this happens. Similar messages about status are conveyed to members of other social groups: women, members of minority ethnic groups and aristocrats all hold socially constructed positions, and in part these constructions are conveyed to each person by means of interpersonal communication, which in turn relates to the structures and institutions of different societies. (It is also possible for interpersonal communications to attempt to subvert these meanings, to which I return later).

The work of my second theorist, Irving Goffman, has provided influential demonstrations of how people come to understand themselves, and the social roles which are appropriate for them, on the basis of social interactions. In his book *Stigma*, Goffman (1968), drawing on his research as a participant observer employed in an asylum, showed that patients accommodated to the roles and characteristics expected of them by staff, which were conveyed by means that included personal communication. In their interactions with staff, patients learned how to be a person with mental illness, living in an institution. This was to learn a discredited and stigmatising position, not quite human, and not in accord with the patient's previous expectations:

> Those who have dealings with him fail to accord him the respect and regard which the uncontaminated aspects of his social identity [that is, before becoming a patient] have led them to anticipate extending, and have led him to anticipate receiving. (Goffman 1968, p.19)

However, over time the patient comes to a state of 'acceptance' of a new identity: significantly, the subtitle of Goffman's book, *Stigma*, is *Notes on the Management of Spoiled Identity*. Of equal importance, Goffman argues that the values of the wider society, which holds people who are mentally ill in low regard, are channelled through the interactions and communications between staff and patients in mental health hospitals and, indeed, in other of life's circumstances.

Social pedagogy and interpersonal communication

So if it is known that interpersonal communication is a central meaning making process, which has great consequence for people's lives, and that professionals can be trained in 'effective' communication, how does this relate to social pedagogy? Other chapters in this book describe and discuss social pedagogy in some detail. Here I would like to summarise a few points to indicate aspects of social pedagogy that relate to 'effective' interpersonal communication. Throughout, we shall see that today's social pedagogy is seen as an ethical practice (see other chapters in this book), and it is at the level of ethics that it is primarily effective or not.

The term 'social pedagogy' relates to three distinct, but connected, fields: social policy, professional practice and theory. All are relevant to this discussion. The adjective 'social' is significant for all three. For social pedagogues, the people with whom they work are seen as social both in their immediate relationships and in that they are members of the larger society. Social pedagogy is deeply concerned with the connectedness of human beings. An important early theoretician, Paul Natorp (see Chapter 2), saw social pedagogy as a form of education in which the intrinsic social nature of human beings is fully acknowledged and prioritised.

At one level, the term 'social pedagogy' refers to broadly educational measures, implemented by government or by the private sector, whether historically or today (Hämäläinen 2003; Petrie 2002). For example, the state addresses areas such as poverty, unemployment and disease by means such as employment, public health and benefit measures. It can also employ social pedagogy, which makes use of measures and practices that are, in broad terms, both educational, often based on ideas of learning, and social, performed as they are on behalf of society, for the benefit of society as well as for the benefit of the individual as a member of society. The aim is often for 'social inclusion'.

Social inclusion is a difficult term; it is questionable that anyone living in a society can ever, in fact, be excluded from it. A description such as 'excluded from the advantages of society' seems to describe more appropriately the position of less powerful social groups. As discussed above, social meanings about people's status in society, and characteristics associated with that status, are conveyed through their relationships and interchanges with others. Social policy is political in its aims and social effects, intended and unintended, and develops out of the systems of power and control in a society. With cultural and economic factors, it contributes to the macrosystem and provides the context for the microsystem (see Bronfenbrenner, above), the level at which interpersonal communication takes place.

Social pedagogic theories arise out of political and economic systems, maintaining them or seeking to modify or reform them or, in the case of radical social pedagogy, to undermine them (see, for example, Sünker (2003) discussing social work, but using the term to apply equally to social pedagogy). These theories often address the balance between the power of the state and the autonomy of the individual. In turn, such theories affect the social pedagogy practice which contributes to the institutions that Goffman describes, the microsystems in Bronfenbrenner's terms. In the different service settings in which children and adults lead some, much or all of their lives, they learn who they are, and who they might be, in the social order, and they do so through interpersonal communication.

Another way of looking at this is that, at the level of the microsystem, the practice of social pedagogy is always, knowingly or otherwise, political. It either mediates or mitigates systems of power and the effects of these on both the individual person and on social groups (by which I mean social constructions based on characteristics such as disability, social class, gender and ethnicity). Today, in much of Europe, social pedagogy practice seeks to be emancipatory, rather than oppressive: empowering people, seeking the benefits of social participation for them and not keeping them 'in their place'. But whether emancipatory or otherwise, it can only achieve its ends via the relationships and interpersonal communication that are the foundation of the work.

The pedagogic relationship is both formed and expressed through interpersonal communication, often in a group context. Where there is a commitment to democracy and empowerment, an important pedagogic principle is that young people's associative life is a central resource and that the peer group has a positive value. Research (Cameron and Petrie 2007) has described the strong focus on group theory and processes in the education of pedagogues. Pedagogues usually work with and in groups of service users. They are trained to be conscious of the dynamics and conditions of group life, including the interpersonal communications which take place there. They also position themselves as members of the group, not as supervisors standing outside the children's experience. Inhabiting the same 'lifespace', children and pedagogues do not exist in separate hierarchical domains.

As noted earlier, effective communication is about achieving desired ends. If the aim is for the furtherance of democratic values in service settings and in the wider society, then the interpersonal communication which takes place there should itself be based on democratic principles. The recognition that the people with whom they work are different from themselves in many ways, yet of equal worth as fellow human beings, is important for social pedagogy as a democratic process. Democratic dialogue (see below) does not subjugate other perspectives, but allows them to be expressed and listens to them. In social pedagogic terms, acknowledging difference and seeking to understand 'where the other person is coming from' relates to a particular body of social pedagogic theory and practice. The German theoreticians Klaus Mollenhauer and Hans Thiersch (1986, 1992) developed theories such as *Alltagsorientierung* (an orientation towards everyday life) and *Lebensweltorientierung* (literally, living world orientation) (see Chapter 2). These take into account both the perspectives of the other person and the social, economic and political forces which – whether he or she is aware of them or not – impact on him or her in everyday lives. Understanding the world-view of service users and appreciating the validity of their decisions, and therefore respecting their social agency, are seen as parts of an emancipatory process.

Ideas of learning underlie much pedagogic practice and the professional education of pedagogues today. Most characteristically, the subject of social pedagogic learning is about life as a member of society, participating in its responsibilities and benefits, while at the same time being respected as an individual, with one's own social agency. Nor is this learning about social life seen as a matter of instruction about facts – what Paulo Freire, the Brazilian educationalist, called the banking model of learning in which the child is a receptacle for information, to be filled by the educator. Instead, he sees both as parties to pedagogic dialogue, both as simultaneously teachers and students, both as 'subjects' in the process, meeting in a cooperative endeavour, not with one aiming at the indoctrination and subjugation of the other (Freire 1972).

To sum up, in democratic social pedagogic settings, human beings are not to be forced to conform, and the interpersonal communication on which they are based both models and recognises this. Social pedagogues encourage these different perspectives to be expressed, so that the whole group can discover new solutions to intellectual, emotional and moral dilemmas together.

> The models and values upon which social pedagogy builds are those of democracy and citizenship with children and young people (Petrie 2010). Pedagogy is, after all, what Payne (2005) refers to as a 'reflexive' practice, in which all participants are seen as affecting each other and as affecting those processes in which they are jointly involved. (Petrie 2010, p.136)

Just as the service user is not seen as a receptacle for facts about the world, similarly the social pedagogue does not preach homilies about morals and 'right' attitudes. To do so would undermine the non-hierarchical, democratic aims of much of today's social pedagogy. Instead, learning is seen in terms of dialogue: interpersonal communication and meaning making, in which the pedagogue is on a journey with others, learning together: 'We make the road by walking...together' (Horton and Freire 1990). Dahlberg, Moss and Pence (2007, p.124) cite an influential document from the Swedish Childcare Commission: '[dialogue pedagogy] starts from the idea that there should be a continuous dialogue between the child and the adult, on both an inner and outer level, which implies a reciprocal giving and taking of emotions, experiences and knowledge' (SOU 1972, pp.26, 46).

Reciprocity is central to such ideas of dialogue in a democratic, pedagogic process and applies to the varied settings in which pedagogues work. The pedagogue is open to learning from the people with whom she works, sharing their perspectives and together constructing new meanings and knowledge. The quotation from the Swedish Childcare Commission also acknowledges that pedagogic dialogue is an encounter in which feelings as well as thoughts and perspectives are important. Being aware of another person's feelings gives the listener a glimpse of that person's perspective on life: how he or she feels and thinks about his or herself and circumstances.

The social pedagogue has to be a good listener, and this is a complex role (see also the discussion of listening in Chapter 9). A theoretical understanding of listening relevant to social pedagogy is of listening as an interpretive process (Bostrom 1997). A skilled listener actively supports the person to whom she is listening, perhaps by reflecting back what she has heard, or by encouraging words and body language, such as nods and smiles. In addition, a skilled listener, as well as comprehending the literal meanings conveyed by words, has to take into account the various visual and vocal cues of the other person, which may convey other or additional meanings and relate to unspoken feelings. In working in this way, pedagogues need to be aware of the part that their own feelings play in relating to others and in their communications with them.

On hearing someone else's story, a listener's own feelings may also be aroused, whether because what she is hearing resonates painfully with her own experience, or because the other person's understandings and values are very different from her own. Unless she is aware of her own feelings, this may diminish the social pedagogue's capacity to listen responsively to another person. In interpersonal communication terms, the listener's feelings are a source of 'interference' in the communication, blocking the messages which the other person is sending. Another way of thinking about this is that, without self-knowledge, a social pedagogue is less capable of accepting another person, his or her experience and perspectives on life:

> Danish [social pedagogy] students and others referred to
> the term *rummelighed*, (meaning literally space or capacity),
> which derives from psychoanalysis and relates to notions
> of containment. This term implies the capacity to accept
> others, because of self-knowledge, an awareness of one's
> own reactions, and the dimensions of one's own personality
> which may resonate with those of the other person... To have
> *rummelighed* implies being able to work with difference and the
> capacity to involve the self in the other's life (Jensen, 2000).
> (Petrie *et al.* 2006, p.24)

Rummelighed (discussed further in Chapter 6) has something in common
with the concepts of empathic understanding and unconditional positive
regard, as developed particularly by Carl Rogers and applied to the work
of the therapist who should take on:

> the internal frame of reference of the client, to perceive the
> world as a client sees it, to perceive the client himself as he is
> seen by himself, to lay aside all perceptions from the external
> frame of reference while doing so and so communicate
> something of this empathic understanding to the client.
> (Rogers 1951, p.29)

Just as it is for a Rogerian therapist, accepting the other person is
important for the pedagogue and the basis of the pedagogic relationship.
However, social pedagogy is not therapy. In many ways, a therapeutic
relationship differs from a pedagogic relationship. In part, this is because
the pedagogue and the child are, ideally, in dialogue, each contributing
to the construction of meaning as they make sense of life together. For
social pedagogues, the settings in which they work are 'living spaces',
with children and staff sharing each others' company on a democratic
footing. The medium for their relationship is everyday activities, not
a matter of following bureaucratic procedures on the one hand, nor a
problem-focused or 'therapeutic' relationship on the other. Everyday
activities – play, eating together, homework, creative activities and
holidays – are seen as meaningful, not routine. Such activities are often
referred to in Denmark as 'the common third', activities belonging to
both the pedagogue and the child; they are neither 'you' nor 'I' but, as it
were, a 'third party'.

The common third provides a mutual focus for the pedagogue and
child, or indeed a group consisting of pedagogue(s) and children,
together intent on the same task. Activities are the medium in which the

relationships between young people and between young people and their pedagogues are formed and the medium for dialogue. A further element is that engagement in the common third builds trust between pedagogues and children. This trust stems from children's experience of successfully engaging in activities, whether individually or as members of the group. It is trust that fosters children's self-confidence and feeling of being of value. Pedagogues accept children, valuing them as persons in their own right; they do not judge them solely on the basis of their performance, achievement or, indeed, behaviour in the course of any activity. In social pedagogy, being valued is viewed as important for all children and especially essential for work with those whose life circumstances have affected their confidence and self-esteem.

Reference to the common third raises the place of creative activities in the education and practice of social pedagogues. Research (e.g. Petrie *et al.* 2006) describes how, in many European countries, a substantial part of social pedagogy training is in areas such as music, drama, the visual arts, outdoor life and sport. In Denmark, alongside academic studies and practice placements, pedagogy students spend 25 per cent of their three-and-a-half-year course engaged in one creative field (see Petrie and Chambers (2010) for a fuller description and discussion). This participation in creative activities allows the pedagogues to make use of some of these participatory experiences in their work with children. First and foremost, pedagogues bring *themselves* to such activities, as well as being in a professional relationship, in which the pedagogue has certain responsibilities, understandings and skills.

Activities based on music, drama, theatre, the visual arts and other activities can sometimes provide the medium for the relationship between pedagogues and children and between children and each other. Seen as the common third, such creative activities can be means of enjoyment and of making friends, not just of talking about doing so. The spirit in which creative activities are approached by social pedagogues should be that of joint exploration, with interpersonal communication as dialogue, a dialogue which takes place through words, sounds, visual representation and actions. The 'hundred languages of children', a concept originating in Reggio Emilia (see Chapter 9), expresses the many forms of expression and communication available to children, but also to adults. At the outset, neither the pedagogue nor the children know in any detail how the activity will proceed nor what the outcome will be, but all contribute to it.

Creative activities may, at the same time, allow children to shape or 'realise' previously unexpressed experiences, both to make sense of these experiences for themselves and to express them to others. Drama, visual arts, song and singing are means by which children's voices are heard, whether about important and difficult matters or as a way of conveying their own particular perspectives on everyday life. They may also be safer ways of approaching difficult experience. The forms and boundaries of artistic activities and, sometimes, their less direct, more symbolic, communications can provide an element of personal distance, while still allowing people to express individual or group feelings and experience.

End thoughts

I started by asking how do social pedagogy and interpersonal communication link; what do they have to offer each other? Achieving effective interpersonal communication is not an end in itself, because judgements about whether communication is effective must always be in terms of the communicator's intentions and answer the question: does the communication further desired ends – in this case, social pedagogic ends?

As mentioned above, throughout its history and between different countries, social pedagogy has had various ends, and different judgements are to be made about the values on which these are based. Given oppressive social policies and/or unscrupulous professionals, effective communication skills can be used to manipulate feelings, indoctrinate beliefs and produce or confirm disadvantaged social status. In fact, manipulating others to behave in a democratic way could also be seen as oppressive, being somewhat contradictory in the clear mismatch between its means and ends. In any case, the democratic pedagogue cannot entirely escape the power relations inherent in interpersonal relations, particularly, perhaps, those involving children and young people and especially those children in difficult life circumstances. Nevertheless, pedagogues' education, and the personal and professional reflection (often in groups) characteristic of social pedagogy, should lead them to be aware of such imbalances and to guard against them.

The aims of social pedagogy are primarily about the pedagogue's own professional practice and how she seeks to relate to others. Social pedagogy, as described today (see other chapters in this book), is an ethical, rather than an instrumental practice. Given that they are skilled communicators, social pedagogues can only be effective communicators to the extent that they work in accordance with their own ethical framework. As a profession, they live and work alongside others – children and young people and adults – not as teachers or therapists, but in dialogic practice. It is this practice that both seeks and allows a deeper appreciation of other people's 'life-world' (*Lebensweltorientierung*): their perspectives, personal histories and the wider social forces which shape these.

Dialogic, democratic practice accepts the social agency, the actions and communications of others as arising from particular 'life-worlds'. Such pedagogic practice is prepared to challenge and to point out to others the possible outcomes of any particular action and to enter a dialogue about it. The pedagogue will also present other relevant perspectives – for example, the pedagogue's own views, those of peers, of a service provider, of the wider society. But, finally, the underlying pedagogic response is not to deny the other person's capacity for social agency: people are responsible for their own actions, for their own creativity, for their own ideas.

Such understandings, informed by democratic and emancipatory intentions, allow the social pedagogue to accept the people with whom she works, open-heartedly, respecting and supporting their autonomy and avoiding stereotyping or stigmatising them on whatever grounds. Goffman's 'Spoiled Identity' has no place in democratic social pedagogy and the interpersonal communication on which it is based.

References

Barnett Pearce, W. (2007) *Making Social Worlds: A Communication Perspective*. Oxford: Blackwell Publishing.

Bostrom, R.N. (1997) 'The Process of Listening.' In O. Hargie (ed.) *The Handbook of Communication Skills*. New York, NY: Routledge.

Bronfenbrenner, U. (1979) *The Ecology of Human Development: Experiments by Nature and Design*. Cambridge, MA: Harvard University Press.

Bronfenbrenner, U. and Morris, P.A. (1998) 'The Ecology of Developmental Processes.' In W. Damon (series ed.) and R.M. Lerner (volume ed.) *Handbook of Child Psychology: Vol. 1. Theoretical Models of Human Development*. New York, NY: Wiley.

Cameron, C. and Petrie, P. (2007) *Implementing the Social Pedagogic Approach for Workforce Training and Education in England*. Unpublished report to Department for Children, Schools and Families, London, Thomas Coram Research Unit.

Dahlberg, G., Moss, P. and Pence, A. (2007) *Beyond Quality in Early Childhood Education and Care: Languages of Evaluation* (2nd ed.). London: Routledge.

Freire, P. (1972) *Pedagogy of the Oppressed*. Harmondsworth: Penguin.

Goffman, I. (1968) *Stigma.* Harmondsworth: Penguin.

Hämäläinen, J. (2003) 'The concept of social pedagogy in the field of social work.' *Journal of Social Work 3*, 1, 69–80.

Hargie, O. and Dickinson, D. (2004) *Skilled Interpersonal Communication: Research, Theory and Practice* (4th ed.). Hove: Routledge.

Horton, M. and Freire, P. (1990) *We Make the Road by Walking: Conversations on Education and Social Change.* Philadelphia, PA: Temple University Press.

Jensen, J.J. (2000) *Social Pedagogy and Residential Care in Denmark.* Unpublished report for the Thomas Coram Research Unit, Institute of Education, University of London.

Payne, M. (2005) *Theories of Social Work* (3rd ed.). Basingstoke: Palgrave Macmillan.

Petrie, P. (2002) 'Social Pedagogy: An Historical Account of Care and Education as Social Control.' In J. Brannen and P. Moss (eds) *Rethinking Children's Care.* Buckingham: Open University Press.

Petrie, P. (2010) 'Children's Associative Spaces and Social Pedagogy.' In P. Foley and S. Leverett (eds) *Children and Young People's Spaces: Developing Practice.* Basingstoke: Palgrave Macmillan.

Petrie, P. and Chambers, C. (2010) *Richer Lives: Creative Activities in the Education and Practice of Danish Pedagogues: A Preliminary Study: Report to Arts Council England.* London: Institute of Education, Available at http://eprints.ioe.ac.uk/6415, accessed on April 2011.

Petrie, P., Boddy, J., Cameron, C., Simon, A. and Wigfall, V. (2006) *Working with Children in Residential Care: European Perspectives.* Buckingham: Open University Press.

Rogers, C.R. (1951) *Client-Centered Therapy.* London: Constable.

SOU (1972) *Förskolan del 1 och 2 (The Preschool, Volumes 1 and 2).* Stockholm: Allmänna Förlaget.

Sünker, H. and Otto, H.-U. (1997) *Education and Fascism.* London: Falmer Press.

Sünker, H. (2003) 'The Politics of Social Welfare: Critical Perspectives on Contemporary Social Work.' In H. Sünker, R. Farnen and G. Széll (eds) *Political Socialisation, Participation and Education.* Frankfurt am Main: Peter Lang.

Thiersch, H. (1986) *Die Erfahrung der Wirklichkeit.* Weinheim: Juventa.

Thiersch, H. (1992) *Lebensweltorientierte Soziale Arbeit: Aufgaben der Praxis im sozialen Wandel.* Weinheim: Juventa.

CHAPTER 5

Social Pedagogy as Relational Dialogic Work: Competencies in Modern Society

INGE M. BRYDERUP AND ANNA KATHRINE FRØRUP

Introduction

In this chapter we discuss the applicability of relational dialogic approaches in social pedagogical work for the purpose of acquiring competencies that are of use in modern society. A relational dialogic approach means that the relational work takes place in dialogue with another or others. We will take as our focus social pedagogical work carried out at residential childcare centres in Denmark. We examine Danish research, critique the approaches and thinking used in social pedagogic practice, particularly in relation to a major trend in modern society – that of individualisation – and question whether these approaches accommodate the demands for competencies in modern society marked by individualisation. But, first, it is necessary to understand the Danish context.

Understanding social pedagogy in a Danish context

There is relatively little specifically social pedagogic research in Denmark – that is, equating to what in England might be referred to as child welfare research. Most research about the placement of children and young people in care has had a focus on the placement itself (as an action) and not on the processes which take place during a stay at a residential care centre or on the everyday life and practice within these centres (Bryderup 2000; Egelund and Hestbæk 2004).

Regardless of how social pedagogy is approached, it is always defined within a context. It is founded on different historical conditions and situated within particular societal conditions, existing social problems and particular social policies (Bryderup 2005a). The history of child welfare cannot be separated from the history of society.

Three defining features of the Danish context must be outlined. First, one of the defining characteristics of the child welfare service in Denmark is that it is organised in one unity. In most other countries it is divided into two parts. One part is a welfare service that provides care and support to children and young people without parents or children who have been experiencing neglect or abuse. In English-speaking countries, such a service is often called 'child welfare' or 'child protection'. The other part is a *service* that consists of youth courts. In this type of provision, judges determine the conditions for young people with behavioural problems as well as those engaging in criminal behaviour. These judges also supervise the placement of young people at special residential care centres or in youth prisons in order to undergo punishment and education. For many years, children and young people have been placed under the same existing law and often at the same residential care centres irrespective of the reasons for them being placed in care.

Second, patterns of placements are very different in Denmark compared to other countries. For example, in Denmark more than half of young people in care are placed in residential care centres. In other countries, such as England and Sweden, around three quarters are placed in foster care.

Third, the education of those who work in Danish residential care centres is very different from other countries. Social pedagogy at residential care centres in Denmark is carried out by skilled workers with a bachelor's degree; in other countries this work is often carried out by unskilled workers who are supervised by one qualified social worker. Denmark has a strong social pedagogic tradition, while some other countries, such as Ireland, Portugal and Greece, can be characterised as being without such a tradition. The difficulties of European norms in the related field of social work education were raised by Lorenz (2001), and Kornbeck and Jensen (2009) similarly pointed to the diversity of social pedagogy in Europe at large.

Research contends that it is not possible to ascribe an original core or essence to social pedagogy (Bryderup 2005a; Erlandsen 2006; Hegstrup 2005; Madsen 2005; Schmidt 1999), and therefore it is difficult to write *the* history of social pedagogy, because it has developed in different directions. Moreover, it is difficult to give an exact definition of (Danish) social pedagogy.

From a theoretical and academic perspective, there are disagreements regarding the definition of the concept, as well as how to use and understand the term social pedagogy. Examining its history, Grue-Sørensen (1975) asks what social pedagogy is: is it a pedagogical approach or method? Or an opinion or an orientation based on certain values? Or a specific pedagogical field? Grue-Sørensen does not answer the question but rather gives examples of all three approaches from social pedagogical praxis in the 1960s and early 1970s (Grue-Sørensen 1975). Other researchers argue that two historical traditions and discussions can be identified within social pedagogical praxis and research in Denmark. These follow either a narrow or a broad tradition (Madsen and Perthou 2002; Schmidt 1999; Bryderup). The *narrow tradition* springs from social policy and is inspired by Herman Nohl and Gertrud Bäumer (Holst and Madsen 1998). From this perspective, social pedagogy relates to the social and to situations of social concern. The focus is on social conflicts and social problems. In this tradition, social pedagogy is defined in terms of the distinction between normality and deviation from this normality.

The *broad tradition* comes from general pedagogy and is inspired by Paul Natorp (Holst and Madsen 1998). From this perspective, social pedagogy is about socialisation and the development processes of all social individuals within several fields: school, pre-school, the family and social work (Madsen 2005; Mathiesen 2000; Schmidt 1999).

The *narrow tradition* deals with the question of the 'social' and considers the concept of social pedagogy as a pedagogical field that involves working with a specific target group. This work is carried out with the aim of solving social problems and, according to the perspective of Grue Sørensen (1975), this can be considered as being 'a specific pedagogical field'. The *broad tradition*, however, considers the concept of social pedagogy as orientation, where it is the core of any pedagogical activity aimed at all children and not only children with special needs and social problems. According to Grue Sørensen this tradition can be considered as being 'a pedagogical approach or method and an orientation based on certain values'.

In Denmark, the narrow concept appears to have a longer history and is still the most commonly used concept among pedagogues. The broad tradition, however, belongs to discussions and praxis which took place in the 1960s and 1970s. Having said this, the use of the narrow concept only answers the question 'What is social pedagogy?' up to a point. A more fruitful question might be: what ingredients and processes are part of social pedagogy and how can these be analysed?

Analysis requires a choice of methods that is suitable for the topic under study. The complexity of social pedagogy is such that research methods with a focus on 'what works',[1] that establish targets or objectives for treatment and practice, are unsuitable (Bryderup 2005b, 2008b; Madsen 2005; Schwartz 2001) because in social pedagogy many correlations and problems come into play, creating opposites and conflicts. According to Schwartz (2001), social pedagogical methods and approaches are constructed in the specific context of the everyday organisation and relational work which takes place with the children.

Given these considerations, it is difficult to find unambiguous and generally agreed definitions of the characteristic practices and ways of thinking that define the social pedagogue profession, even from a national perspective. Nevertheless, the question about what social pedagogy is can be answered in another way. This way involves describing and analysing: a) the target group, b) the aims of social pedagogy and c) its methods. Furthermore, it can involve analysing the strategies and ways of thinking that are reflected in a combination in these three elements. We will now look more closely at this way of answering the question.

Approaches and educational thinking in social pedagogy

Current Danish legislation relates to individuals whose needs require the use of 'special provisions' in order that those needs are met so as to give them the same opportunities for personal development and growth as their peers.

Understandings of children and young people's special needs are usually based on descriptions of the target group and are rooted in the definition of tasks within particular residential care centres (Bryderup 2004, 2005a, 2005b). Concrete descriptions of tasks in such centres are often based on the needs of the target group or on the actual aim of the intervention – or on both. The task is defined as social pedagogy and includes such elements as methods, content, activities, setting and so on. These elements and relations are illustrated in the following figure.

---

1   *What works* refers to an agenda subscribed to the use of different types of (quantitative) methods to systematise knowledge and/or measure effects of interventions (e.g. evidence-based knowledge, randomised controlled trial (RCT), etc.).

SOCIAL PEDAGOGIC APPROACH

– approaches, methods, content, activities, setting, etc.

TARGET GROUP   AIM

(special needs/potential)   (competence in modern society)

LEARNING PROCESSES OF CHILDREN AND YOUNG PEOPLE

Figure 5.1 The relationship between target group and pedagogical aims

Figure 5.1 is an analytic model that illustrates a process which links the conception of the target group with the aim of the social pedagogical approach, which is to give the young person the skills, or competencies, to live in modern society. This linkage, in turn, evolves simultaneously and in accordance with the learning processes of children and young people. As a result, the social pedagogical approach is conceived as synthesising an understanding of the target group's needs and the aim of the intervention. Perspectives on the person's or the group's past and their likely future, therefore, form part of the present social pedagogy intervention.

This figure can be used to analyse the question of how different residential care centres and approaches integrate the three elements of the target group, the aim and the learning process, and how this integration is reflected in their social pedagogical methods.

The target group: Views on children and young people in care

As noted above, Danish legislation views children and young people in care as in need of special provisions; their needs must be met in order to function effectively in social and educational contexts. Social pedagogic institutions, or other kinds of special provision, are intended to compensate for troubled backgrounds and inadequate learning conditions in such a way as to afford these children and young people the same opportunities as their peers regarding personal development and growth. Special needs are thus viewed as various forms of 'deficiencies' that must be compensated for through the use of special provisions. Legislation specifies the requirements for such special provisions, namely that they must be based on individual assessment and planning. The individual is conceived as a carrier of needs or characteristics that are seen as more or less static.

The same view pervades the literature on this issue (Bryderup 2005b; Killen 1993). The focus is on the child as a bearer of problems in the form of psychological defects. Such a view results from a diagnostic description of the problem and of its causes, which can be traced back to the family. It is important to ask: What are the consequences of this view and what difference does it make to think in terms of potentials and resources?

Personal development is characterised by increased choice and possibilities for action and is determined by an individual's participation in specific social and cultural contexts (Bryderup 2004, 2005a, 2005b). Development cannot be reduced to a question of upbringing or personal traits and instead must be related to concepts such as competence and potential. Linking development to competence facilitates the identification of two related processes. If a planned developmental process rests solely on the (usually troubled) background of children and young people, learning and development is not likely to take place. If, on the other hand, the developmental process takes as its point of departure children's potential, it can be argued that they will develop new competencies as a result of social interaction with social pedagogues. Such interaction should provide space where the actual possibilities contained in their potential can be realised through communication and cooperation. Potential is, therefore, a socially determined developmental phenomenon that can only be recognised and described through nurturing and communicative processes (Bryderup 2004; Bryderup et al. 2002). The desire to find this potential must already lie at the heart of the view of the target group's situation, background and reactions, and, as such, at the heart of the social pedagogical approach.

Several studies show that social pedagogues in residential care centres focus on the personal, social and learning difficulties of the target group (Bryderup 2004, 2005b; Bryderup, Madsen and Perthou 2001; Bryderup et al. 2002). The focus is usually placed on individual and personal problems, which are often described in terms that range from psychiatric diagnoses, such as personality disorders, ADHD (attention deficit and hyperactivity disorder) and Asperger's syndrome, to more mundane expressions such as lack of concentration, confusion, frustration, identity weakness, uneasiness and so on.

Furthermore, social pedagogues in residential care often focus on young people's lack of social skills. For instance, they use expressions such as lack of empathy, selfishness and anti-social attitudes. These 'lacks' are viewed as the result of children and young people's personal and emotional problems or are ascribed directly to their troubled backgrounds. An example is that some of the children are described as coming from resource-weak or ruptured families or as having been exposed to adult neglect in their upbringing (Bryderup and Andsager 2006).

Staff in these centres often ascribe the difficulties these children and young people experience to their troubled backgrounds and various labels are attached: concepts such as 'neglect' and 'early trauma' are common. There is a widespread tendency to focus on the problems and deficiencies of individuals who attend special provision such as social pedagogic institutions due to their special needs.

Social pedagogy approaches: Compensatory vs prospective orientation

Research shows that educational thinking and social pedagogical practice can emphasise an understanding of the target group's needs and thus social pedagogy is viewed as a compensatory device for deficiencies (Bryderup 2004, 2005b; Bryderup *et al.* 2002). In such a *compensatory* approach, the emphasis is on individual deficiencies and troubled backgrounds and the social pedagogic task is to compensate for these deficiencies (Bryderup 2004). The approach results from a *focus on the past*, which has led to shortcomings in children and young people's backgrounds becoming the subject of social pedagogy. One example of a compensatory approach is to give the child in question the opportunity of experiencing success to compensate for low self-esteem. Another example of compensatory thinking, targeted at remedying a child's previous life experience, is to describe the child's background in terms of adult neglect and then to define the social pedagogic solution as providing stable adult relationships.

If, however, the focus is placed on the aim of the social pedagogical intervention (see Figure 5.1), the result is a prospective orientation that mainly relates to children's personal and cognitive development.

The focus of this broader perspective is *on the future*, with the aim of empowering children and young people to achieve autonomy and enjoy a high quality of life as adults. The social pedagogic answer to such aims is often normative,[2] based on a preconceived notion of what might constitute a high quality of life for these children and young people. Is it the ability to enjoy a trip to the cinema or to learn to prepare a healthy meal? Is it earning vast amounts of money and having wild parties every weekend? Or is it starting a nuclear family where the young person first needs to acquire the practices of 'normal' family life?

The formulation of these aims is more or less concrete, and they may assist in understanding children and young people's needs or cast doubt on the possibility of their attainment. For instance, learning to go to the cinema and to prepare a healthy meal can be difficult if you are unable to read subtitles and recipes. In this case, learning to read must be part of the intervention. In other words, social pedagogical approaches synthesise an understanding of the target group and the aims of the intervention where the past, present and future merge together.

Social pedagogy, linked to compensatory thinking, may result in the aim of the intervention becoming itself compensatory – that is, where only the present and the past are taken into consideration. One example is a view of children and young people as having had an upbringing characterised by adult neglect. The social pedagogical solution to this problem is, as mentioned above, the provision of stable adult relationships. The content of the approach can become an aim in itself, namely for children and young people to feel safe and learn to trust adults. Neglecting to formulate prospective aims may obstruct a process where the children and young person's present developmental needs can find concrete expression in relation to their future options (Bryderup 2004). We would argue, therefore, that the 'ideal' social pedagogical intervention consists of formulating future goals in collaboration with children and young people, and formulating the approach in such a way as to connect the past, the present and the future.

---

2   Normative here means that norms and values form part of the formulation of the aim of an educational intervention. This may occur either at an institutional level, where a certain educational approach is chosen, or it may occur at an individual staff level, where social educators more or less consciously impose their own norms and values on children or young people. The concept of relational education is fundamentally based on the individual social educators' normative conceptions (Bryderup 1999a, 1999b).

Approaches and educational strategies in social pedagogy

Different approaches or methods in social pedagogy are based on implicit views of the target group and views regarding the social pedagogy intervention. Here we outline some examples of such differing social pedagogic approaches.

In the literature on the subject, *milieu or environmental therapy* is described as a form of treatment that encompasses all aspects of children and young people's lives in residential care centres, since both planned and informal situations form part of treatment. This form of treatment includes a number of established methods, all of which build on an implicit instrumental rationality (Bryderup and Andsager 2006; Kvaran 1996; Rasborg 2005). The educational approach used focuses on the personality/psychological/emotional life of the target group, all of which are traced back to certain aspects of their upbringing. In other words, there is a focus on the past and the present emotional life situation.

An example of such an approach could be the daily activity of meals because they provide the possibility to work with group dynamics and being together. Meal times yield insights into the problems and thoughts of the children or young people. Observing and analysing the way they eat and how they experience the food, as well as the eating situation, is one way social pedagogues use everyday situations and activities to intervene and handle the problems of children and young people.

To a large extent, the same kind of instrumental rationality characterises the approach of *structured social pedagogy*. This approach begins with the notion that the inner life of a child, who has been damaged early in life, is characterised by psychic chaos and fundamental psychological damage to such a degree that he or she is dependent on external control in the form of many clear rules, structures and adult presence (Schwartz 2001). Structured social pedagogy focuses on the background of each individual in the target group as well as on his or her personality/psychology/emotional life. Nevertheless, in its social pedagogic practice, it focuses also on aspects relating to behaviour, that is to say rules, structures and adult control, in order to provide a social pedagogical intervention.

The everyday life of children and young people within a structured social pedagogy approach is dictated by structure, regulations and rules defined by social pedagogues. Everyday activities are scheduled and need to be followed; otherwise, different kinds of sanctions are imposed. Examples of such sanctions would be suspension of free time such as playing time, sports or other activities of great value to the children or young people.

Social pedagogy with a focus on relations and dialogue is built on a close relationship between the child and professional social pedagogue. Here, the approach is founded on an individual and differentiated view of a particular child and young person's background and difficulties, and the social pedagogic intervention seeks to compensate for this by means of the relationship. Research shows that the content of the approach – that is, building close relationships – often becomes an aim in itself, namely for children and young people who are viewed as persons who need to learn to trust adults (Bryderup 1999a, 1999b). Such an approach is explicitly based on both the background of the target group and their personality/psychology/emotional life, and the social pedagogic 'solution' is the establishment of relationships with social pedagogues. All this happens through dialogue.

The special needs of the target group can thus be viewed in various ways and on different levels which has a bearing on both the social pedagogical 'solutions' and asserted aims. At times this influence can even occur in the reverse sequence, where the choice of social pedagogy approach fundamentally affects the view of the target group's special needs (Bryderup and Andsager 2006).

Studies show that the social pedagogical approach that focuses on relations and dialogue, with its compensatory thinking, dominates Danish residential care centres (Bryderup 2004, 2005a; Bryderup et al. 2001, 2002). It is thought of as the solution to children and young people's problems and troubled backgrounds. And it tends to focus on backgrounds and difficulties – that is, on the past, rather than on the competencies needed to develop to function successfully in the future.

The same research reveals that social pedagogues in residential care centres with a focus on relational dialogic work describe the aim of the intervention mainly at an individual level, paying particular attention to the development of personal and social skills. Attempts to integrate the young people into society are often described in general and rather abstract terms such as 'normal and ordinary', 'citizenship' or 'the ability to lead an autonomous existence'. A further characteristic in the research is that the aims are rarely integrated into the social pedagogical approach and view of the target group. The children's past tends to be ascribed significant importance in conceptions of the social pedagogic aim at the expense of a prospective orientation. Again, the focus is on problems and deficiencies caused by past adult neglect and broken relationships, rather than on acquiring new competencies (Bryderup 2010).

This view of the target group has consequences for children and young people's development and learning conditions. Traditionally, the concept of integration has played an important role in discussions about how it is possible for children and young people in care to obtain developmental conditions that correspond to those of their peers of the same age.

In the next section we will look more closely at a number of tendencies in modern society in order to clarify the competencies that enable young people to take part in society.

Competencies in modern society

The societal task of social pedagogy has often been defined as a strategy that is used to contribute to marginalised groups' integration in society (Bryderup 2003). In order to navigate in a modern society, the individual has to regard him or herself as an agent and take responsibility for his or her own life. The task is to find opportunities that can contribute to lifelong learning. Hence, successful integration means that the individual is enabled to lead an ordinary life.

Anthony Giddens (1990) and Ulrich Beck (1992) highlight individualisation and increased reflexivity as significant aspects of modern society and, therefore, it is seen as necessary to develop these competencies in order to take part in a modern society. Giddens's concept of reflexivity concentrates on the individual's reflection and focuses on cognitive development, while Beck's consideration is primarily linked to reflexive action in the sense that the individual must constantly respond to him or herself and at the same time respond to others' perceptions of him or her.

Ziehe and Stubenrauch (1983) argue that in modern society an upbringing is linked to subjective examination and testing processes that are dominated by diversity and ambivalence. They regard education as a process that is incorporated into the societal processes of modernity. Pedagogy and learning are characterised as the tools for these societal processes of modernity.

Integration endeavours to create conditions conducive to the development of marginalised groups by integrating them into the normal contexts of life. Integration has been associated with normalising the living conditions of marginalised groups and giving them access to the resources characterising ordinary life. From this perspective, residential care centres have the task of providing normal conditions for learning and development, in spite of young people's individual difficulties. The purpose of social pedagogy is closely related to normalisation because it is described as adapting individuals or groups to society's norms and rules. The task of social pedagogy has as its starting point contributing to society's stability. The ideal is a coherent and homogeneous society, but also a society that is marked by an agenda of individual choice and decision making.

Societal and social policy changes can be summed up by the concepts of individualisation and tendencies towards holding families responsible (Bryderup 2007a, 2007b, 2008a, 2010). It is largely the family's own task to participate actively in the state's different forms of control mechanisms through involvement in contracts, injunctions and sanctions as well as being part of problem solving (Bryderup 2010). When social policy turns its gaze to the individual and the family's internal social relations, the result is a focus on the children and young people's reactions, behaviour and development. Such a focus can be explained by two types of individualisation:

1. Individualisation as a result of modernity where the individual no longer has any tradition to rely on, which results in everybody assuming an individual responsibility to choose and act.

2. Individualisation caused by social policy, containing new institutional demands, forms of control and hindrances. At the same time all states – also the so-called welfare states – set demands on their citizens to lead and control their own lives.

The first type of individualisation relates to general societal tendencies that are placing individuals in a different situation from in the past. In the past, the individual's life was largely determined by clearly marked cultural, employment and social reference points and adherence to preordained social categories. In current times, however, there are many opportunities at the disposal of individuals which place them in a new position of being required to make life choices. Reflexivity is increased with the possibility of choosing a life pathway, as the individual assumes a responsibility to independently decide and act upon the possibilities that are in place. In order to be able to live in a modern society, the individual must see him or herself as an agent of his or her own life. The key concepts here are reflexivity and personal responsibility, described by (among others) the sociologists Ulrich Beck (1992; Beck and

Beck-Gernsheim 2002a, 2002b); Anthony Giddens (1984, 1990, 1991); and Zygmunt Bauman (2000, 2001).

Hermann Giesecke (1985, 1998) argues that *all* children and young people in the Western world grow up in a pluralistic society. These children and young people are educated not only within their families but also in other institutions such as day care centres and schools, as well as by the media and their peers. Society is divided into different areas, each with diverse and divergent values. All the things that children need to learn in their present and future life cannot be taught in one place. Knowledge and rules for behaviour cannot be transferred from one place to another. According to Giesecke, such a background paves the way for discussions regarding individualisation. In his view, no clear-cut educational practice can be found that relates to the whole person. In a pluralistic society, the responsibility for the development of values and norms is largely an individual project. As a result, individuals must create meaning in their own lives and find their own values.

This diversity of opportunities and lack of traditions to adhere to can, on the one hand, be seen as opening and creating opportunities. On the other hand, it can also be experienced as restraining and creating insecurity because it is the individual who has to take chances and navigate through life without being guided by any traditions. These tendencies, with their twofold individualisation, are captured well in Beck and Beck-Gernsheim's words: *risky freedoms* (2002b).

In a highly individualised society, integration also gives individuals access to vital resources and independent choices. Conditions around integration in individualised society have changed critically with respect to *the social* (Beck and Beck-Gernsheim 2002b; Satka 1995; Skehill 2004). The result is that a development of the capacity to participate in social communities has to come on to the agenda in an actual discussion of social work in order to integrate marginalised and individualised children and young people (Bryderup 2010).

The social aspect should become internalised and form part of an identity, although the individual remains distinctive. Individualisation is, therefore, the story of children and young people loosening the hold of traditional social and institutional communities, but simultaneously extending those social networks and communities which support their choices and actions. Such a process ensures the development of an identity that is integrated into society and one which continuously gives the child or young person the opportunity to participate and gain access to vital resources.

The second type of individualisation relates to the political arena and also the social political arena. An individualisation has emerged that consists of new institutional demands or ways of exercising power and control. These new institutional demands are exercised through contracts and by specifying goals. A case in point is the implementation of rules regarding individual evaluations and action plans for children and young people, which are required in residential care centres. These plans increasingly contain a justification for the choice of particular goals and the resultant outcome of each type of intervention (Bryderup 2005a, 2007a).

These changed societal and social political conditions position the individual in a fundamentally different situation. Coinciding with the breakdown of traditions has been a loss of fixed outer poles of orientation and horizons of meanings, against which individuals can understand themselves and evolve in their own lives. Young people have no set traditions but assume a responsibility for choice and action in their own lives, which can be problematic and demanding.

Beck's focus on constructing an individual biography (Beck 1992) is in line with a critical approach to relational thinking. Accordingly, this approach can ensure children and young people's participation in social and societal communities. Beck emphasises the tendency towards an individualisation of social risks on two levels: where a) social problems are perceived in terms of psychological dispositions; and b) social crises appear as individual crises connected to traits such as disabilities considered as being independent of social identification (Beck 1992).

Following this argument, the competencies demanded in modernity can be characterised as:

- responsibility for one's own learning across the lifespan

- individual learning in collective communities

- one's own responsibility to develop identity, social relations and network

- one's own responsibility to develop self-esteem, continuity and meaningfulness

- continual reflection upon one's own situation (past, present, future)

- social and capability mobility

- on-going social, cultural and societal integration.

Thus, the competence of social pedagogues focuses on these requirements of modernity: lifelong learning, individual learning in collective (life-) community, the development of self-esteem, continuity and meaningfulness, the ability to reflect, social and capability mobility and on-going social, cultural and societal integration. We will shed further light on these competencies in the next section.

Perspectives on relational thinking vs competencies in modernity

The objective in this section is to discuss the applicability of the relational dialogic approach in social pedagogical work to the acquisition of competencies which children and young people in residential care centres can use in modern society.

The relational dialogic and compensatory approach contributes on the one hand to the development of social relations. The purpose of establishing this relationship and taking part in dialogue is to prepare the young person to take part in social communities. But it also enhances the development of an asymmetrical relationship. In other words, the relationship is not based on the child or young person's reflexion on his or her own situation and does not take its point of departure in his or her potential; it is based instead on a preconceived notion of quality of life, for example. This orientation has a focus on the past and the future but not on the present situation or potential.

According to this perspective, relational dialogic thinking does not directly correspond to the competencies demanded in modern society, because developing responsibility with a lifelong and prospective orientation is about seeking out and finding openings for oneself. In other words, such responsibility creates openings that can contribute to one's future life, lifelong learning and building up a biography of life. The key word is reflexivity: the ability to reflect and take the past, present and future into account.

This prospective orientation diverges from the normative orientation that characterises the relational dialogic approach, based on a preconceived notion of what might constitute a high quality of life for children and young people. It not only weakens the development of social skills through children and young people's mutual relations, but it also weakens the possibility of development of these relationships within a network. Furthermore, it weakens the possibility of developing competencies aimed at future participation in the social and societal communities found in the 'real' world. A number of consequences ensue, which impact on the formulation of legislation seeking to prepare young people for an autonomous existence in the educational system and on the labour market. This group of children and young people lack the necessary social skills to function in a modern society on equal terms with their peers. They also lack the necessary social and cultural skills to be integrated into society.

We strongly refute the claim that it is more difficult for so-called marginalised children and young people to make choices, take chances and test their grounds. Instead, we propose that a focus should be directed towards increasing resources that will enhance their capacity to choose and towards setting up or developing networks supporting these choices. And it is important to consider what resources and learning environments, including stable settings and networks, constitute the prerequisite for developing the capacity to reflect and make choices at the expense of anxiety (Giddens 1991).

There is, in short, a need for social pedagogical approaches that emphasise participating in social communities as a group member rather than those focusing solely on a one-to-one relationship with social pedagogues. This need arises from the demand of being able to reflect on and take into account the past, present and future in order to create and develop mobility regarding networks and social communities.

The social pedagogic intervention may thus be clarified by formulating future goals in collaboration with children and young people. Furthermore, the social aspect should largely become internalised within social pedagogical approaches. Interventions supporting the choices and actions of marginalised and disadvantaged children and young people and their capacity to participate in social communities have to be brought on to the agenda in social pedagogical approaches which aim to integrate them into society.

A pedagogy of past, present and future: Concluding thoughts

In this chapter we have demonstrated that social pedagogical approaches tend to focus on children and young people's backgrounds and difficulties – that is, on the past, rather than on the competencies they need to develop to function successfully in the future. To focus on the past, present and the future calls for an approach that simultaneously combines these three orientations. Such an approach could include: a focus on background and past difficulties; a focus on the present potential of the children or young people according to their reflection on their opportunities (to be able to choose, make decisions, create meaning and find one's own values in life); and a focus on (developing) competencies in order to participate fully in society and function successfully in their future lives.

In summary, we conclude that competencies in modern society and the social aspect should largely become internalised within social pedagogical approaches. The capacity for socially disadvantaged children and young people to participate in social communities has to come on to the agenda in an actual discussion of social pedagogy to ensure that they are integrated into, rather than marginalised from, modern society.

References

Bauman, Z. (2000) *Liquid Modernity*. Cambridge: Polity Press.

Bauman, Z. (2001) *The Individualized Society*. Cambridge: Polity Press.

Beck, U. (1992) *Risk Society: Towards a New Modernity*. London: Sage.

Beck, U. and Beck-Gernsheim, E. (2002a) 'Individualisering i moderne samfund – en subjektorienteret sociologis perspektiver og kontroverser' ['Individualization in modern society – perspectives and controversies of a subject-oriented sociology']. *SLAGMARK nr. 34*.

Beck, U. and Beck-Gernsheim, E. (2002b) *Individualization: Institutionalized Individualism and Its Social and Political Consequences*. London: Sage.

Bryderup, I.M. (1999a) *Drop Afmagten – socialpædagogisk arbejde, De Unges Hus, Roskilde Amt [Quit powerlessness – Social pedagogy, The Youngsters House, Roskilde County]*. København: Danmarks Pædagogiske Institut.

Bryderup, I.M. (1999b) *Forskning I socialpædagogisk arbejde med unge [Research in Social Pedagogical Work with Young People]*. In *Tidsskrift for Social Pædagogik, nr. 3*.

Bryderup, I.M. (2000) 'Socialpædagogikken – et forskningstyndt område' ['Social Pedagogy – an area of insufficient research']. In *Danmarks Pædagogiske Institut 2000*. København: Danmarks Pædagogiske Institut.

Bryderup, I.M. (2003) 'Pædagogisk sociologi – forholdet mellem individ og samfund' ['Educational Sociology – the relationship between individual and society']. In I.M. Bryderup (ed.) *Pædagogisk sociologi – en antologi*. København: Danmarks Pædagogiske Universitets Forlag.

Bryderup, I.M. (2004) 'The educational principles of social education and special education for children and youngsters in care – a Danish study.' *Young, Nordic Journal of Youth Research 4, 3, 337–356*.

Bryderup, I.M. (2005a) *Børnelove og socialpædagogik gennem hundrede år [Child Act and Social Pedagogy through one hundred years]*. Århus: Forlaget Klim.

Bryderup, I.M. (2005b) 'Beskrivelser af socialpædagogisk arbejde – et dokumentationsprojekt' ['Descriptions of Social Pedagogical Work – A Documentation Project']. In I.M. Bryderup (ed.) *Socialpædagogisk arbejde med børn og unge*. København: Socialpædagogernes Landsforbund.

Bryderup, I.M. (2007a) 'Socialpolitikkens indflydelse på socialpædagogikkens udvikling – fra tvangsfjernelser til kontraktstyring' ['The influence of social policy on the development of social pedagogy – from removal to contract management']. In K. Jensen and N.R. Jensen (eds) *Staten og den institutionelle pædagogik, Pædagogisk Sociologi*, bind 1. København: Danmarks Pædagogiske Universitetsforlag.

Bryderup, I.M. (2007b) 'Kvalitet i indsatsen over for socialt udsatte børn og unge – et historisk blik på normativitet i socialpolitik og forskning' ['Quality in Intervention of Marginalised Children and Young People – A Historical Perspective on Normativity in Social Policy and Research']. In *Social Årsrapport 2007 Kvalitet i den offentlige sektor*. København: CASA.

Bryderup, I.M. (2008a) 'Socialpolitik, socialforskning og socialpædagogik' ['Social Policy, Social Research and Social Pedagogy']. In I.M. Bryderup (ed.) *Aktuelle udfordringer i socialpædagogikken*. København: Danmarks Pædagogiske Universitetsforlag.

Bryderup, I.M. (ed.) (2008b) *Evidence Based and Knowledge Based Social Work*. Århus: Aarhus Universitetsforlag.

Bryderup, I.M. (2010) *Ungdomskriminalitet, socialpolitik og socialpædagogik. Biografiske interview med unge om straf og behandling [Youth Crime, social policy and social pedagogy. Biographical interviews with young people about punishment and treatment]*. Århus: Forlaget Klim.

Bryderup, I.M. and Andsager, G. (2006) *Skolegang for anbragte børn og unge [Schooling for Children at Residential Care Centres]*. København: Danmarks Pædagogiske Universitets Forlag.

Bryderup, I.M., Madsen, B. and Perthou, A.S. (2001) *Specialundervisning på anbringelsessteder og dagbehandlingstilbud [Special Education at Residential Care Centres and Day Care Centres]*. København: Danmarks Pædagogiske Institut.

Bryderup, I.M., Madsen, B. and Perthou, A.S. (2002) *Specialundervisning på anbringelsessteder og dagbehandlingstilbud – en undersøgelse af pædagogiske processer og samarbejdsformer [Special Education at Residential Care Centres and Day Care Centres – A Study in Pedagogical Processes and Forms of Collaboration]*. København: Danmarks Pædagogiske Universitet.

Egelund, T. and Hestbæk, A.D. (2004) *Anbringelse af børn og unge uden for hjemmet. En forskningsoversigt [Placement of children and young people outside home – a research review]*. København: Socialforskningsinstituttet.

Erlandsen, T. (2006) 'Hvem navngav "socialpædagogerne" i Danmark' ['Who named "the Social Pedagogues" in Denmark']. *Tidsskrift for Socialpædagogik nr. 17*.

Giddens, A. (1984) *The Constitution of Society*. London: Polity Press.

Giddens, A. (1990) *The Consequences of Modernity*. Cambridge: Polity Press.

Giddens, A. (1991) *Modernity and Self-Identity – Self and Society in the Late Modern Age*. Cambridge: Polity Press.

Giesecke, H. (1985) *Das Ende der Erziehung*. Stuttgart: Klett-Cotta.

Giesecke, H. (1998) 'Socialpædagogik og skolen' ['Social pedagogy and the school']. *Tidsskrift for Socialpædagogik nr. 1.*

Grue-Sørensen, K. (1975) *Almen pædagogik – En håndbog i de pædagogiske grundbegreber [General pedagogy – a handbook in the basic concepts of pedagogy]*. København: Gjellerup.

Hegstrup, S. (2005) 'Socialpædagogikkens forsvinden og mulige genkomst' ['The disappearance and possible reappearance of social pedagogy']. *Tidsskrift for Socialpædagogik nr. 16.*

Holst, J. and Madsen, B. (1998) 'Socialpædagogik og det senmoderne' ['Social pedagogy and late modernity']. *Tidsskrift for Socialpædagogik nr. 2.*

Killen, K. (1993) *Omsorgssvigt er alles ansvar [Neglect is Everybody's Responsibility]*. København: Hans Reitzels Forlag.

Kornbeck, J. and Jensen, N.R. (eds) (2009) *The Diversity of Social Pedagogy in Europe*. Bremen: Europäischer Hochschulverlag.

Kvaran, I. (1996) *Institusjonsarbeid med barn og ungdom [Institutional Work with Children and Young People]*. Kristiansand: HøyskoleForlaget.

Lorenz, W. (2001) 'Social Work in Europe – A Portrait of a Diverse Group.' In S. Hessle (ed.) *International Standard-Setting of Higher Social Work Education*. Stockholm: Stockholm University, Stockholm Studies in Social Work, bd. 17.

Madsen, B. (2005) *Socialpædagogik – integration og inklusion i det moderne samfund [Social Pedagogy – Integration and Inclusion in Modern Society]*. København: Hans Reitzels Forlag.

Mathiesen, R. (2000) *Sosialpedagogisk perspektiv [The Perspective of Social Pedagogy]*. Hamar/Norge: Sokrates AS.

Rasborg, L. (2005) *Miljøterapi med børn og unge [Environmental Therapy with Children and Young People]*. København: Akademisk Forla.

Satka, M. (1995) *Making Social Citizenship: Conceptual Practices from the Finnish Poor Law to Professional Social Work*. Jyväskyla: Jyväskyla University Printing House.

Skehill, C. (2004) *History of the Present of Child Protection and Welfare: Social Work in Ireland*. Ireland: Edwin Mellen Press.

Schmidt, L.-H. (1999) 'Socialpædagogikkens genkomst' ['The Reappearance of Social Pedagogy']. In *Diagnosis III*. København: Danmarks Pædagogiske Institut.

Schwartz, I. (2001) *Socialpædagogik og anbragte børn [Social Pedagogy and Placed Children]*. København: Hans Reitzels Forlag.

Ziehe, T. and Stubenrauch, H. (1983) *Ny ungdom og usædvanlige læreprocesser [Plädoyer für ungewöhnliches Lernen] [Modern Youth and Unusual Learning Processes]*. København: Politisk Revy.

CHAPTER 6

The Supportive Relationship in 'Public Care': The Relevance of Social Pedagogy

Janet Boddy

What care in 'public care'?

The word 'care' – as it is used to describe provision for children looked after away from home – implies the centrality of the relationship between 'carer' and child. But what does this mean? Are relationships the central feature of care for looked after children? Should they be? And what *sort* of relationships should they be?

These questions are both practical and conceptual, underpinned by fundamental considerations about the importance of supportive relationships for the upbringing of children and young people in 'public care'. Social pedagogy, as a theoretical and professional approach to work with children, offers a conceptual framework that provides rich possibilities for reflecting on the nature of the supportive relationship between carer and child. A substantial body of research highlights the importance of relationships with carers, for children who are separated from their families (e.g. Bullock *et al.* 2006; Gilligan 2007; Sinclair, Wilson and Gibbs 2005a). In England, however, training for work in residential or foster care is not, fundamentally, an education in work with relationships; rather, it has tended to be focused on practical competencies (Cameron and Boddy 2006). Social pedagogy is of interest in this context as a theoretical discipline – and professional qualification – for work with, and through, relationships (Boddy, Cameron and Petrie 2006). In this chapter, I examine this approach and some key parts of its conceptual framework, and consider why a social pedagogic approach is so well suited to meeting the often complex relational needs of children and young people in 'public care'.

The importance of relationships: Attachment theory

Interest in the importance of relationships for the well-being and development of children in care has been strongly influenced by John Bowlby's attachment theory. First set out in his 1951 monograph for the World Health Organization (Bowlby 1951), the theory posits that the primary function of attachment is biological – to ensure the child's survival. But attachment between the child and the carer offers more than simply protection from harm: attachment theory highlights the importance of recognising that children grow up *within relationships*. Bowlby argued that the child's attachment experiences formed the basis of their understanding of relationships – their 'internal working models', or mental representations of the self and the attachment figure. These understandings were said to inform their perception of, and response to, any subsequent relationships.

Bowlby's original theory, as set out in his monograph, was based on three small studies and has inevitably been subject to criticism over the years since it was first proposed. Not least, it can be seen to idealise motherhood, in accounts that are very much located in the post-war period in which they were written (Holmes 1993), while neglecting children's capacity to form multiple attachments (Schaffer and Emerson 1964). Attachment theory has, of course, developed and been refined over the intervening years – by Bowlby himself and others – and a review of its theoretical developments over the last 60 years is beyond the scope of this short chapter. That said, recent research has emphasised the need to recognise that relationships are culturally and contextually situated: there are no universal 'norms' in patterns of attachment nor direct pathways between measured attachment 'styles' and individual outcomes (e.g. Shaver and Mikulincer 2010; Simpson and Rholes 2010).

Attachment and children in care

Despite the criticisms and caveats noted above, attachment theory is valuable in emphasising the need to consider the ways in which important relationships influence our lives. Howe (2005) conducted a comprehensive review of the application of attachment theory to work with children and young people who have been abused or neglected. His discussion of the implications of past childhood experiences for current relationships is highly relevant to our concern here with supportive relationships with children in care. For example:

> Many maltreated children do not feel safe when they allow the carer to be in charge of the relationship. After all, this is the relationship associated with hurt and danger, fear and pain… Controlling strategies empower children. They help them disown representations of the self as helpless, vulnerable and needing comfort. (Howe 2005, pp.42–44)

Such strategies are described by Howe as 'self-preservational', developed as an adaptive response to the adverse situation in which the child is living. But, according to attachment theory, these internal working models of relationships, developed through their early care experiences, do not just apply to their interactions with the maltreating parent. They also guide the child's perceptions of – and response to – new interactions and relationships with others. Thus, for children in care, the child's internal working models, developed from their existing relationship experiences, will continue to influence the relationships they form when they are accommodated in substitute care. To take Howe's example above, if it feels unsafe for a child to allow the carer to be in charge, he or she is likely to feel threatened by – and to resist – any attempts by a substitute carer to exert control.

Studies of children placed for adoption can help to illuminate the considerations involved in building supportive relationships with children in substitute care. Hodges and colleagues (2005) interviewed children and young people who were adopted from public care, to examine children's understandings and expectations of relationships as they moved from care into adopted families and over the subsequent two years. They observed:

> a child who avoids showing attachment needs makes it very hard for the new adoptive parents to recognise the times when they could respond to the child's needs by offering comfort and security – responses that disconfirm the child's underlying expectations of rejection and that could help the child begin to develop new and happier expectations. (Hodges *et al.* 2005, p.108)

Over the two years of this study, children formed new and more positive representations of relationships than they expressed at the beginning of the research, although these new representations did not automatically transform, nor did they replace, established ones. This finding is critical in highlighting potential misconceptions about supportive relationships for children in care. No matter how adverse children's early experiences, it is inappropriate to conceptualise a child as 'damaged' irrevocably by early adversity. Children's relationship models *are* open to change, and 'the attachment system is sufficiently flexible to operate even in late placements of children with adverse histories' (Rushton *et al.* 2003, p.397).

Nonetheless, it is likely to be challenging for new carers to establish relationships with children who have been maltreated – precisely because the understandings and strategies developed in adverse relationships had an adaptive or protective function for the child in that adverse context. As Rushton and colleagues (2003) concluded, 'good parenting' alone may not be enough to establish mutual attachment. They cautioned that adoptive parents may need help to build and maintain relationships with children who respond with defensive strategies and note that these considerations have implications for the likely success of the placement. Such considerations are equally likely to apply to placement in residential or foster care. For example, a review by Munro and Hardy (2006) of the literature on placement stability quoted a young person interviewed by Skuse and Ward (2003, p.115), who observed: 'they [foster carers] got annoyed with you because you didn't know how to take them or anything'.

As summed up by this young person, a child in public care may not easily know how to 'take' the supportive relationship that the carer seeks to build. This observation has critical implications for the way in which relationships within public care are conceptualised.

Relationship stability

Attachment theory emphasises the importance of stability and continuity in relationships. For example, Bowlby (1958/2003, p.237) cites Winnicott's (1948) analysis of the 'vitally important' qualities of the mother. The first quality he cites is that 'she exists, continues to exist…'.

Recent research and policy has placed similar emphasis on continuity in relationships for children in public care. Munro and Hardy's review observed that 'Placement instability…may compound existing difficulties and further reinforcement of insecure patterns of attachment' (2006, p.2). Moreover, the development of meaningful relationships takes time, perhaps especially for young people for whom earlier relationship experiences are characterised by adversity. Holland and colleagues observed that 'sustained relationships are needed in order to communicate successfully with children and young people in care' (Holland *et al.* 2008, p.19). Similarly, Howe (2005, p.218) commented on the need to 'proceed very gently' in establishing relationships. Studies of adoptive placements have also demonstrated that relationship development can be a slow and complex process (see Rushton 2007).

These observations raise an important question, about how to ensure that carers and children have enough time to establish stable and meaningful relationships. The English public care system prioritises swift return home from care, and care statistics are characterised by frequent movement in and out of the system (Boddy *et al.* 2009a; Sinclair *et al.* 2007). For example, over half of 10–15-year-olds who ceased to be looked after in 2008 had been accommodated for less than eight weeks, and many of those who return home subsequently re-enter care. These are systemic issues – and so are arguably out of the control of the individual practitioner – but they can still be informed by a social pedagogic perspective on public care, a perspective that emphasises the supportive relationship.

In the Continental European countries where I and colleagues from the Thomas Coram Research Unit have conducted research, policy and services for children and families – including placement of children in care – are informed by social pedagogic theory and principles (Boddy *et al.* 2009a, 2009b; Petrie *et al.* 2006). This understanding can be seen in legislative frameworks, as well as in policy makers' and practitioners' understandings of the purpose of care, and the role of care work (Boddy *et al.* 2009a). Thus, for example, in Germany, public care is defined in law[1] as a form of 'help with upbringing' – *Hilfe zur Erziehung* – and children have a legal right to assistance and support for their personal and social development, and to an upbringing that supports this development. Similarly, in France, the social pedagogic intent of placement was illustrated by the manager of a French voluntary sector organisation, discussing a secure residential unit for young people who have been involved with crime:

---

1 Book VIII of the 1990 Child and Youth Welfare Act, *Kinder- und Jugendhilfegesetz* (KJHG).

It's very important to give them back a *'cadre de vie'*,[2] to give
education through sport, art, culture and so on, to give them
back their confidence and an aim for their lives, as these
children are not always responsible for their actions because
of their family backgrounds and their environment. (Boddy *et
al.* 2009a, p.131)

That is likely to depend, in no small part, on achieving stability in
placement, beginning with careful placement matching. It also depends
on investing in a workforce – of residential and foster care workers – that
is adequately equipped to meet the relationship needs of children and
young people within the care system. These arguments are not new, but
they reflect aspirations which are still not easily achieved.

In 1989, Aldgate wrote that 'perhaps the most serious problem [facing
the care system] has been the low expectation of success' (p.32). This low
expectation is still apparent today and is in itself problematic: 'The more
we say that anything to do with care is bad, the more you reinforce the
notion that it's a last resort' (national policy advisor, England, quoted in
Boddy *et al.* 2009a, p.134).

In England, public 'care' away from the parental home has primarily
been conceived of as a service of last resort, only to be invoked when
preventive work has failed, with swift return home prioritised wherever
possible (Biehal 2007; Boddy *et al.* 2009a). As noted above, in other
European countries, interviewees in our research at Thomas Coram
Research Unit have described a social pedagogic objective for placement:
to support the young person's upbringing and education in the broadest
sense through work within supportive relationships (Boddy *et al.* 2009a).
This objective was achieved through careful placement matching, with a
professionalised workforce in which social pedagogy was the predominant
professional education for direct work with children and families (e.g. for
residential care work in institutional settings, or in training and support
for foster carers). Although there is some cross-country variation in the
content of education, and in the levels of qualification required for the
work, our research has consistently shown important commonalities in
understandings of the aims and key theoretical principles of the work,
including a focus on the supportive relationship across diverse forms
of placement, tailored to children and young people's individual needs
(Boddy *et al.* 2009a, 2009b; Petrie *et al.* 2006).

---

2   An environment for life.

The role of relationships in public 'care'

Attachment theory has had a formative influence on policy and service provision for children in public care (e.g. Rutter and O'Connor 1999), and, in line with this, foster care is prioritised for looked after children in England. For example, in 2009, 73 per cent of the 61,000 children in care were accommodated in foster care.[3] This English emphasis on foster care is set out in a range of English policy guidance measures (e.g. Department for Education and Skills 2006; Department of Health 1998). As Sinclair and colleagues (2007, p.140) noted, it 'fits the family agenda of children's services', and accords with the UN Convention on the Rights of the Child (1989), which established the child's right to live with a family. Overall, this emphasis on family, and on foster care, is intended to offer children and young people the best chance of benefiting from supportive caring relationships – including the provision of alternative attachment figures for children and young people whose attachment experiences have been disrupted by the circumstances that led to their placement in public care.

Accounting for diversity

Children in public care comprise a heterogeneous population (Boddy *et al.* 2009a; Sinclair *et al.* 2007). Sinclair and colleagues (2007) analysed care records from 13 English councils, and commented on 'the great variety of the children and of their experiences', noting that 'there is very little that is true of all the children who are looked after by the state'. Similarly, another analysis of data on looked after children, living in England in 2005, also showed striking differences between subgroups in the care system (Boddy *et al.* 2009a). This research was particularly concerned with services for 10–15-year-old children. Compared with younger children in the care system, these young people experienced less stability. They moved in and out of care more quickly; almost half of those leaving care had been accommodated for less than eight weeks, compared to just over 30 per cent of younger school-aged children. Compared to younger children, 10–15-year-olds also experienced more changes of placement while in care, with 50 per cent recorded as having three or more placements in a year.

---

3   This figure includes the 11 per cent of looked after children who are fostered by family or friend. Source: Department for Education, http://www.education.gov.uk/rsgateway/DB/SFR/s000878/index.shtml

These statistical trends are relevant to the present discussion because they have implications for the way in which we understand the carer–child relationship. Sinclair and colleagues (2007) reported that social workers interviewed for their study saw placement in a family as more 'normal' than other forms of care. But the patterns noted above – of transition into and out of care, of placement breakdown and of use of residential accommodation – challenge any assumption that the carer–child relationship can be conceptualised as a 'normal' substitute parent–child relationship for many children in care.

Munro and Hardy's (2006) review of placement stability, as noted above, indicated that not all children want, or know 'how to take', that 'normal' substitute parental relationship. One model of care does not fit all, and not everybody who is accommodated away from home will want to live in family-based care. Even in an English policy context that prioritises foster care, family-based care may not be appropriate for – and may not be available to – all children and young people who are accommodated away from home. For example, there are documented difficulties in finding appropriate foster care placements for sibling groups and for older children (e.g. Fostering Network 2006; Munro and Hardy 2006), with 10–15-year-olds more likely to be placed in residential care than younger children.

Foster care itself is, of course, not a uniform provision, and not all foster care relationships are intended to offer substitute parenting (Sinclair *et al.* 2005a). Indeed, Courtney and Thoburn (2009) noted that most foster care relationships are neither wholly personal nor focused on care and upbringing. Rather, they argued, for most children and young people in foster care, the carer is task- or role-oriented.

These authors distinguished between foster care that lasts 'days or weeks, but usually less than two or three years' and 'de facto parents' who care for a single child or sibling group from early childhood through to adulthood. This first group encompasses a variety of placement models, including respite and emergency accommodation as well as specialist or treatment foster care, and parent and baby assessment placements. Courtney and Thoburn described these carers as 'task-centred', in fulfilling a particular role or task, in contrast to 'de facto parents' who provide long-term or permanent 'care and upbringing'. Both groups may include friends or relatives providing foster care, indicating that blood ties are not in themselves sufficient for a substitute parenting relationship.

The heterogeneity of public care, and of children and young people in care, raises a new question: how to conceptualise the relationship between carer and child in different forms of placement. Are relationships still of primary importance for children and young people in residential care, for example, or for those in emergency, short-term placements? Can such placements still offer the benefits posited by attachment theory, of positive alternative relationship models? How can the potential benefits of supportive relationships be made available to *all* children in public care?

A 'professional heart'?

The research outlined above suggests that normative conceptions of the care relationship as a form of substitute parenting are problematic. There is a fundamental tension in the relationship between the personal and the professional. Placements, whether in residential or foster care, are often short-term and/or task-focused. Even in long-term and adoptive placements, 'good parenting' in itself may not be sufficient to ensure the development of mutual attachment with children who have experienced early adverse relationships. Equally, studies of children and young people's views of their care experiences highlight the fact that – however positive relationships might be – children remain aware that the foster care family is not their birth family. In line with many other researchers, Sinclair and colleagues (2005a) noted that this awareness is reinforced by factors such as differences in the surnames of child and carer, the bureaucracy associated with placement, and the 'style' of upbringing by foster carers. These authors noted ambiguity for many young people in the extent to which foster care felt like family, even when very positive about their care. They quoted one young person who summed up this tension by saying: 'Although it feels like my family, there's always that part of me that knows that it's not' (p.151).

Personal *and* professional?

If, by its nature, the carer–child relationship cannot be wholly personal, and if it cannot rely on instinctive or experiential understandings of 'good parenting', there is a need to make explicit, and address, the tension between the personal and the professional. In this context, Bowlby's original attachment theory could be seen to have exerted an unhelpful influence, in its concern with the 'instinctual response' in the attachment relationship (Bowlby 1958/2003). This emphasis could be taken to imply that substitute care does not require professional knowledge, but rather depends on instinctual qualities of care.

In English public care, the tension between the personal and the professional could be exacerbated by the low knowledge base for the work, relative to other European countries, where qualifications in social pedagogy form a common foundation for work with children in residential care. Most looked after children in England (whether in residential or foster care) are cared for by adults who are unqualified or who have low levels of formal qualification (see Cameron and Boddy 2006; Petrie *et al.* 2006). It seems likely that these workers have to rely more on tacit and experiential knowledge – on the personal – because they do not have the resource of professional reflection on the relationship.

Social pedagogues participating in cross-European research undertaken by the Thomas Coram Research Unit have explicitly addressed the tension between personal and professional in their education, working with the concept of the 'professional heart'. This phrase was coined by a Danish student, interviewed in our first study of social pedagogy, but it refers to a concept that was described by students and workers, across countries and consistently across a range of studies (see Boddy *et al.* 2006; Petrie *et al.* 2006). It is, perhaps, hardly surprising that the meaning of the professional relationship should be well considered by pedagogues, because the relationship is fundamental – it is the basis of the pedagogue's work. As Eichsteller and Holthoff write in Chapter 2: 'Social pedagogy is brought to life through the relationship between the professional and the subject' (p.42).

The concept of a 'professional heart' allows for a relationship that can be both personal *and* professional. In this vein, social pedagogues in our research have described their work as being about 'head, hands, and heart'. Hands and heart – practical engagement and empathy – are seen as necessary but not sufficient for work with the complex needs and difficulties of young people in or at the edges of care, and their families. The heart also needs the head – the balance brought by professional knowledge and reflection on a relationship. Danish interviewees (Petrie *et al.* 2006) have referred to the concept of *rummelighed* (literally, space or capacity), which derives from psychoanalysis and refers to notions of containment (see also Chapter 4). Interviewees spoke of having 'room in your heart' for someone, even if they are challenging to work with and even if you do not like them, because you have the self-knowledge and skills to balance the personal and the professional.

In social pedagogic terms, as Eichsteller and Holthoff observe in Chapter 2, a professional relationship is *authentic* and informed by the professional's personality, but it differs from a private relationship in the way the self is used. The worker may use her personal life experience, but only to support the professional focus on the child, and his or her upbringing, within the relationship. Thus, tacit and experiential knowledge remain relevant, as part of the pedagogue's *Haltung* (defined by Eichsteller and Holthoff in Chapter 2 as attitude, mindset or ethos). But these forms of knowledge are not sufficient for the work. Rather, they are used reflectively, in conjunction with professional understanding and theoretical knowledge.

The key to the relationship is therefore the *combination* of personal and professional in the relationship. The recognition that both are necessary, but neither sufficient, becomes critical in addressing the challenges inherent in bringing up children away from their families of origin. In relation to foster care, it addresses the concern raised by Rushton *et al.* (2003) in their discussion of adoptive placements: for some children who are accommodated in care, understandings of 'good parenting', and love and affection, may not be sufficient to meet their needs.

In Boddy and colleagues' (2009a) study of work at the so-called 'edges' of care, foster placement was seen as a preferred option for young people in England. Although there was recognition that residential care was necessary for some children, it was considered an option of last resort, in part because it was seen as lacking in the supportive relationships that foster care can provide. But foster care was not an inevitable first choice in France, Denmark or Germany, nor was residential care seen as a failure or last resort. Interviewees in all those countries emphasised the use of residential care when necessary to meet a young person's needs and spoke of the use of residential care as an intervention for young people with complex and challenging needs that needed greater professional expertise than could be offered by foster care. For example, a senior manager in Denmark discussed the way in which choice of placement would be tailored to a young person's specific needs and preferences:

> It depends on the kind of problems the child has. If a child has [significant] emotional difficulties, you have to be very careful about a placement in a foster home. It can cause difficulties, for example with the family's own children. They [can] test the family, to see how much love they can give. So [you] don't place a child with significant emotional difficulties in foster

care, you would use *opholdssteder.*[4] And if [their problems] were very severe, you would place them in residential care for treatment. (Boddy *et al.* 2009a)

The key point here is that, because the work is social pedagogic, the *relationship* remains at the centre, whatever the form of provision. Residential care is not assumed to be less able to provide the child with a supportive relationship. But, because the relationship is both personal and professional, it is, in itself, an intervention of 'help with upbringing' – *Hilfe zur Erziehung*, to adopt the German term. This is a key distinction. Belgian researchers (Coussée *et al.* 2010; see also Chapter 3) rightly note that social pedagogy is not simply a *method* of intervention; it is a complex theoretical discipline, as the writing collected in this volume clearly shows. But, nonetheless, social pedagogic theory underpins intervention, as social pedagogues work with relationships to intervene in children's lives.

In England, Clough (2006) argued for a reconceptualisation of residential care for children as a positive resource for intervention, within provision differentiated by levels of need. That might be achieved, not just in residential care, but across forms of provision, by a conceptualisation of the care relationship in social pedagogic terms, as a supportive relationship that is both personal and professional. In relation to English foster care, there is already interest in the professionalisation of the supportive relationship, for example, through treatment and specialist foster care (e.g. McDonald and Turner 2007).

An equal relationship

In interviews, social pedagogues have consistently emphasised equality as a cornerstone of the social pedagogic relationship (e.g. Petrie *et al.* 2006). A relationship between adult and child is nonetheless a relationship between two people. The relationship aims to be equal, not hierarchical, and this is enabled by the pedagogue through dialogue and listening. This emerges in students' drawings of a 'good pedagogue', such as can be seen in Figure 6.1. The pedagogue has 'the ability to keep kids in my heart' (as discussed above), but she is also shown with big ears, 'to listen to the kids' needs'. It is also important to note that the notion

---

4   *Opholdssteder*, literally translated, means 'a place to stay'; it is a small-scale alternative to residential care, staffed by social pedagogues and usually provided by the independent (non-profit) sector.

of equality in the relationship is not seen to negate, or undermine, the adult's professional knowledge and experience. The 'good' pedagogue in this picture is saying, 'I'm here to help and support you. Please let me take care of you. I know what I'm doing!'

Figure 6.1 A 'good' pedagogue

This understanding of equality means that the conception of the young person's rights in that relationship goes beyond what is stipulated in procedures and legislation. Their participation in, and responsibility for, decision making is enabled by the pedagogue through dialogue and listening – as one person in relation to another. In interviews, pedagogues have commented that both residential care staff and young people need to reach agreements that the young person understands, one putting the agreement like this: 'As adults we are always afraid to give authority to children, but it's not authority, it's responsibility' (Petrie *et al.* 2006, p.35). In France, the conception of equality is expressed in the term *accompagnement*. Literally meaning 'accompaniment', in the context of the supportive relationship between pedagogue (*éducateur*) and child, it connotes the idea of 'going alongside' the child through his or her everyday life – it is support, but it is not hierarchical (Boddy *et al.* 2009a).

The social pedagogic emphasis on dialogue and equality, as foundations of the relationship between carer and child, resonates with findings from other research with children in public care. With reference to attachment-focused interventions, Howe (2005, p.219) argued that '(d)ialogue is therapy. It is mind-engaging. It provokes self-reflection and thoughts about the other.' Thus, he argued, dialogue is critical in establishing and maintaining the development of an emotional relationship between carer and child.

Equally, there is a need to caution against adult-centric understandings of young people's needs and to recognise young people in their own right, as individuals with voices and opinions. Holland and her colleagues (2008, p.20) cautioned that the young people who participated in their research could often feel that professionals asked about their lives 'because of a bureaucratic routine, rather than because the questioner is genuinely curious about how they are'. This is not a dialogue of equality: it may be professional, but it is not personal. McLeod (2010) highlights similar concerns in her account of interviews with young people in public care, who described the attributes of a 'good' social worker as being like 'a friend' or 'an equal'. Again, the tensions of the 'professional heart' in an English context are apparent in her comments:

> In a world in which maintaining appropriate professional boundaries is stressed, in which a relaxed and informal approach can be seen to be collusive, and in which social care staff fear that any display of warmth or intimacy may be construed as exploitation, how can the front line representative of the child's corporate parent also be their friend? And how can a reflective worker, who is aware of inequalities and sensitive to the risks of oppressive practice, deny the significance of differences in age, class, status, income, education, professional power and perhaps even physical size, and claim to be a young person's equal? (McLeod 2010, p.773)

She goes on to argue that the concept of the social worker as a 'friend' and an 'equal' to a child in the care system should not be a professional impossibility, but can be seen to be consistent with social work values, evidence-based practice and childcare theory. Equality does, however, require a framework that addresses the tensions between personal and professional that are outlined above. Within a social pedagogic framework, such tensions are directly addressed through the pedagogue's stance (*Haltung*), formed by the combination of her professional knowledge, reflective practice and emotional connection to the child.

Everyday relationships

Research on the importance of attachment can be criticised for focusing too much on the implications of early relationships for long-term measurable 'outcomes' (Holmes 1993). Similarly, researchers studying children in public care risk prioritising long-term outcomes over children's everyday lived experiences, when arguably the two are inseparable (Berridge *et al.* 2008). The importance of an everyday perspective was highlighted by Holland and her colleagues (2008) in their study of the everyday lives of children in care. They noted the need to focus on children's own views of their experiences, in order to 'understand their identities in all their messy complexity and avoid narrow or stereotypical constructions of young people in care' (p.19). Children and young people should be recognised 'as active members of society...rather than just focusing on outcomes – the adult they will become' (p.20).

Figure 6.2 Doing, and doing 'with'

As discussed elsewhere in this volume, work with the everyday is a cornerstone of social pedagogic theory; an emphasis on the relationship means also an emphasis on everyday life. As such, social pedagogy is not simply about dialogue, about talking and listening. Students' drawings of 'good' pedagogues often had 'big hands' or were shown engaged in activities with the child: the relationship is rooted in action as well as words (see Figure 6.2, and Boddy *et al.* 2006). A French pedagogue interviewed for Boddy and colleagues' (2009a) study of work with young people at the 'edges' of care commented that the supportive relationship is about *doing*, and doing *with* someone (*c'est le faire avec*) as well as working with relationships (*travailler avec des relations*). In Germany, this understanding of a relationship based in everyday life is expressed in part through a social pedagogic concept introduced earlier in Chapter 2: *Lebensweltorientierung*, meaning 'life-world' orientation (e.g. Thiersch and Grunwald 2001), which can also be thought of as an 'everyday world orientation' (Colla *et al.* 2006).

Conclusion

The research presented in this chapter has indicated the complexities involved in developing supportive relationships with children and young people in public care. There is substantial evidence of the importance of strong and supportive emotional relationships for children's current and future lives. But there are also likely to be particular challenges involved in establishing positive supportive relationships between carers and children and young people whose understandings of relationships are influenced by previous adverse experiences.

The work of public care is not wholly personal, and it is not ordinary 'good parenting'. Most provision, in residential or foster care, does not comprise substitute parental care. Consequently, a model of care and the supportive relationship that is predicated purely on attachment theory, conceived in terms of 'normal' family life and instinctual 'good parenting', is problematic. It is unlikely to meet the diverse needs of children who live within the care system.

The English government's *Care Matters* implementation plan (Department for Children, Schools and Families 2008, p.29) spoke of the need to 'ensure that children in care are provided with the one thing they have told us makes the single biggest difference to their lives: being in the right placement'. It quotes a young person saying, 'Give me a choice about my placement and, unless it is an emergency, let me meet my new carers before I move. Things can work out if we are a good match.' To achieve that good match is not a matter of chance. Rather, it relies on a conceptualisation of care, and of the supportive relationship, that can span forms of provision – whether short- or long-term, residential or foster care – to address the heterogeneity of the care population. This requires a differentiated model of care, with a cohesive objective – to provide a positive relationship-based intervention for children whose needs cannot be met within their family of origin. Arguably, such a conceptualisation is possible in other countries, such as Denmark, France or Germany, because care and the supportive relationship are conceived of in social pedagogic terms.

Thus, the supportive relationship is a mutual relationship, of one person in relation to the other. As a relationship that is equal, not hierarchical, it can be seen as 'accompaniment': the adult 'goes alongside' the child, valuing the everyday and the child's 'life-world' as well as his or her aspirations for the future. In doing so, the social pedagogue must balance professional knowledge and theoretical understanding with experience, and reflection. However, the relationship is also explicitly personal *and* professional, informed by the concept of a 'professional heart'. Critically, it is rooted in an emotional connection between carer and child, a connection which neither undermines nor substitutes for the worker's professionalism. In social pedagogic terms, therefore, public care is an intervention of upbringing, supporting the child's education (in the broadest sense of that word) through the supportive relationship between carer and child.

References

Aldgate, J. (1989) 'Foster families and residential care for older children: Some interpersonal dynamics.' *Children and Society* 3, 1, 19–36.

Berridge, D., Dance, C., Beecham, J. and Field, S. (2008) *Educating Difficult Adolescents: Effective Education for Children in Public Care or with Emotional and Behavioural Difficulties.* London: Jessica Kingsley Publishers.

Biehal, N. (2007) 'Reuniting children with their families: Reconsidering the evidence on timing, contact and outcomes.' *British Journal of Social Work* 37, 807–823.

Boddy, J., Cameron, C. and Petrie, P. (2006) 'The Professional Care Worker: The Social Pedagogue in Northern Europe.' In J. Boddy, C. Cameron and P. Moss (eds) *Care Work: Present and Future.* London: Routledge.

Boddy, J., McQuail, S., Owen, C., Petrie, P. and Statham, J. (2009a) *Working at the 'Edges' of Care? European Models of Support for Young People and Families.* London: Thomas Coram Research Unit, Institute of Education, University of London.

Boddy, J., Statham, J., Smith M., Ghate, D. *et al.* (2009b) *International Perspectives on Parenting Support: Non-English Language Sources.* DCSF Research Report DCSF-RR114. Available at www.education.gov.uk/publications//eOrderingDownload/DCSF-RR114.pdf, accessed on 5 May 2011.

Bowlby, J. (1951) *Maternal Care and Mental Health (World Health Organization Monograph Series).* Geneva: WHO.

Bowlby, J. (1958/2003) 'The Nature of the Child's Tie to his Mother.' In A.C. Furman and S.T. Levy (eds) *Influential Papers from the 1950s. International Journal of Psychoanalysis Key Papers Series, Papers from the Decades.* London: Karnac.

Bullock, R., Courtney, M.E., Parker, R., Sinclair, I. and Thoburn, J. (2006) 'Can the corporate state parent?' *Child and Youth Services Review 28,* 1344–1358.

Cameron, C. and Boddy, J. (2006) 'Knowledge and Education for Care Workers: What Do They Need to Know?' In J. Boddy, C. Cameron and P. Moss (eds) *Care Work: Present and Future.* London: Routledge.

Colla, H.E., Tetzer, M., Jansen, A., Renk, F. and Sieburg, J. (2006) *Supporting Families of Young People Entering Public Care: European Models.* Unpublished report on Germany for *Supporting Families of Young People Entering Public Care: European Models.* Lüneburg: Institüt für Sozialpädagogik, Universität Lüneburg.

Clough, R. (2006) 'What works in residential care.' *NCB Highlight 227.*

Courtney, M. and Thoburn, J. (eds) (2009) *Children in State Care.* Aldershot: Ashgate Publishing.

Coussée, F., Bradt, L., Roose, R. and Bouverne-De Bie, M. (2010) 'The emerging social pedagogical paradigm in UK child and youth care: Deus ex machina or walking the beaten path?' *British Journal of Social Work 40,* 3, 789–805.

Department for Children, Schools and Families (2008) *Care Matters: Time to Deliver for Children in Care. An Implementation Plan.* London: DCSF. Available at www.education. gov.uk/publications/standrad/publicationdetail/page1/DCSF-00279-2008, accessed on 5 May 2011.

Department for Education and Skills (2006) *Care Matters: Transforming the Lives of Children and Young People in Care.* London: HMSO.

Department of Health (1998) *Quality Protects.* London: HMSO.

Fostering Network (2006) *Improving Effectiveness in Foster Care Recruitment: An Interim Report of the Innovation in Foster Care Recruitment Study.* London: Fostering Network.

Gilligan, R. (2007) 'Adversity, resilience and the educational progress of young people in public care.' *Emotional and Behavioural Difficulties 12,* 2, 135–145.

Hodges, J., Steele, M., Hillman, S., Henderson, K. and Kaniuk, J. (2005) 'Change and Continuity in Mental Representations of Attachment after Adoption.' In D. Brodzinsky and J. Palacios (eds) *Psychological Issues in Adoption: Research and Practice.* Westport, CT: Praeger.

Holland, S., Renold, E., Ross, N. and Hillman, A. (2008) 'The Everyday Lives of Children in Care: Using a Sociological Perspective to Inform Social Work Practice.' In B. Luckock and M. Lefevre (eds) *Direct Work: Social Work with Children and Young People in Care.* London: BAAF.

Holmes, J. (1993) *John Bowlby and Attachment Theory.* London: Routledge.

Howe, D. (2005) *Child Abuse and Neglect: Attachment, Development and Intervention.* Basingstoke: Palgrave Macmillan.

McDonald, G.M. and Turner, W. (2007) *Treatment Foster Care for Improving Outcomes in Children and Young People.* The Campbell Collaboration Social Welfare Group. Available at www.sfi.dk/graphics/Campbell/reviews/TFC%20REVIEW%20 Macdonald.pdf, accessed on 6 August 2010.

McLeod, A. (2010) '"A friend and an equal": Do young people in care seek the impossible from their social workers?' *British Journal of Social Work 40*, 3, 772–788.

Munro, E.R. and Hardy, A. (2006) *Placement Stability: A Review of the Literature.* Loughborough: CCFR.

Petrie, P., Boddy, J., Cameron, C., Wigfall, V. and Simon, A. (2006) *Working with Children in Care: European Perspectives.* Maidenhead: Open University Press.

Rushton, A., Mayes, D., Dance, C. and Quinton, D. (2003) 'Parenting late-placed children: The development of new relationships and the challenge of behavioural problems.' *Clinical Child Psychology and Psychiatry 8*, 3, 389–400.

Rushton, A. (2007) 'Outcomes of adoption from public care: Research and practice issues.' *Advances in Psychiatric Treatment 13*, 305–311.

Rutter, M. and O'Connor, T.G. (1999) 'Implications of Attachment Theory for Child Care Policies.' In J. Cassidy and P. Shaver (eds) *Handbook of Attachment.* New York, NY: Guilford.

Schaffer, H.R. and Emerson, P.E. (1964) 'The development of social attachments in infancy.' *Monographs of the Society for Research in Child Development 29*, 3.

Shaver, P.R. and Mikulincer, M. (2010) 'New directions in attachment theory and research.' *Journal of Social and Personal Relationships 27*, 2, 163–172.

Simpson, J.A. and Rholes, W.S. (2010) 'Attachment and relationships: Milestones and future directions.' *Journal of Social and Personal Relationships 27*, 2, 173–80.

Sinclair, I., Wilson, K. and Gibbs, I. (2005a) *Foster Placements: Why They Succeed and Why They Fail.* London: Jessica Kingsley Publishers.

Sinclair, I., Baker, C., Wilson, K. and Gibbs, I. (2005b) *Foster Children: Where They Go and How They Get On.* London: Jessica Kingsley Publishers.

Sinclair, I., Baker, C., Lee, J. and Gibbs, I. (2007) *The Pursuit of Permanence: A Study of the English Child Care System.* London: Jessica Kingsley Publishers.

Thiersch, H. and Grunwald, K. (2001) 'Lebensweltorientierung.' In H.U. Otto and H. Thiersch (eds) *Handbuch Sozialarbeit/Sozialpädagogik.* Köln: Hermann Luchterhand Verlag.

United Nations (1989) *UN Convention on the Rights of the Child.* Geneva: United Nations.

CHAPTER 7

Communication and Conflict: An Important Part of Social Pedagogic Relationships

STEFAN KLEIPOEDSZUS

Introduction

This chapter is about two terms that are linked closely, even though this link is not always obvious: communication and conflict. As a part of upbringing, communication and conflict play a crucial interconnected role in the interaction between adults and young people. It is in the nature of the relationship between the older generation tasked with educating the younger generation and the younger generation that there are disagreements between their different perspectives on the world.

From a social pedagogical point of view, conflict should be seen as part of the disposition to grow that is characteristic for human beings (Vogel 2010) and not necessarily as a means to address trauma that an individual has experienced in the past. Conflicts in a social pedagogical context are part of the overall aim of social pedagogy to help to develop the rich potential that each child and young person contains within him or her.

Challenging someone else's perspective, behaviours and attitudes is, generally speaking, a positive thing and helps to understand the other person. At the same time, being challenged is helpful for reflecting on one's perspectives and attitudes and, therefore, is potentially a source of personal growth and learning.

With challenge often comes conflict. If this conflict is resolved through good communication, based on a supportive relationship between the young person and the professional, it will not only help the young person to become more conflict literate, but it will also contribute to achieving the educational aim of the professional.

It has to be highlighted here that conflicts in this sense are not only positive for the interaction between the young person and the professional, but that conflicts between professionals are also crucial for the constant development of good practice. In this chapter the focus is mainly on the interaction between a young person and a professional. However, the same ideas can be applied to interactions between professionals.

Challenging young people means that the professional is likely to risk causing a conflict. This chapter argues that taking this risk is worthwhile, because a conflict resulting from a challenge can be a positive element of a pedagogical relationship between the professional and the young person; rather than avoid conflicts, the pedagogue should see them as an opportunity for growth. I will discuss conflicts and the positive role they can play as part of the upbringing of children and young people, looking in particular at upbringing within pedagogical settings such as children's homes. The chapter will also look more broadly at the issue of communication itself, identifying some of the dimensions that the pedagogue should be aware of. The chapter ends with some consideration of the role that the social pedagogue plays in the dynamic between the pedagogue, the young person and the wider societal context of the upbringing of children and young people.

The assumption underlying this chapter is that social pedagogical practice is closely linked to the passionate rapport of a mature person to a nascent person (Nohl 1935). This rapport is based on communication between two persons who can see each other as equal human beings. Adding passion to this means that pedagogical rapport is not necessarily about unconditional acceptance of each other. Rather, it highlights the fact that there will always be differences of opinions, values and beliefs between the mature and the nascent person, and that these offer the prospect of growth for both if the opportunities raised by conflicts in communication are being taken.

Communication

Communication forms the basis of human interaction, but understanding communication is difficult. It is 'an extremely dynamic phenomenon with a rapid rate of change of levels and of functions, which range from evaluation to transmission and conduction' (Ruesch and Bateson 2008, p.274). The individuals involved in processes of communication constantly change their roles and transmit and receive messages and statements in many different ways. One has to assume that it is difficult to analyse communication because it is probably impossible to say what the actual reality in communication is compared to the perceived reality (p.273).

What needs to be considered when communicating?

The first thing that the pedagogue needs to consider is the idea that processes of communication involve objectifications – that is, the assignment of meanings to actions. So, as Berger and Luckmann (1973, p.37) explain, the reality of the everyday is only made real because of these objectifications, or meaning makings, in our communication. This means that objects that may indicate the subjective intentions of other individuals constantly surround us. For example, a plate thrown at the dinner table may be the objectification of anger. Unfortunately, one cannot be 100 per cent sure if this is really the case or if the plate has been thrown for other reasons.

Speech has become the most decisive method for the understanding of our everyday world. The basis for the use of speech is the inherent ability of humans to express themselves through vocal language. Speech began only when vocal expressions became detachable from the here and now of subjective feelings. Howling, snarling or hissing is not speech even though it can become part of it.

The common and general objectifications of the everyday world – widely agreed meanings – are maintained mainly because of their representations in speech. Living together and cooperation in the everyday world is only possible because of the language that we share with each other (Berger and Luckmann 1977, p.39). But speech is not the only form of communication, and it is worthwhile emphasising the axioms of Watzlawick, Bavelas and Jackson (1967) to highlight the fact that it is important to consider more than just one dimension of communication when interacting with other individuals.

The axioms of Watzlawick

The axioms defined by Watzlawick et al. (1967) provide an important basis for understanding the different dimensions of communication that the pedagogue has to be aware of when working with children and young people.

1. Axiom: One cannot *not* communicate.

   This means that all behaviour has to be seen as communication. Even not reacting to another person sends a message that the other can react to.

2. Axiom: Every communication has a content and relationship aspect such that the latter defines and qualifies the former and is therefore a meta-communication.

   This means that all communication includes more information than what is said; information on how the speaker says something suggests how he himself sees his relation to the receiver of his information.

3. Axiom: The nature of a relationship is dependent on the punctuation of the partners' communication procedures.

   Both parties in communication, the speaker and the receiver of information, structure the communication flow differently and therefore interpret their own behaviour during communicating as merely a reaction to the other's behaviour (i.e. every partner thinks the other one is the cause of a specific behaviour). Human communication cannot be dissolved into plain causation and reaction strings; communication rather appears to be cyclic.

4. Axiom: Human communication involves both digital and analogue modalities.

   Communication does not merely involve spoken language (digital communication), but non-verbal, analogue communication as well (e.g. facial expression, gestures, body language).

5. Axiom: Inter-human communication procedures are either symmetrical or complementary.

   Symmetrical communication is based on equal power while complementary communication is based on differences in power relations. A healthy relationship will have both types of power. Too much of one type of power can lead to possible conflicts. (Watzlawick *et al.* 1967)

It is necessary to discuss what this might mean in practice. To do so, it is useful to introduce the model of communication that Schulz von Thun (2001, 2003) has developed. The benefit of this model is that it has been developed with a focus on practical use, which means that it can be easily adapted to the needs of the individual situation.

The four dimensions of a message

Let us imagine a fairly simple situation involving two people. A residential childcare worker and a young person are sitting together in a meeting room. The young person says: 'I want more pocket money to go to the cinema!' The residential childcare worker answers: 'Don't you think you are already getting enough?'

What happens on a factual level appears to be quite clear. The young person transmits the message that he wants more money. The social worker receives and processes this message and transmits the response. But the reality is more complex. Schulz von Thun (2001, p.25) argues that the message 'I want more pocket money' contains at least four different statements:

- Fact: It is a fact in life that money is needed to pay for cinema tickets.

- Appeal: The young person hopes, with the help of the social worker, to have a good time in the cinema: 'Please let me have a good time.'

- Relationship: The young person is asking the social worker because he hopes that the social worker somehow cares about the young person. If there were no relation between the young person and the social worker, the message would make no sense.

- Self-revelation: The young person shares something about himself – for example, the fact that he enjoys going to the cinema. It may be that he is meeting friends that are important to him. Also the young person might reveal that he finds it difficult to manage money on his own.

Communication is a two-way and multidimensional process and the recipient – in this case the residential childcare worker – can react to one or more of the statements within the young person's message – which is, in effect, not one but four messages. Schulz von Thun explains that each individual should have at least four ears corresponding to each of the different messages that were just outlined: an ear to hear factual messages, another to hear appeals, one for messages about relations and one for self-revelation. Things get more complicated as the receiver of a message can 'choose' with what ear he or she is listening and send a message that again contains at least four dimensions.

Usually the message that the sender has produced and the message that the receiver has decoded are similar enough to achieve a successful communication. Success can be supported if both use a number of checks that can tell how a message should be received, such as facial expression, gestures or even verbal checks ('Did I understand you right?').

Another dimension that needs to be considered is whether or not the verbal messages are congruent with other statements being made. In most cases, statements sent as part of a message have the same directions. If someone says, 'I am happy', one would normally expect a smile that supports the factual statement. These are congruent messages. Messages where the different statements do not fit together or are contradicting each other are called incongruent messages.

What does this mean for the pedagogue? The pedagogue has to make decisions in a very short timescale about the different contents of a message, using all four ears to decode a message and send a message back using the most appropriate channel. At the same time, the pedagogue has to be able to reflect on the use of explicit and implicit messages and consider the issue of congruent and incongruent messages. All this can be very difficult. It needs the support of others who can offer feedback from their observations of the interactions between the pedagogue and the young person.

This is important in conflict situations, which may be the object, the cause or the result of a communication process. Before this is discussed in greater detail, the importance of conflicts for the development of the individual has to be highlighted, because it appears that conflicts are often avoided in pedagogical settings despite the benefits that they might have.

Conflicts

Conflicts are not only relevant in the immediate situation within the pedagogical setting. As shown in the pedagogic triangle in Figure 7.1 (Badry and Knapp 2003), the institutional setting and the societal political context have to be considered as well to understand fully how conflicts are positive for the young person. At the centre of this triangle is the relationship between the pedagogue and the young person linked by the task that has to be fulfilled. In this case, it is the conflict that has to be resolved. Within the inner circle – the pedagogical setting – the discussion about the pocket money might only be a short dispute that can easily be dealt with. The young person can either accept that there is not going to be more pocket money or challenge this decision and negotiate it. The residential childcare worker might just give in and give more pocket money in order to keep the situation calm.

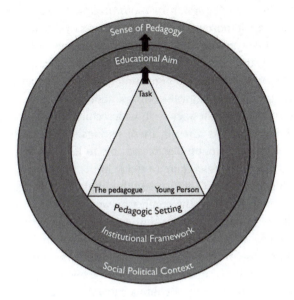

Figure 7.1 The sense of pedagogy

However, from a pedagogical point of view, the institutional framework also has to be considered. Could the pedagogue make these decisions or is it necessary to discuss them with the team, the manager and the allocated social worker, or even with the social worker's team manager? The pedagogue has to communicate these restrictions to the young person to enable the young person to understand decisions being made and maybe even empower the young person to challenge the institutional framework.

But it could reach even further. The pedagogue might need to make references to the wider societal context, which involves the fact that money is not freely available and that one has to work for it; or even that money and access to it are not necessarily distributed fairly. This is where the role of the pedagogue in conflicts becomes even more complicated. Not only must the different aspects of a message be considered; so too must be the different layers that all impact on how the pedagogue might want to deal with this conflict. What this shows is that it is important to look at the wider societal context of conflicts as well as the direct interaction, as all of these levels are interconnected.

Conflict as a source of progress for the individual and for the society
Conflict plays an important role in the progress of human society as progress is based on the diversity and contrariness of that society. According to Dahrendorf (1963), a modern democracy is based on following through conflicts and regulating them, rather than suppressing or denying them. Pedagogical settings should critically reflect the contemporary reality of the society in which children and young people are being brought up. As a result, these settings should become spaces in which children and young people are able to learn how to deal with conflicts and how they emerge in everyday life.

Böhnisch and Schröer (2007, p.203) highlight how the fundamental conflict for young people – the conflict between self-realisation and the reality of life – is hardly ever getting expressed appropriately. So this conflict becomes internalised as part of growing up, in the form of an unspecified feeling of uneasiness, as dissatisfaction, unhappiness and being miserable. If this is right, there can only be two pedagogical ways to address this: the introduction of conflict situations; and the introduction of a practice for the regulation of conflicts on the one hand and, on the other, for formulating, resolving and reflecting upon latent conflicts.

This is supported by Mollenhauer (1968, p.31) who argues that it is unacceptable to speak of a pedagogical approach that avoids the societal reality of conflicts for the sake of well-meaning pedagogical aims. Societal conflicts have to be reproduced in pedagogical settings and a realistic pedagogy has to make use of the educational meaning that these conflicts might have (Böhnisch and Schröer 2007, p.203). For the pedagogical setting, this means that a positive approach to dealing with the societal conflicts experienced by young people in their everyday lives is important. The pedagogical setting can become a space in which the young person learns how to deal with conflicts in a safe way with the support of professionals.

Communicating about conflicts within the pedagogical setting not only helps to build relationships. It becomes a communication about the overarching conflicts in the wider societal context and prefigures potential ways to deal with these conflicts on a larger scale.

Conflict as an opportunity for strong relationships
Conflicts are positive because they prevent the loss of one's own personality that could be the result of a feeling of belonging to another (Prekop 1989). Allowing and developing conflicts helps to create autonomy. The

professional taking a clear position makes it easier for the young person to differentiate him or herself from this position and develop his or her own opinion (Omer and von Schlippe 2002). Different opinions and views support autonomy and present a challenge to the young person. The young person feels that the pedagogue shows unconditional respect, without accepting everything.

To have this experience, the young person needs to have a partner with whom to have this kind of interaction. There needs to be someone who is willing to engage in a conflict and does not avoid it out of fear. Such a partner has to view the young person as strong and competent enough to allow this conflict to happen and use it in a productive way (Farelly and Brandsma 1986). So, for a successful upbringing, the young person is likely to benefit from someone who is able to give honest feedback as to how behaviour affects someone personally and the wider social environment. Pedagogues who do not confront are not able to help the young person to regulate behaviour through feedback (Stiels-Glenn and Glenn 2008, p.168).

Entering a conflict means to take the other seriously as a whole person. Conflicts, therefore, help to build relationships. Engaging in a conflict with a young person assumes that one believes that the young person is strong enough and capable enough to endure this conflict and to use it for his or her own development.

According to Stiels-Glenn and Glenn (2008) pedagogues often avoid conflicts because they are afraid of the emotions and aggressions involved. In these cases, they seem to be occupied with their own agitation and fear, which they try to hide and control. As a result, awareness of what is happening in the relationship between the young person and the pedagogue decreases. In order to control his or her fear, the pedagogue tries to satisfy the young person by supporting the young person's view of the world. In order to avoid these consequences, the pedagogue has to take an active role in the conflict (p.162).

The Theme-Centred Interaction developed by Ruth Cohn (Cohn and Terfurth 1997; Farau and Cohn 1984) gives more reasons for embracing conflicts proactively. In Cohn's view, 'disturbance' take precedence, disturbance meaning all influences that hinder the interaction between two individuals, thereby preventing learning from each other. This means that conflicts should be acknowledged and discussed in order to be able to move on to the underlying issues of a conflict (Stiels-Glenn and Glenn 2008, p.170).

Conflict as the basis for communication

Conflicts can be seen as the emergence of a disturbance that prevents further development of the individual or of the group. Cohn (1975) writes that these disturbances on your path have to be acknowledged and need to take precedence as the lack of a solution hinders and prevents growth. Disturbances, she argues, do not ask for permission to occur; they are just there (Farau and Cohn 1984, p.360). Disturbances are real conditions that work against the conscious aims and tasks of a group or an individual. They waste energy and hinder active learning. But they also direct attention to important aspects that could be lost if they are not picked up in personal interaction (Hoffmann 2010, p.101).

As already discussed, the human capacity for expression has the power of objectification. Human activities manifest themselves in objects that are comprehensible to the producer as well as to other individuals. These objects allow the individuals engaging in a conflict to apprehend the other's intention and action. Berger and Luckmann (1977, p.36) use the example of anger. They explain that the subjective feeling of anger becomes evident in numerous physical ways: through gesture, mimicry, the movements of arms and feet, etc. These indicators of anger are comprehensible as long as the situation lasts. Therefore, they are ideal to gain access to the other as a subject: in this sense, a conflict can become the basis for communication.

The problem is that young people are often conflict-illiterate despite the benefit that conflict literacy could have for them. Gerzon (2006) highlights that virtually entire generations in contemporary societies are word-literate as a result of the education they receive 'yet they often are taught virtually nothing about conflict' (p.227). The result is that many adults are conflict-illiterate and are not able to communicate across differences.

Communication about conflicts in everyday situations can help to resolve this problem and there needs to be discussion how this could be achieved. Gerzon (2006) comments that it is necessary to think of ways to transform conflict into opportunity: 'it is we, the tool users, who must hold the vision… Our challenge is to see the seed or opportunity buried in the soil of conflict' (p.225). This is where it becomes important to introduce the role of the social pedagogue as a person.

The role of the pedagogue when communicating in situations of conflict

Managing conflict and facilitating communication about it becomes a critical role for the pedagogue. So far it has been argued that conflict should be seen as a positive chance for personal growth and as a potential learning situation. In order to ensure that a conflict actually can become something positive, the pedagogue has to take an active role in managing the conflict. How can this be done? What must the pedagogue look out for in order to help a young person to benefit from a conflict situation?

In a conversation or in a conflict, vocal signs (words) are often produced at the same time as the speaker becomes aware of his or her subjective intentions. This means that often one only knows what one wants to say the same moment one speaks. This is made even more complicated by the reciprocal nature of communication in a vis-à-vis situation (Berger and Luckmann 1977, p.39). This is what makes it different from any other method of communication. In a conversation, the continuous production of vocal statement is synchronised to the individual's subjective intentions of the speaker. One speaks and thinks at once, as does the other person involved in a conflict. Both hear at the same time what each one says. That allows for an ongoing, immediate and relational access to each other as subjects, a closeness between two subjects that cannot be improved by any other system of communication. Or, in other words, the direct face-to-face conversation is superior to any form of conversation that draws a line between thinking and saying.

In this sense, it becomes important to understand the role that the social pedagogue as a person, as a professional and as a private being has in this process. The reason for discussing this is simple! The pedagogue needs to be aware of the 'inner team' to facilitate successful communication, especially in situations of heated debate. The model of the three pedagogues appears to be helpful in this respect.

The three pedagogues

It has already been argued that the success of communication is, amongst other things, determined by the choices that the receiver makes in deciding with which ear he or she is listening. In order to achieve successful communication, it is necessary that the sender is to some degree aware that each message has at least four different dimensions and can contain congruent and incongruent statements as well as explicit and implicit elements. This is a difficult role for the professional and it needs a great amount of reflection to be able to ensure that a message is heard in all its dimensions. It is made more difficult by the observation that people tend to listen better with one ear than another – for example, better with the 'factual' than with the 'relational' ear.

This could be explained further by the idea that the pedagogue has three different identities: professional, private and personal. The *professional* pedagogue is using the various theories available to explain the behaviour of a young person. The *private* pedagogue is the person outside work, the person that one is at home or with friends. The *personal* pedagogue is the person that one is at work, someone with personal interests, likes and dislikes. This is the person who can offer something to the young person, who can share ideas, hobbies and interests.

Each one of these three pedagogues is likely to hear the same message with different ears. The private pedagogue might hear a message as an appeal, hearing it with the appellate ear because the young person reminds the pedagogue of her own child. The professional might hear the factual message, as she looks for evidence to be used to explain behaviour. The personal pedagogue might listen better to the relational messages because she is looking for chances to engage a young person. These three pedagogues come together in one real person. What role they play depends on personal history and development.

It is necessary for a pedagogue to understand how these three pedagogues come together to be able to reflect about the impact that a conflict is having on her and to ensure that reactions to challenges are well balanced between these three pedagogues. These three pedagogues are forming the inner team that enable the pedagogue to facilitate communication about conflicts successfully, which will help the young person to grow. The pedagogue has to develop the skills to ensure that all members of this team are being heard in order to manage conflict.

Managing conflict

In order to manage conflict successfully, it is not only necessary to listen to the inner team but also to be aware of the potential variety of conflict styles. Conflict styles 'provide an overall picture of a person's communication orientation toward conflict. Individuals have a predominant conflict style'. It also has to be acknowledged that 'the conflict style is a combination of traits (e.g. cultural background and personality) and states (e.g. situation)' (Oetzel and Ting-Toomey 2003, p.601).

The pedagogue, therefore, needs to consider the personal history of the young person and look for indicators that could be telling about the individual's conflict style. According to Oetzel and Ting-Toomey, there are three basic conflict styles:

• control, forcing, or dominating

• solution-oriented, issue-oriented or integrating

• non-confrontational, smoothing or avoiding.

Again, it is important to emphasise that the pedagogue needs to understand her own conflict style in order to communicate successfully in conflicts with young people. The pedagogue needs to become a role model for the other actors the conflict:

> People are also influenced by the models to whom they are exposed, especially those of higher status (Bandura 1986). Thus, the behaviour of third parties who intervene in conflicts is extremely important. Mediators and facilitators need to model the same types of behaviours they wish to have the parties to the conflict display. (Stephan 2008, p.34)

Stephan goes on to explain that there are three types of psychological process that can have a beneficial impact on conflict resolution and, therefore, can help the young person to become conflict literate. He writes:

> ...these processes can operate separately, more commonly they occur simultaneously. These processes do not refer to the substantive issues involved in the conflict, nor do they refer to the actual techniques and procedures employed to successfully resolve conflicts. Rather, they can be used to create a climate in which people gathered in small groups can come to understand the positions of others, change their own positions, and work toward resolving intergroup conflicts. (Stephan 2008, p.34)

These processes, which are so important for pedagogues, can be described as follows:

• *Affective processes* create emotional empathy, involving the capacity to feel the same emotions as others. Empathising can lead to a concern for the welfare of others and, therefore, can lead to a more positive attitude to them.

- *Cognitive processes* let the individual experience cognitive empathy by taking the role of another. This enables the individual to understand the other's perception of the conflict.

- *Behavioural processes* are working with the observation that cooperation in the pursuit of common goals, equality and the approval of relevant authority figures allow people to get to know one another. They use the benefits of mutual interdependence. (Stephan 2008, p.34)

What do these ideas about conflict and communication mean for social pedagogy? First, the potential of communication and conflict has to be recognised and embedded in pedagogical settings, which means embracing conflicts to enable growth. Second, this is not a one-way process. As has been discussed, the person of the pedagogue is crucial in this. The pedagogue has to reflect on her own role in communication about conflict using knowledge about the different parts of a message, the inner team and the individual's conflict styles. The pedagogue can become a great resource if she understands these links and develops skills to support the cognitive processes that can help to manage conflicts.

Conclusion

Communication and conflict are two closely entangled concepts, with communication often being the trigger for conflict (if communication goes wrong) and the solution to conflict. It has to be understood that constructive conflict on the basis of working communication is of great importance for the individual's disposition to grow. And, in this sense, communication and the ability to manage conflicts is a key skill for social pedagogues alongside the ability to reflect on practice in order to identify one's own communication skills and to understand how one reacts in situations when there is conflict.

Communication and conflicts have many different dimensions and this makes it very complicated to manage these situations successfully. As a result, social pedagogues and other practitioners often try to avoid conflicts. This means, however, that it is more difficult for the young person to learn from responsible adults how to engage and resolve a conflict successfully without having to refer to ways of avoiding conflicts or resolving them through means other than communication. Engaging in conflicts when working with young people, including conflicts with other professionals, means the possibility to initiate learning situations where the young person can learn and experience a great range of social skills that are important for his or her future.

References

Badry, E. and Knapp, R. (2003) 'Grundlagen und Grundfragen des Pädagogischen.' In E. Badry, M. Buchka and R. Knapp (eds) *Pädagogik – Grundlagen und sozialpädagogische Arbeitsfelder*. München: Luchterhand.

Bandura, B. (1986) *Social Foundations of Thought and Action: A Social Cognitive Theory*. Englewood Cliffs, NJ: Prentice-Hall.

Berger, P. and Luckmann, T. (1977) *Die gesellschaftliche Konstruktion der Wirklichkeit: Eine Theorie der Wissenssoziologie*. Frankfurt am Main: Fischer.

Böhnisch, L. and Schröer, W. (2007) *Politische Pädagogik: Eine problemorientierte Einführung*. Weinheim: Juventa-Verl.

Cohn, R.C. (1975) *Von der Psychoanalyse zur Themenzentrierten Interaktion*. Stuttgart: Klett-Cotta.

Cohn, R. and Terfurth, C. (1997) *Lebendiges Lehren und Lernen: TZI macht Schule*. Stuttgart: Klett-Cotta.

Dahrendorf, R. (1963) *Gesellschaft und Freiheit: Zur soziologischen Analyse der Gegenwart*. München: Piper.

Farau, A. and Cohn, R. (1984) *Gelebte Geschichte der Psychotherapie. Zwei Perspektiven*. Stuttgart: Klett-Cotta.

Farelly, F. and Brandsma, J. (1986) *Provokative Therapie*. Berlin: Springer-Verlag.

Gerzon, M. (2006) *Leading through Conflict: How Successful Leaders Transform Differences into Opportunity*. Boston, MA: Harvard Business School Press.

Hoffmann, S.G. (2010) 'Störungspostulat.' In M. Schneider-Landolf, J. Spielmann and W. Zitterbarth (eds) *Handbuch Themenzentrierte Interaktion (TZI)*. Göttingen: Vandenhoeck & Ruprecht.

Mollenhauer, K. (1968) *Erziehung und Emanzipation: Polemische Skizzen*. München: Juventa.

Nohl, H. (1935) *Die pädagogische Bewegung in Deutschland und ihre Theorie*. Frankfurt am Main: Schulte-Bulmke.

Oetzel, J. and Ting-Toomey, S. (2003) 'Face concerns in interpersonal conflict: A cross-cultural empirical test of the face negotiation theory.' *Communication Research 30*, 6, 599–624.

Omer, H. and von Schlippe, A. (2002) *Autorität ohne Gewalt*. Göttingen: Vandenhoeck & Ruprecht.

Prekop, J. (1989) *Hättest du mich festgehalten…: Grundlagen und Anwendung der Festhalte-Therapie*. München: Käsel.

Ruesch, J. and Bateson, G. (2008) 'Individual, group, and culture: A review of the theory of human communication.' In J. Ruesch and G. Bateson (eds) *Communication*. New Brunswick, NJ: Transaction Publishers.

Schulz von Thun, F. (2001) *Miteinander reden 1 Störungen und Klärungen*. Reinbek bei Hamburg: Rowohlt-Taschenbuch-Verl.

Schulz von Thun, F. (2003) *Miteinander reden*. Reinbek bei Hamburg: Rowolhlt-Taschenbuch-Verl.

Stephan, W.G. (2008) 'Psychological and communication processes associated with intergroup conflict resolution.' *Small Group Research 39*, 1, 28–41.

Stiels-Glenn, M. and Glenn, P. (2008) 'Stirn And Stirn: Streiten Lernen Helfen.' In J. Weidner and R. Kilb (eds) *Konfrontative Pädagogik*. Wiesbaden: VS Verlag für Sozialwissenschaften/GWV Fachverlage GmbH Wiesbaden.

Vogel, P. (2010) 'Humanismus.' In M. Schneider-Landolf, J. Spielmann and W. Zitterbarth (eds) *Handbuch Themenzentrierte Interaktion (TZI)*. Göttingen: Vandenhoeck & Ruprecht.

Watzlawick, P., Bavelas, J. and Jackson, D.D. (1967) *Pragmatics of Human Communication: A Study of Interactional Patterns, Pathologies, and Paradoxes*. New York, NY: Norton.

CHAPTER 8

Understandings of Danish Pedagogical Practice

JYTTE JUUL JENSEN

Understanding understandings

Achieving some understanding of how pedagogues themselves, or any other group of workers, understand the nature of their work and the defining features of their practice can be difficult; often what is most central is so self-evident and taken for granted by practitioners that they may find it difficult to see and to talk about it. This chapter attempts to make visible and audible some central understandings of pedagogical practice in Denmark, by an innovative visual method that involves showing films of work in children's services in a number of countries as a 'provocation' to reflection. It builds on an ongoing research project, funded by a Danish trade union for pedagogues (BUPL 2008), the aim of which is to examine pedagogues' understandings of some basic values in Danish pedagogical practice.

As my research study is focused on early childhood centres, I talk about pedagogical practice and not social pedagogical practice. In Denmark, a new qualification was introduced in 1992 – a bachelor of education as pedagogue. This new education integrated three formerly separate educations for pedagogues: kindergarten pedagogue (mainly for those wanting to work in early childhood services), leisure-time pedagogue (mainly for those wanting to work in 'out-of-school' services for school-aged children) and social pedagogue (mainly for those wanting to work in a range of social welfare services for children, young people and adults). The post-1992 integrated education is a generalist education and we talk about a generic pedagogue profession. There were several reasons to call the new profession a 'pedagogue' rather than a 'social pedagogue'. One reason was that the term 'social pedagogue' was associated with only one of the three pre-1992 educations; another, and related to the first reason, was that the terms 'social pedagogy' and 'social pedagogical practice' are used to refer only to certain types of work, in particular in residential care for children and young people, among adults with disabilities and with other people with special needs. On the other hand, a disadvantage of using the basic word 'pedagogue' is that it is not clearly distinguished from teaching in schools and adult education.

Pedagogues is a widespread profession in Denmark with a three-and-a-half-year BA education leading to work in a range of settings. The pedagogical practice in this study is from early childhood services for young children from one year up to six years, though, as noted above, Danish pedagogues can also be found working with older children, young people and adults with disabilities. Pedagogy, therefore, plays a central role in the Danish welfare state and pedagogues constitute a numerous and important part of the workforce. In doing this research, a number of themes emerge, which may help to define the identity of the pedagogue's work in Denmark. The chapter will focus particularly on three of them: everyday life, *kropslighed* (perhaps best translated into English as 'embodiment') and outdoor life. It will more briefly touch on two more: child–child relations and participating adults.

The empirical study

The research is a qualitative study. The data gathering uses a research method where focus groups of pedagogues and others involved with pedagogical work are shown half-hour films of everyday life and practice in early childhood centres in Denmark, England and Hungary; these films were made for an earlier European project in which I participated, *Care Work in Europe: Current Understandings and Future Directions* (Cameron and Moss 2007). Each film focuses in particular on two members of staff, pedagogues in the case of the Danish centre. The method was inspired by Tobin, Wu and Davidson (1989), then developed further in the European project where we called it SOPHOS: Second Order Phenomenological Observation Scheme (Hansen and Jensen 2004). The films pose an open interview question: What do you think when you see this? And through the responses of the focus groups to this question, what the pedagogues and others talk about and discuss – what we might call the provocation of the film – it is possible to investigate and create a picture of their ideals and their understandings of central values in pedagogical practice.

The power of this method to give insight into understandings partly arises from its aesthetic form – the immediacy and power of the medium of film – and partly from the 'exotic' nature of the two films showing practice from abroad. The films involve, so they may get under the skin; they may affect the pedagogues. They provoke two types of verbal response: on the one hand, viewers talk about what they see on the films; and, on the other hand, they talk about notions of how pedagogues as a profession should act ideally in practice.

In the course of a day, the films could be shown to and discussed by a group of four pedagogues. Altogether five groups participated in such one-day sessions, with these groups selected from different types of centres, geographically spread; among those participating were the two pedagogues who are the focus of the Danish film. Other groups of informants have also seen and discussed the films, including educators of pedagogues and academics in pedagogy; some of their statements also appear in this chapter. The discussion of the three films in each focus group has been recorded and transcribed, and these transcriptions are the primary empirical data.

It is important to underline that the focus of the research is not the three countries' practice per se. The research is not a cross-national study, but a study into Danish understandings of good pedagogical work using films of practice from other countries (and also Denmark) to provoke discussion and reflection; the films could, of course, be used in the same way to study understandings of good work in any country. So it is important to bear in mind that the Danish pedagogues' understandings do not necessarily tell us something about English and Hungarian practice. Rather, they say something about how these practices are interpreted through Danish eyes. Through the practice of other countries and Danish practice viewed on film, as well as their professional knowledge and experiences, the pedagogues formulate and articulate how they view good practice.

It is, however, also important to bear in mind that by using films of practice in other countries as a way of getting data, it turns out – in my empirical data anyway – that the Danish pedagogues do talk a lot about contrasts between the three countries. It was the English practice that was most likely to generate comment, it being seen as very different to Danish. Another point to notice is that interpretations of practice differences may be rooted in wider cultural differences. An example, discussed later, is meals, which have high value in Danish centres as they also do in families.

This chapter focuses on some critical themes, which particularly stood out in the focus group discussions. There are more themes, but space precludes discussion here. The themes have emerged by using a grounded theory approach, interpreting and being open to the pedagogues' and other informants' understandings, language and their categorisations and concepts.

One way of creating generalisability is by analytic generalisation. By using my knowledge of Danish practice, as the researcher I reflect on whether the understandings of the pedagogue informants may be typical of the profession – in other words 'through logic, thoughtful and problem oriented reflection instead of through statistics and probability' (Jensen and Johnsen 2005, p.230; see also Kvale and Brinkmann 2009, pp.262–265). I have been further confirmed in my interpretations having shown the films to several cohorts of students and having presented my results around Denmark, and finding much agreement about the themes expressing basic values. It seems that these themes are typical of pedagogues' understandings of good pedagogical practice.

Three sets of institutional logic

There is a general agreement among the Danish pedagogues and other informants that the practice shown in the three films each has its own logic, which I have chosen to name as follows:

- pre-school logic

- home/family logic

- childhood logic.

These concepts are derived from my analysis that reflects the general understandings of the pedagogues. The logic represents the rationality that generally underpins the institutional practice of the centre in each country. The three sets of institutional logic are reflected in various critical areas such as aims and objectives, pace/rhythm/atmosphere, staff role, view of the child, oral communication, and the 'meeting' between children and adults. It is also reflected in the themes I highlight below: everyday life, embodiment (*kropslighed*), outdoor life, child–child relations and participating adults. The logics can be further seen in the material and the physical environment. The three sets of institutional logic will briefly be mentioned, followed by an analysis of the five themes; the main contrasts that emerged from the Danish pedagogues' responses to the three films are summarised in Table 8.1.

Table 8.1 Three institutional logics on the basis of the Danish pedagogues' understandings of pedagogical practice

Country / Critical themes	The English film	The Hungarian film	The Danish film
General institutional logic or agenda	Pre-school logic	Home/family logic	Childhood logic
Age of children	2–4 years	2 years	0–6 years
Role of staff	Pre-school teacher	Educator (careful 'mother')	Pedagogue
Child view	The learning child	The fragile child (partly)	The playing child Participant
The interaction between children and adults	By way of learning	By way of adults and things	By way of appreciative relations
Oral communication	Dictating	Instructing	Dialoguing
Tempo/rhythm/ atmosphere	Several shifts Group activities	Regularity Order Calmness	Absorption Unpredictability Humour
Play, planned learning by activities and everyday life	Planned learning by activities	Everyday life	Playing Planned learning by activities Everyday life
Embodiment The use and expression of the body	Bodily discipline Focal point: the child's head	Body care A quiet and calm body Calm activities	Embodiment Development A free and natural child
Outdoor life	Low priority Activities as indoors	Priority Calm and quiet activities	High priority Calm and wild activities
Child–child relations	Less important	Important	Very important
Participating adults	Teaching tone	Instructing tone	Dialoguing

The Danish pedagogues' statements about the Danish, English and Hungarian films reflected, directly and indirectly, a number of values and understandings of practice in *Danish* services for young children. They saw the Danish institutional logic as a 'childhood logic', where an underpinning idea is that children are experts in their own lives. The aim assumed by this rationality is children's acquisition of experiences and experiences gained by children on their own terms. The staff role includes the pedagogue viewing the child as a playing and participating child. The interaction between children and adults takes place by way of respectful relations with dialogic communications ('appreciative relations'). The pace, rhythm and atmosphere in day-to-day life are characterised by absorption in certain activities, unpredictability and humour.

In contrast, the Danish pedagogues saw a 'pre-school logic' in the film of the *English* nursery, with a school rationality in control of practice. The aims and objectives are seen to be formal teaching and learning. The role of the staff is that of a pre-school teacher who views the children as learning children. The interaction between children and adults involves alternating activities, with adults dictating to children as the dominant form of communication. The pace, rhythm and atmosphere are characterised by a high number of shifts over the day, from one activity to another, and activities involving the entire group of children.

In the film of the *Hungarian* nursery, the pedagogue informants found an institutional logic characterised by the good family life/home and where an image of the good family or home shapes the practice. The aim is upbringing. The role of the staff is the careful 'mother' and educator who sees before her, in part at least, a fragile child. The interaction between the children and adults takes place by way of the adults taking the initiative and through different activities, and the dominant type of communication is instruction. The pace, rhythm and atmosphere are characterised by regularity, order and calmness. The observers viewed the institution as a highly female universe.

Within this framework, of three institutional logics, five critical themes stood out from my analysis of the responses of pedagogues to the films, themes that reveal key features of pedagogues' understandings of good practice.

Critical theme 1: Everyday life

A day in a Danish early childhood centre involves many activities and situations. In the Danish pedagogical debate of recent years, the conceptual pairing of 'play and learning' has been put forward as core activities and situations during a day in a centre. But from the pedagogues' statements in this research, a third activity or situation can be put forward: everyday life. These three activities or situations do not appear in pure form, as there may be overlaps and multiple purposes. However, describing a particular situation and activity as belonging, for example, to play means that the relation and situation are dominated by play.

Children's play has always been a central part of the Danish pedagogic practice, probably reflecting the historical heritage of Fröbel, whose thoughts lay behind the establishment of the first kindergarten in Denmark in 1870, which led to the first education as a 'pedagogue' in the late 19th century. Children's play is here understood as involving informal relations between the children and where the children possess the power of definition: here they decide, by and large, who they want to play with, where and how. Play is considered a process and as important in its own right. The role of the pedagogue in each play situation is to choose between leaving the children to play unobserved, being the observer or being the supporter and initiator of the play. In play, too, the child of course learns.

Since a national government requirement in 2004 that every early childhood centre must work with and prepare written pedagogical learning plans, learning has come more into focus. Learning can be defined broadly so it includes all activity which has a developmental perspective. But many understand learning more narrowly. Here I speak of learning in planned activities, where adult–child relations are more formal.

Everyday life is togetherness and necessary activities in day-to-day life, such as eating, sleeping, going to the bathroom, going for a walk, saying hello and goodbye to parents. Some are routines and are repeated every day. It is a mix of informal and formal child–child and child–adult relations. Such everyday life actions are a core value in Danish practice even though they take place in the centre's institutionalised context. Much time and space is given over to them. They are important, among other reasons, for the child becoming resourceful, independent and capable of living in society.

Play, learning in planned activities and everyday life, the pedagogue informants say, carry equal importance in Danish pedagogical practice. In their view, however, this was not the case in the practice shown in the English film, where the learning in planned activities was pivotal, and play and everyday life only had peripheral importance. This was reflected in the general pace and atmosphere of day-to-day life with a large number of adult-controlled and alternating activities for the entire group of children.

According to the following statement by an academic in pedagogy, the practice in the English film shows that meals are pieces of everyday life to which no particular importance is attached:

> What really stands out is the lack of involvement in everyday situations in [the English film]. The Danish centre is based on an everyday approach. We bring food and plates to and fro. It is a project that goes on alongside everything else. In [the English film] it is all about other things, and about learning stuff.

As the pedagogues saw it, eating as well as visits to the toilet seem to be less important, the consequence being that the staff are simply servicing the children.

The Danish pedagogues interpret the English film as showing little importance being given to the resourceful and independent child. Visits to the toilet must be done very quickly – for example, the adult pulls up the older child's trousers as a very natural thing – because the current activity is more important. Before meals some of the staff lay the table with glasses and open lunchboxes, while stories are read for the children. During the meal the staff sit by the table, but distanced and with no 'real' dialogue, only a little about the food, but in a tone of teaching rather than of dialogue; Palludan (2008) elaborates these two types of tone, which pedagogues use in their communication with children, in her anthropological study in a Danish centre.

So at the English meal time, the adult does not pick up on the children's initiatives, but is sitting a bit back with her bottle of water. Other adults stand up behind the children and give the children a choice between milk and water, but then they pour from behind. These adults behind the children also wipe the table clean over the child's shoulder if that child spills something. The adults, too, by and large, clean up after the children as if these everyday activities should be over and done with in a hurry, and no value is assigned to the children themselves being able to do those things.

Lise Ahlmann (1998), through development work in Danish centres for young children, finds that many of these centres also have the service-oriented approach to meals that the pedagogues saw in the English film. Alternatively, they adopt a 'prefect' approach, where children take it in turns to be in charge of laying the table and cleaning up. Ahlmann, like the pedagogue informants in my research, is critical towards both approaches. The meal should be organised in such a way that both adults and children participate and the children become independent and resourceful. Ahlman also argues for the use of the word 'meal' instead of 'meal-situation'. The name 'meal' indicates that the purpose is to eat together and a strengthening of the community. This meaning is cosy and social. 'Meal' is a name used in the family, whereas 'meal-situation' is a concept used in an institutionalised context and indicates that the purpose is to 'give children a feed' and then move on to the next planned activity. One pedagogue talks about how in her centre they make the meals cosy and home-like – for example, by laying the table with plates and knives, forks and spoons, instead of letting the children eat directly from their lunchboxes.

Everyday life activities, such as having a meal, going to the bathroom, sleeping and so on, are emphasised not only in Danish pedagogical work with young children but also in the pedagogical work with other groups, such as children and young people in residential care and adults with severe disabilities living in shared accommodation. In all such settings, these activities take up much time and space. The great importance given to the everyday life in Danish centres also underlines the importance attached to the life here and now instead of instrumental ideas about future outcomes. What is important – what matters – is children and adults living *together*. This attitude may originate from the history of Danish services, many of which started out from civic society, looking more at the family setting than the school setting as a reference point, but it also reflects pedagogical ideas about the importance of group living and community.

Underlining the everyday life also reflects a notion that daily life cannot be split up, with different activities and situations given to different levels of worker. Physical caring, such as blowing a child's nose or taking a child to the bathroom, is considered to be an important part of pedagogical work. Physical caring tasks themselves do not define what pedagogical work is, but how the tasks are performed does, so the tasks cannot be left to less educated staff. One consequence is that Danish settings tend to be less hierarchical than in some other countries, such as England, because many staff are pedagogues with the same high level of education. For example, around 60 per cent of the staff working in Danish early childhood centres are qualified pedagogues with a graduate education (Oberhuemer, Schreyer and Neuman 2010); they blow children's noses and take children to the bathroom, rather than delegating such tasks to various levels of assistant and confining themselves to pedagogical 'leadership'.

Critical theme 2: *Kropslighed* or embodiment

It is striking that all pedagogue informants talk so much about how they see children's and adults' *kropslighed* expressed differently in the three films. 'Embodiment' is perhaps the nearest English translation for this important Danish pedagogical term, which is about the use and expression of the body. I will use this English word in the remainder of this section.

The different embodiments are probably especially visible when looking at staff and children on film. The pedagogues find that both children and adults show few expressions of embodiment in the English and Hungarian films. One informant, an academic in pedagogy, put it this way:

> ...you can say that the children have their body in a different way in the Danish film, and the pedagogues as well. The children's bodies are much more present. The body is allowed to be there... Nursing of the body is a focal point in [the Hungarian film] and one way or the other the body has been reduced to a head in the English film.

The Danish view of the child is a child who must be allowed to express himself with his body and to show his feelings. Danish pedagogues put great emphasis on the child's natural expression as a child and it is part of the child's embodiment to run, jump, laugh, cry, scream out loud and so on. It is this image of the child that the pedagogues elaborate and work with in creating the physical and mental environment of their centres, and it is one of the reasons why outdoor life is so important for the pedagogues.

One informant who educates pedagogues elaborates on this framing of the centre's mental atmosphere and stresses that 'it is of basic importance for children [to have an]...atmosphere of joy and lightness'. And for this the pedagogue's personality is important. The educator continues by talking about one pedagogue's relations with the children in the Danish film:

> Yes, an incredible contact. She makes them blossom. She shows confidence and respect and creates space for them to express themselves. They both cry more here, laugh more, and

move, and communicate much more with each other. In the other two films there was much interaction between adults and children, but here we see how children communicate with each other.

The two pedagogues focused on in the Danish film are critical, on viewing the film, of their own actions and behaviour, and their self-criticism is precisely about body-related and emotional issues. They look, they say, too sour and stiff; they usually have more fun and fool around more with the children. Here they touch on the role of humour in pedagogic work. The academic informants pick up on this too. They find that feelings are curbed in the Danish film, which, as one observes, 'results in neutral child-friendliness, where one smiles and stimulates'; by which he means that the pedagogues practise the philosophy that children are experts on their own lives and must be listened to, but in a too routinised and unemotional way. Another informant says she misses 'those intensive moments where everything swings and everybody is deeply involved', indicating the value she attaches to relations being at a passionate level of involvement.

The criticism voiced by pedagogues and other informants about the lack of embodiment expresses their understanding of pedagogical work and of how Danish centres should be less institutional and more about real life. They should be places where people get involved with each other in a genuine, intense, emotional manner – as we do in real life.

Critical theme 3: Outdoor life

The outdoor life – in the playground and exploring the world outside the early childhood centre – is central in Danish practice. Children and adults spend much of their time in the playground, and daily trips out of the centre with a group of children are common. Many of the trips are to the forest or beach, but normal city life, museums, the library and so on are also visited. The basic elements – earth, fire, water and air – are used in Danish pedagogy, and visitors from abroad are always surprised at the importance given to outdoor life (Jensen 1999). A classic example is the amazement that very young children have their naps outdoors, even in the coldest weather. Another example is the so-called 'forest' kindergarten, a widespread type of early childhood provision in which children spend the entire day outdoors (found also in other Nordic countries).

Outdoor pedagogy is partly dominated by informal relations where children can hide, get dirty, run around almost naked during summer time, and play without interruption: play with mud and sand, play with water, play in trees, play football. Nearly every playground has a fireplace for cooking and getting some warmth in winter time. Although some Danish centres are only for children under three years old or only for children from three to six years old, many others are age-integrated, taking in children from one up to six years of age, and the playground is used for all ages without fencing off different age groups. Small groups of children are in the playground by themselves; they climb trees, use sharp knives and real saws, light bonfires. Children can walk around on their own, outside and inside their centre, without needing an adult's permission.

Within the framework of outdoor life, both children and adults can express embodiment more wildly and with less inhibition: 'it is also here that one can shout really loud because it is high to the sky', a pedagogue says. The conflicts are few and even pedagogues working with the youngest children, those under three years, notice this. Outdoor life has a good effect on all of us.

The pedagogue informants provide various examples of a good playground. It must be big with a varied landscape, flat areas with large and small hills, so that even small children's motor function can be challenged, and with caves, bushes and trees. There should be hiding places so children get the feeling of being lost and that it is a bit dangerous, and places where they are out of sight from adults. And the obligatory sandbox – a Danish invention, as one informant knew! – must be physically challenging – big, with a high edge over which the children have to crawl – and children must feel that they can dig a hole which never stops.

The use of the great outdoors is sometimes mentioned as an extra pedagogical 'room' and forms an important part of the education of pedagogues. Many pedagogical ideas are behind the layout of each playground in Denmark, where over the last 20 years much effort has been put into developing new outdoor opportunities. Playgrounds have been transformed from areas with fixed equipment and manufactured toys into nature-oriented spaces with much use of natural materials. These natural materials appeal to the children's imaginations and creativity.

Not only play dominates outdoor life; pedagogues plan certain activities here. It can be plays or bonfire food or knowledge of nature – for example, children themselves experiencing snails on leaves or filling up half a bucket with snails; or to be out on a rainy day; or to experience the alternation of the seasons. A pedagogue tells how she and her colleagues walked along the same path with the children each week for half a year, where they sensed, noticed and talked about the seasonal changes such as how the apples started as flowers until they finally ripened, then were picked and eaten.

Outdoor life is also important for getting outside the centre. It is a core value that the centre does not become a ghetto without contact with the outside world. Children must go out and look and feel a part of the wider world, and the world should see them. The centre as a childhood place should participate in the many public spaces in its area. Here pedagogues express their view that the centre should not be like a closed classroom and should not take the school as its model.

Outdoor life is seen as being given priority in the Hungarian film, but with a different approach to that in the Danish film. The layout of the playground encourages calm and quiet activities supported by the adults. Some of the pedagogue informants compare it to a fine suburban lawn where it is unthinkable that the playhouse gets muddied by the children. Wilder and more expressive *kropslige* movements from children and adults are not to be seen.

The agenda for the outdoor life in the English film is a limited physical environment, a small asphalt playground, no flowers, trees or natural materials. According to the pedagogues watching the films, the playground in the English nursery is seen as an extra indoor space, the activities in which could just as well have taken place inside. Everything is clean, nice and orderly, and the adult control is dominating. That children must sense nature and the distinctive features of outdoor life seems to be given low priority, looking at the English film. Hence, the logic of the three institutions also feeds through to the understanding of how outdoor life should be prioritised and take place in the pedagogical practice.

Critical theme 4: Child–child relations

One of the most valuable benefits of being together in a centre is, from a Danish pedagogical perspective, the formation of relations between children and adults. These relationships and appreciation of their importance take up much space in the pedagogue education (Nørgaard 2008). Also, relations between children are highly valued. All the time, the pedagogues encourage the formation of relations between the children not only in play or planned activities but also in everyday life activities, from which the examples below are drawn.

Let me give an example from the Hungarian film. A child observes an adult wipe the nose and eyes of a child who has been crying, and the watching child, around the age of two and a half years, without being asked, walks and gets tissues for the child and adult, which means that the child has registered the needs of another child and adult, as one pedagogue informant notices. If a child must be comforted, the pedagogues draw the nearby children's attention to the fact by talking about it, so the children learn how to register others' feelings. One pedagogue talks about how she mostly goes to the bathroom with a couple of children and not only with one child, because she is then able to invite the children to help each other. She tells how, the day before, she was in the bathroom occupied by other things, and a two-and-a-half-year-old child went without being asked up to a younger child and started to pull down the child's pants: 'How wonderful it was that they can help each other,' she said. One misses this opportunity if there is only one child and adult present.

Of course, others might say that this is an example of the younger child's privacy being invaded. To which a pedagogue might answer 'it depends', on the context and situation. This also shows how powerful this type of method, using film, can be for opening up discussions during the education or continuing professional development of pedagogues and other workers.

During a meal shown on the Danish film, a pedagogue sits at a small table with three children between two and three years old, each with their lunchboxes, and one child asks another if she wants to taste his dried bananas. The child nods and gets a taste in her mouth. The pedagogue asks if the third child also gets a taste, and immediately a piece of banana is also put into his mouth. At another table with children under three years, one child is pouring water into his glass, then asks the child sitting beside him if he wants some water, too. This takes place without being asked by the pedagogue. This example illustrates the Danish approach, and although taken directly from the film, this sequence is also picked up on and discussed by the pedagogue informants, who express strong approval of what is going on here between the children.

A special part of child–child relations is the formation of friendships among children. It is a strong ideal that children must have friends in the centre, and they must be allowed to cultivate these friendships. If a child does not have any friends or playmates, he or she is considered a marginalised child and tends to be excluded from the community. Ellegaard (2004) finds in his research that the most excluding factor for children is not being able to relate to other children.

The pedagogues have an eye for these important child–child relationships. Children must be attentive to each other, register each other and their needs, and help each other. This can be seen as an example of how pedagogues in their practice work on the formation of an inclusive community, which is one of the aims for the services in Denmark, set out in law. One pedagogue expresses it in this way: 'The weight one assigns to the collective. How to become a social individual and show consideration and have empathy…we did not see that so much in the Hungarian and English films.'

Critical theme 5: Participating pedagogues

It is important for the pedagogue informants that they themselves participate in activities and situations together with the children. They must put on an apron and participate in the painting, too. During a rest time with three- to six-year-old children, where the children lie down on the floor to a background of relaxing music, the Danish pedagogue on the film is criticised by some of the pedagogue informants for not lying down together with the children. At the small bridge by the stream, where some children lie down to peer over, the pedagogues must do the same and look at the stream with its floating leaves (sharks!) and other exciting things. They must sit down in the sandbox with their feet in the sand. And they must sit at the children's eye level and join the meal.

The pedagogues watching the films give many such examples. They also give several reasons why this matters. If pedagogues do not participate, then they distance themselves from the children. The adults are role models, too. Sometimes it can be hard for children to understand a verbal message or what is going to happen; it is easier if the pedagogue does the things herself. Not least, participation is used to build relations. Closeness and engagement can be used to talk not only about what is happening in the activity, but also about everything else. Through this the pedagogue can grasp the moment where the child tells or does something.

Each child's individual needs, wants, feelings and initiatives are important and interesting. Pedagogues try to listen to their ideas, to understand their feelings and to see things from their perspective, grasping opportunities that arise during the day. They expect active children, who want something and who express feelings. That's why the 'appreciative relations' with the children, which I referred to earlier, are of great importance in pedagogues' understandings of good practice.

Concluding remarks

In response to films showing practice in early childhood centres in Denmark, England and Hungary, Danish pedagogues see three types of institutional logic or rationality: pre-school, home/family and childhood logic. Those logics run through a number of themes that stood out in the pedagogues' discussions and statements about the three films, of which five are chosen for this chapter: everyday life, embodiment, outdoor life, child–child relations and participating adults.

The themes highlight some basic values in and understandings of pedagogical practice in Denmark. As we have already seen, pedagogical work is a very complex profession, and practice raises all sorts of questions about how the pedagogue should act. What does follow from these different themes is how pedagogical practice requires pedagogues to make situated judgements in complex situations. During the course of a day in a centre, there are many such complex situations where the pedagogue has to use her judgement. No situations are the same and no 'objective' rules or guidelines can tell the pedagogue how to act in a specific situation. It will depend on the context and special character of each situation.

The complex everyday life demands the exercise of judgement by the pedagogue. Each time she must decide what action should be taken, and her decisions will depend on a range of conditions. The complexity of the situation and the pedagogue's professional judgement are products of the specific knowledge of the profession, the pedagogue's personality, the voice of the children, and the political and administrative system.

The introduction in Denmark since 2004 of pedagogical learning plans has led to an increase of national and local control in services for children, and more demands for documentation and evaluation. Too much external prescription and control can undermine the pedagogue's ability to practise knowledgeable judgements in complex situations arising in everyday life, as well as undermining children's voices. This is potentially a route to 'de-professionalisation' and is also a worry shared by the pedagogues in this study.

References

Ahlmann, L. (1998) *Små børn og de voksne*. København: Christian Ejlers' Forlag.

BUPL (2008) *Research Programme*. Available at www.bupl.dk/paedagogik/udvikling_ og_forskning/forskningsprojekter_stoettet_af_bupl?opendocument, accessed on 5 May 2011.

Cameron, C. and Moss, P. (2007) *Care Work in Europe: Current Understandings and Future Directions*. London: Routledge.

Ellegaard, T. (2004) *Et godt børnehavebarn?* Roskilde: Roskilde Universitetscenter. Available at http://rudar.ruc.dk/bitstream/1800/825/3/Rev.%20afhandling%20 (090405).pdf, accessed on 8 August 2010.

Hansen, H.K. and Jensen, J.J. (2004) *A Study of Understandings in Care and Pedagogical Practice: Experiences using the Sophos Model in Cross National Studies*. Available at http://144.82.31.4/reports/WP10%20consolidated%20report%20full.pdf, accessed on 9 August 2010.

Jensen, J.J. (1999) 'Hvad så når snottet fryser til is? – Udlændinges reaktioner på danske daginstitutioner.' *Vera 9*, 50–57.

Jensen, T.K. and Johnsen, T.J. (2005) *Sundhedsfremme i teori og praksis*. Århus: Philosophia.

Kvale, S. and Brinkmann, S. (2009) *Inter Views: Learning the Craft of Qualitative Research Inter Viewing*. London: Sage Publications.

Nørgaard, B. (2008) 'Hvorfor fylder "anerkendelse" og "relationer" så meget i uddannelsen?' In K. Tuft and C. Aabro (eds) *Faget pædagogik*. Værløse: Billesø & Baltzer.

Oberhuemer, P., Schreyer, I. and Neuman, M.J. (2010) *Professionals in Early Childhood Education and Care Systems: European Profiles and Perspectives*. Farmington Hills MI: Barbara Buddich Publishers.

Palludan, C. (2008) *Børnehaven gør en forskel*. København: Danmarks Pædagogiske Universitets Forlag.

Tobin, J., Wu, D.Y. and Davidson, D.H. (1989) *Preschool in Three Cultures*. New Haven, CT: Yale University Press.

CHAPTER 9

Early Childhood Education in Reggio Emilia and Social Pedagogy: Are They Related?

Peter Moss

A local cultural project of childhood

Since the early 1960s, Reggio Emilia has become one of the most important experiences of early childhood education in the world. Tens of thousands have visited the city to learn more about this experience. Since 1981, its exhibitions – first, *The Hundred Languages of Children*, followed recently by *The Wonder of Learning* – have travelled the world. There are Reggio networks in more than 20 countries, including all five Nordic countries, Australia, Korea, the United Kingdom and the United States. There is a large and growing literature about this educational project, both by educators in Reggio Emilia and by outsiders.

This educational project of Reggio Emilia has resonated with people from around the world: it has a global appeal. Yet it is a very local experience, undertaken and sustained by one relatively small urban community. It is what might be termed a local cultural project of childhood, to borrow the term used to me by the head of early childhood services in another Italian city about that city's work on early childhood education, a reminder that Reggio Emilia was and is part of a wider 'municipal school revolution' in northern Italy (Catarsi 2004). In this chapter I want to offer my reading of this local experience, my interpretation of the distinctive identity of Reggio's thought and practice.

What has this to do with social pedagogy? As my interest in both Reggio Emilia and social pedagogy has grown over time, I have been increasingly struck by certain similarities in both thinking and practice. So,

I shall finish by drawing out some of these similarities, between the local educational experience of Reggio Emilia and its 'municipal schools' on the one hand, and the far more widespread approach of social pedagogy on the other, and speculate about the relationship between them. Can we say, in any way, that Reggio is an example of social pedagogy applied to the education of young children? And, if so, can this help us to explore future possibilities for the relationship between education and social pedagogy?

What is Reggio?

Reggio Emilia is a city of about 150,000 people in the Emilia Romagna region of northern Italy, one of the wealthiest parts of Europe, some 60 kilometres to the west of Bologna. Like many Italian cities, it has a long history made visible in old buildings, streets and piazzas. At the same time, it is very modern, with a post-industrial economy and an influx of immigrants from around the world, contributing to what Sandra Piccinini (responsible for educational policy in the municipal administration from 1990 to 2003) calls a 'new Reggio'. But what makes Reggio world-famous is its local educational project, the decision made in the early 1960s to develop 'municipal schools' providing early childhood education and care for young children, from a few months old to six years. Today, the municipality is responsible for a network of 54 schools – 28 for children under three years, 26 for three- to six-year-olds – that provided in 2009–10 for just over 3500 children, and are managed through an agency of the municipality with a high degree of autonomy, the 'Istituzione' (Istituzione of the Municipality of Reggio Emilia and Reggio Children 2010).

As with the rest of Italy, there are also state-run and private (mainly church) schools for three- to six-year-olds in the city, and 58 per cent of this age group of children attend them. But it is the municipal schools where the extraordinary project in early childhood education has taken place, an example of how local government can, at its best, become an agent of what Roberto Unger terms 'democratic experimentalism':

> The provision of public services must be an innovative collective practice, moving forward the qualitative provision of the services themselves. That can no longer happen in our current understanding of efficiency and production by the mechanical transmission of innovation from the top. It can only

happen through the organisation of a collective experimental practice from below... Democracy is not just one more terrain for the institutional innovation that I advocate. It is the most important terrain. (Unger 2005, pp.179, 182)

Such experimentation is, for Unger, an essential element of what he terms 'high energy democracy', which should include 'vastly expanded opportunities to try out, in particular parts of the country or sectors of the economy, different ways of doing things' (Unger 2005, p.78; for a fuller discussion of the concept of 'democratic experimentalism', see Moss 2009). The link between education, experimentation and democracy is, as will become apparent, a defining feature of Reggio Emilia's educational experience.

This local educational project emerged from a particular political context, with its origins in left-wing politics and an early women's movement:

The first school for young children in our area, the Villa Gaida, was opened in 1912, inspired by the Socialist mayor of Reggio. He wanted a school that clearly expressed important ideas in socialist thinking – education as a tool, a weapon against poverty, ignorance, arrogance; education as a tool for freedom... Especially after the end of the Second World War, the women's movement developed the idea of a school for young children as a public place... [I]t was also supported by farm workers, an exploited group who were influenced by left politics. It was in this very lively atmosphere that the municipality of Reggio (which had a Communist party majority) took the decision to innovate and open the first municipal school [in 1963], the beginning of 40 years of experience. (Rinaldi 2006, pp.178–179)

The project was also a reaction to the Fascist regime, which, on coming to power in the early 1920s, had closed the pioneering nursery schools in Reggio and elsewhere in the province. Decades of fascism, a former Mayor of Reggio has commented, 'taught them that people who conformed and obeyed were dangerous, and that in building a new society it was imperative...to nurture and maintain a vision of children who can think and act for themselves' (Dahlberg 2000, p.177).

This project, to create an education for young citizens, was not, however, confined to Reggio Emilia. In the 1960s, similar projects were initiated in a number of other towns and cities in and around Emilia

Romagna, in particular in those controlled by left-wing parties (Catarsi 2004). So today there remains in northern Italy a network of innovative local educational experiences, sharing much in common but also with local variations (for another example of municipal action, San Miniato in Tuscany, see Fortunati 2006, whose book is tellingly titled *The Education of Young Children as a Community Project*).

A leading figure in the Reggio project was Loris Malaguzzi (1920– 1994), one of the last century's greatest educationalists and first head of Reggio's early childhood services. While deeply interested and well read in the work of educationalists and psychologists, Malaguzzi's thinking was shaped by boundless curiosity that constantly took him into new territories in search of new perspectives:

> In analysing his philosophy and his work, we have found the presence of past and contemporary pedagogical thinkers and psychologists. But we also find philosophers, historians, artists, sociologists, scientists, linguists, poets and anthropologists...
> His method of study was like that of a person working on a jigsaw puzzle without knowing the final picture. In reality he was not a prisoner of anyone's ideas; he enjoyed, as a humanist, drawing from all sources to construct his thoughts.
> (Hoyuelos 2004, pp.6–7)

His influence is everywhere in Reggio, even today more than 15 years after his death. It can be seen, for example, in the continued willingness to cross borders into new disciplines and theories; in a desire to make connections and find new relationships; in a rejection of the theory/ practice divide; in a scepticism about certainties and linear progression, a refusal to be bound by predetermined outcomes, and a love of complexity, experimentation and thinking differently; and in the continuing exploitation of the fantastic and democratic theory of the hundred languages of children (of which more below).

But Reggio was and is more than a one-man (or woman) band. The project has shown remarkable powers of organic growth and sustainability, thriving for more than 40 years. A strong and cohesive company of educators, with a capacity to produce new thought and practice, enabled it to survive the body blow of Malaguzzi's death. It is built on the strong foundations of political commitment, public support, a reflective, researching, experimenting and democratic workforce, and an effective organisation that supports rather than regulates what gives Reggio its identity and strength: a body of educational thought and practice, permeated by explicit values and a recognition that early childhood education is, first and foremost, a political and ethical practice.

What is your image of the child?

The starting point for Reggio's project has been a critical question: What is your image of the child? This is an overtly social constructionist stance that acknowledges the profound significance of how we understand or construct childhood, since our image of the child is highly productive – of policy, provision and practice. The image that Reggio decided on was the rich child: not materially rich but 'rich in potential, strong, powerful, competent and, most of all, connected to adults and children' (Malaguzzi 1993, p.10). The 'connected' part attaches the highest value to relationships, while the rich potential of the child refers, in part, to the child being born with a hundred languages. This theory of the hundred languages of childhood emerged early on in the municipal project, during debates about the privileged position given in traditional education to just two languages – speech and writing – which 'supported the power, not only of certain knowledges, but also of certain classes' (Rinaldi 2006, p.193). The 'hundred languages', a theory that, as Carlina Rinaldi (who succeeded Malaguzzi as the head of Reggio's municipal schools) observes, is full of democracy, refers 'to the different ways children (human beings) represent, communicate and express their thinking in different media and symbolic systems; languages therefore are the many fonts or geneses of knowledge' (Vecchi 2010, p.9). These many linguistic possibilities range from mathematical and scientific languages to the poetic languages, 'forms of expression strongly characterized by expressive or aesthetic aspects such as music, song, dance or photography' (Vecchi 2010). The choice of a 'hundred' does not denote a precise count, but is intended to be 'very provocative, to claim for all these languages not only the same dignity, but the right to expression and to communicate with each other' (Rinaldi 2006, p.193).

But, for Reggio, the hundred languages is a potential too often thrown away by a stifling, monolingual education system. Malaguzzi wrote poetically about how the rich potential with which human beings are born is wasted in childhood, with education and school complicit in this loss:

> The child has a hundred languages
>
> (and a hundred hundred hundred more)

but they steal ninety-nine

the school and the culture

separate the head from the body...

They tell the child that

work and play

reality and fantasy

science and imagination

sky and earth

reason and dream

are things

that do not belong together.

And thus they tell the child

that the hundred is not there.

The child says:

No way. The hundred is there! (Malaguzzi undated)

One further part of Reggio's image of the child should be added: the child as a 'subject of rights', not a 'subject of needs', and as a citizen from birth, here and now and not just in a future adult incarnation.

> Children are not only our future, which we invest in by oppressing their dreams and freedom to be something other than we would wish them to be. They are our present. The child is not a citizen of the future; he is a citizen from the very first moment of life and also the most important citizen, because he represents and brings the 'possible', a statement that for me is completely without rhetoric. The child is a bearer, here and now, of rights, of values, of culture: the culture of childhood. He is not only our knowledge about childhood, but childhood's knowledge of how to be and how to live. (Rinaldi 2006, p.171)

Knowledge and learning

This rich child calls for matching understandings of learning, capable of realising rather than stifling potential, suited to the image of a competent child who, equipped with a hundred languages, strives to make meaning of the world from birth, a co-creator of identities, values and knowledges. One approach to learning is transmission, or reproduction – what Malaguzzi referred to as a 'small' pedagogy; this is learning as knowledge reproduction, learning where the answer to every question is already known, learning where the outcomes are predefined. But Reggio has chosen another approach. The city's educational philosophy is, says Vea Vecchi (2010), one of Reggio's first *atelieristas* (a role described below), based on 'subjectivity, dialogue, connection and autonomy' (p.174). Learning is knowledge building, recognising that knowledge so produced is inescapably partial, perspectival and provisional and not to be confused with information.

Such knowledge building is a process of meaning making or co-constructing an 'understanding of problems through experiment, trial, error and testing' (Vecchi 2010, p.47) where the learner develops and constructs theories, shares them with others, then reconstructs them, in an approach to learning that emphasises the importance of listening and relationships – indeed, is referred to as 'a pedagogy of listening and relationships'. One of the foundations of Reggio's work, says Vecchi (2010, p.29), is 'the careful, respectful, tender "listening" with solidarity to children's strategies and ways of thinking'. Such listening is a complex process, involving:

> listening not just with our ears, but with all our *senses* (sight, touch, smell, taste, orientation)…the hundred, the thousand *languages*, symbols and codes we use to express ourselves and communicate…*emotion*; it is generated by emotions and stimulates emotion…[and] *interpretation*, giving meaning to the message and value to those who offer it. (Rinaldi 2006, p.65; emphasis added)

Attention to relationships recognises the interdependence of individual and group, how both individual and group learn, and how the one contributes to the other in an endless process of knowledge construction (Giudici, Rinaldi and Krechevsky 2001).

This approach to learning attempts to avoid the sterility of predetermined results and to be open to 'the unpredictable results of children's investigation and research' (Rinaldi 2005, p.19). New thinking, new ideas, new perspectives are highly valued, though established knowledge is also respected. Vecchi expresses this desire to keep learning open in a statement that makes it clear that the pedagogy of listening and relationships can apply not only to younger children but also to children and young people in compulsory schooling:

> It is important to society that schools and we as teachers are clearly aware how much space we leave children for original thinking, without rushing to restrict it with predetermined schemes that define what is *correct* according to a school culture. How much do we support children to have ideas different from those of other people and how do we accustom them to arguing and discussing their ideas with their classmates? I am quite convinced that greater attention to processes, rather than only the final product, would help us to feel greater respect for the independent thinking and strategies of children and teenagers. (Vecchi 2010, p.138; original emphasis)

Schools, she adds, consciously need to take a position on '*which knowledge* they intend to promote': in short, there are alternatives, and choices of a political and ethical nature must be made between them. She contests an idea of teaching that chooses to 'transmit circumscribed "truths" in various "disciplines"'. Her choice and position is clear: 'to stand by children's sides together constructing contexts in which they can explore their own ideas and hypotheses individually or in groups and discuss them with friends or teachers' (Vecchi 2010, p.28).

As Vecchi's comments indicate, Reggio places great importance on process, not just product or outcome, which in any case cannot and should not be split and set up in opposition as often happens today. Echoing Morin's call for 'thinking the complex', a 'kind of thinking that relinks that which is disjointed…and tries to discern interdependencies' (Morin 1999, p.130), great importance is also attached to connections in processes of knowledge construction, in clear contrast to much modern education which is structured in a compartmentalised way that divides rather than connects disciplines, subjects and languages, fragmenting reality and making the development of thinking and understanding far more difficult. Reggio puts forward 'proposals for learning that do not hurry to fence the world in more or less rigid categories of thought; but, on the contrary, seek connections, alliances and solidarities between different categories and languages or subjects' (Vecchi 2010, p.32).

The unpredictability of learning in this approach to education, arising from the synaptic dynamic of relationships and new connections, contests the idea of learning as a process of linear progress and development, in favour of learning as an uncertain, unpredictable and intensely creative activity, with new understandings created unexpectedly and shooting off in new directions. Here, as elsewhere, can be seen the pervasive influence of Malaguzzi's pedagogical thinking:

> His pedagogy is complex: 'it allows itself' subjective, divergent and independent interpretations of the world in contrast with the idea of linear and accumulative progress. It takes a sceptical position on past, present and future certainties... It is also aesthetic: in its ability to reveal and show essentials through new relationships, in placing things side by side which might seem far apart. (Hoyuelos 2004, p.7)

Information is not the same as knowledge, 'which is only obtained by organising and placing parts in relation to each other' (Vecchi 2004, p.19). Nor is the image of knowledge like a staircase, a linear pathway where you have to take one step after another, which is similar to the tree metaphor of knowledge that remains so prominent in education. Rather the image is the *rhizome*, something which shoots in all directions with no beginning and no end, but always *in between*, and with openings towards other directions and places, a *multiplicity* functioning by means of connections and heterogeneity, a multiplicity which is not given but constructed. Malaguzzi offered a complementary, but more Italian image, when he described knowledge as like a 'tangle of spaghetti.'

Connections, it should be emphasised, go well beyond developing multilingualism and interdisciplinarity. Equally important are connections between rationality, imagination, emotions and aesthetics, between head, heart and hand. As Vea Vecchi puts it, education involves creating opportunities for 'brains, hands, sensibilities, rationality, emotion and imagination [to] all work together in close co-operation' (Vecchi 2010, p.2). I turn now to how this is done in practice.

Ways of working and organisation

Part of the secret of Reggio's success, its extraordinary power of survival and renewal, has been the project's willingness to combine openness to uncertainty, relishing the unpredictable and experimentation with very rigorous ways of working and attention to organisation. These ways of working and organisational features have created conditions where democracy, experimentation and encounter can be sustained, and where thinking and doing, working hand in hand (for there is a strong antipathy to splitting theory and practice), have constantly been open to evaluation, reflection, dialogue and new directions. But important as these more technical aspects are, they have also been very carefully positioned, ensuring that ways of working and organisation are subject to the images, values and ideas that Reggio has decided upon, that the technical is at the service of the political and ethical.

A simple example was the early decision that each class or group of children should have two teachers, to support collaborative and reflective work in a pedagogy of relationships. But the organisation of the workforce has gone further, involving the introduction and development of new roles. One example is the *pedagogista* or pedagogical coordinator. *Pedagogistas* have a higher degree in psychology or pedagogy, and each works with a small number of municipal schools to help develop understanding of learning processes and pedagogical work through, for example, pedagogical documentation (discussed further below).

Another example is the *atelierista* who works in and from an *atelier* (workshop) found in each municipal school for three- to six-year-olds. This worker has an artistic but not an educational background. She is more artist than teacher, but works closely with teachers in schools, both being engaged with processes of learning. One role of the *atelierista* is to stimulate the role of 'poetic languages', especially the visual ones, in learning: 'if aesthetics fosters sensibility and the ability for connecting things far removed from each other, and if learning takes place through new connections between disparate elements, then aesthetics can be considered an important activator for learning' (Vecchi 2010, p.9).

The *atelierista*, therefore, supports connections, or, as Vecchi more poetically terms it, 'the dance between cognitive, expressive, rational and imaginative', acting as 'guarantor of more complete educational processes' (Vecchi 2010, p.130). An aesthetic sense is fed by empathy, an intense relationship with things; 'it does not put things in rigid categories and might therefore constitute a problem where excessive certainty and cultural simplification is concerned'. The task here is not only to connect but break down the constraints created by monolingualism, closed-off disciplines, preconceived categories, predetermined ends. What is expected of this role is that the *atelierista* and her *atelier* are at the heart of learning, key partners with teachers, not technical specialists who transmit specialised skills and help children produce nice products, nor purveyors of a particular subject that children can dip into every now and then (the twice a week 'art lesson'): 'we always did things in such a way', says Vecchi of her work, 'that the atelier expanded out into the classes and school... We always worked on projects and it was the progress of these that determined children's presence in the atelier' (Vecchi 2010, p.127).

In addition to the *atelierista* as educator (though not teacher), the *atelierista* has other roles and makes other contributions. There is the *atelerista* as a guide for border crossing into the world of art, architecture and design, equipped with a sensitive antennae for contemporary issues; as a go-between and coordinator, working across the school to keep the group of teachers in a school together and acting in solidarity; as a lens for the school community, helping it to see children and adults in a certain, aesthetic way; and as provocateur, the 'persevering defenders of *non-obedient* processes' (Vecchi 2010, p.179: original emphasis).

If a varied workforce, complementary and collaborative, provides one set of conditions for the educational project in Reggio, another set is provided by the tools and ways of working they deploy. Two are of particular importance: pedagogical documentation and project work. Put simply, pedagogical documentation makes learning processes and educational practices visible by being documented in various ways (by means of notes, photographs, videos, recordings, children's artistic or other creations, etc.) so that they can be shared, discussed, reflected upon, interpreted and, if necessary, evaluated. It can and does involve everyone – children, teachers, auxiliary staff, families, administrators and other citizens – and gives 'the possibility to discuss and dialogue "everything with everyone" and to base these discussions on real, concrete things' (Hoyuelos 2004, p.7). It makes education and the school transparent by enabling 'the active and visible exchange of ideas between a school and its surroundings including the families, community members, and political leaders'; and it transforms a school 'to become a meeting place of co-construction...[and] a place of democracy [by inviting] multiple ideas, debate, and negotiation among different points of view of an experience' (Turner and Wilson 2010, p.10).

We could describe this as a tool and process for rigorous, collaborative and democratic reflection, which assumes multiple perspectives, the inescapability of subjectivity and the importance of dialogue, confrontation and co-construction. Vecchi sees it as the origin of the *atelierista*, whose evolution she believes 'together with that of Reggio Emilia pedagogy, stems above all from the birth and diffusion of observation and documentation of learning processes' (Vecchi 2010, p.132). There is today a growing literature on the purpose and practice of documentation, a multi-purpose tool of great value for planning, researching, evaluating, professional development and supporting democratic participation (for other, complementary sources, see Dahlberg, Moss and Pence 2007; Giudici *et al.* 2001; Rinaldi 2006).

Project work is also integral to Reggio's pedagogy and its understanding of learning, and the *atelierista* plays an integral part here also. Project work, Vecchi explains, means 'work in which adults (teachers, *atelierista*, *pedagogista*) make initial hypotheses and seek to have a deeper understanding of an area or topic but where key elements for moving forward come from work with children and careful analysis by adults of what is happening along the way' (Vecchi 2010, p.120). The project then provides a supportive context for learning as knowledge building, evoking:

> the idea of a dynamic process, a journey that involves uncertainty and chance that always arises in relationships with others. Project work grows in many directions, with no predefined progression, no outcomes decided before the journey begins. It means being sensitive to the unpredictable results of children's investigation and research. (Rinaldi 2005, p.19)

A third type of organisational condition is the physical environment of the school, not only the buildings but the furnishings and fittings. This is considered important for a number of reasons: for its contribution to learning; for its contribution to well-being and the aesthetic experience it offers; for its ability to express values, ideas, images and emotions; and for its capacity to allow, encourage and 'educate ways of seeing, exploration and sensibility' (Vecchi 2010, p.89). The educators of Reggio Emilia are fierce defenders of the importance of an environment that is beautiful and well cared for: 'we are convinced of the right to beauty in a healthy psychological relationship with surroundings' (Vecchi 2010, p.82).

Last but not least, good work takes and needs time: time for preparation, time for listening, time for documenting, time for discussion, time for reflection, time for pleasure. Vecchi reserves some of her most scathing comments for those tendencies in modern education that lead to hurried and, therefore, superficial work. This gets to the heart of the matter. If education is about technicians transmitting information and skills and delivering predetermined outcomes against predefined norms, then it needs little time for children or educators to think or work. But if it is a democratic process of building knowledge through complex and creative relationships and processes, using various and varied languages, then education requires commensurate time. Asked once how Reggio had come to achieve such rich and rigorous work, Malaguzzi answered, 'we discuss and discuss and discuss'; and when asked how this was possible, he answered further, 'we prioritise'.

Values

Such educational thinking and practice and the organisation and ways of working that support it are inscribed with a number of strong and explicit values. First and foremost is democracy. This commitment is described below by three Reggio *pedagogistas*, who are quoted at length for the insight they give into Reggio's understanding and practice of democracy:

> [The educational project of Reggio Emilia] is by definition a participation-based project: its true educational meaning is to be found in the participation of all concerned. This means that everyone – children, teachers and parents – is involved in sharing ideas, in discussion, in a sense of common purpose and with communication as a value...
>
> So in the Reggio Emilia experience, participation does not mean simply the involvement of families in the life of the school. Rather it is a value, an identifying feature of the entire experience, a way of viewing those involved in the educational process and the role of the school... The subjects of participation then, even before the parents, are the children, who are considered to be active constructors of their own learning and producers of original points of view concerning the world...
>
> The subjects of participation also include the school staff. The teachers, in particular, do not merely execute programmes established by others, but participate actively in the construction of the knowledge-building processes of each child and group of children, as well as their own... [Participation] is based on the idea that reality is not objective, that culture is a constantly evolving product of society, that individual knowledge is only partial and that in order to construct a project, especially an educational project, everyone's point of view is relevant in dialogue with those of others, within a framework of shared values. The idea of participation is founded on these concepts;

and in our opinion so, too, is democracy itself. (Cagliari, Barozzi and Giudici 2004, pp.28–29)

What emerges here is democracy that goes beyond institutions and processes of governance (though these exist), to a Deweyan understanding of democracy as a 'mode of associated living embedded in the culture and social relationships of everyday life' and 'a personal way of individual life' (Dewey 1939) – democracy as everyday practice and relationships, applied to everyday activities: learning, evaluation, projects, the quotidian life of the school. It is, too, an idea of democracy that assumes irreducible diversity and plurality, partiality and provisionality, and the need to create spaces and times to explore these multiple perspectives, to dialogue, to confront if necessary, and to work on co-construction.

Democracy as a value also leads to particular images or understandings of the early childhood centre: as 'a social and political place and thus as an educational place in the fullest sense' (Cagliari, Barozzi and Giudici 2004, p.29); as a forum, a place of encounter, a construction site, a workshop and a permanent laboratory, a public place 'which is both a community in itself as well as an integral part of a wider community' (Rinaldi 2006, p.12). However, such images, just like the image of the rich child, are not givens; they are not self-evident. They are collective choices, democratic political choices, choices based on values.

Other values are also important. Solidarity is expressed in the city taking responsibility for the education of its children, in the emphasis placed on both individual staff and schools working collaboratively, and in the deep commitment to relationships of respect, trust and care. Research and experimentation are important, not as specialist activities undertaken by experts but as values that permeate everyday practice and produce a habit of mind, 'a way of thinking, of approaching life, of negotiating, of documenting' (Rinaldi 2006, p.192), while the whole approach to learning and evaluation is inscribed with the value given to dialogue, uncertainty and subjectivity. What these and other values have in common is an openness to the new and unexpected, a resistance to governing by normalisation and predicted outcome, and a desire for wonder and amazement. Dialogue, for example, is of absolute importance, but it is an idea of dialogue 'not as an exchange but as a process of transformation where you lose absolutely the possibility of controlling the final result. And it goes to infinity, it goes to the universe, you can get lost' (Rinaldi 2006, p.184).

How does Reggio Emilia relate to social pedagogy?

There is a deeply engrained tendency in the Western world of trying to understand others through applying one's own mindsets, understandings and categories: the will to know by grasping the Other and, in so doing, making the Other into the Same (Dahlberg and Moss 2005). So it is possible to 'pigeon hole' Reggio Emilia, to say it is an example of such-and-such or just like this or that. I have indulged in this myself in a book I wrote with two colleagues, where we argued that Reggio Emilia's educational work might be thought of as postmodern (Dahlberg *et al.* 2007): to which, in a later book, Carlina Rinaldi responded that 'although Reggio may be postmodern in its perspectives, we are not for postmodernism, because "isms" are risky. Because they simplify and lock you in prison again' (2006, p.182).

However, to resist categorisation and acknowledge singularity does not require the denial of connections, relationships and influences. Anyone who reads the other chapters in this book on social pedagogy will, I think, find many resonances between those chapters and many of the features of Reggio Emilia's project outlined in this chapter. Take, for example, Chapter 2, with its discussion of conceptual foundations of social pedagogy, and there are many points of similarity; for example: the importance attached to how children are conceptualised – our image of the child – and the image of the child as full of potential and possibilities (the rich child with a hundred languages proposed by Eichenstellar and Holtoff, who explicitly cite Malaguzzi in their discussion); an understanding of children as active and competent learners, not vessels to be filled; the importance of reflection based on direct observation; the central role of relationships, including the relationship between the individual and the group and the necessity of viewing the child as part of a group; the need to keep head, heart and hands in balance; and deep respect for and commitment to children's rights. I could go on drawing connections between this and other chapters and the Reggio Emilia project, though at the same time sounding a note of caution by recognising that considerable and more nuanced differences may well exist beneath such broad agreement on principles and understandings. But I hope the case is made for the thesis that there is more connectedness than might be expected by chance, a thesis perhaps worthy of more systematic enquiry.

If such enquiry were to confirm extensive connections and overlaps, how might this be accounted for? In many years of visiting, reading and writing about Reggio Emilia, as well as editing books from leading figures in the city's municipal schools project, I have never heard or seen mention of the term 'social pedagogy'. This anecdotal experience is not, of course, conclusive. But if the absence of any direct and explicit relationship were to be confirmed, it is possible that more indirect and complex relationships are at work, notably common influences on both Reggio's local project and the wider European practice of social pedagogy; for example, Maria Montessori, John Dewey and the New Education movement are three influences on social pedagogy cited by Eichstellar and Holttoff and these are also acknowledged by Reggio Emilia. What would be both fascinating and productive would be to go deeper and more rigorously into the study of educational and pedagogical ideas and practices and into the work of leading educational and social pedagogic thinkers to begin to plot and better understand the connections, influences and modes of communication. Apart from its intrinsic interest, such study might help us better comprehend the flows of ideas and their transformation across borders and time.

Social pedagogic theories and practices remain important in the early childhood services of a number of countries, including some Nordic states and Germany. Reggio Emilia already has a substantial influence in all these countries, most of which have national Reggio networks in which pedagogues participate. But the relationship between Reggio Emilia, whose local project is clearly located in an educational context, and those countries, whose early childhood services are located in a social pedagogical context, deserves more attention. Not least, it might throw light on a key issue and subject for the next chapter: the wider relationship between school-based education on the one hand and, on the other, social pedagogy or what some have termed education in its broadest sense – and the possibility of creating a dialogue.

References

Cagliari, P., Barozzi, A. and Giudici, C. (2004) 'Thoughts, theories and experiences: For an educational project with participation.' *Children in Europe 6*, 28–30.

Catarsi, E. (2004) 'Loris Malaguzzi and the municipal school revolution.' *Children in Europe 6*, 8–9.

Dahlberg, G. (2000) 'Everything is a Beginning and Everything is Dangerous: Some Reflections on the Reggio Emilia Experience.' In H. Penn (ed.) *Early Childhood Services: Theory, Policy and Practice.* Buckingham: Open University Press.

Dahlberg, G. and Moss, P. (2005) *Ethics and Politics in Early Childhood Education.* London: Routledge.

Dahlberg, G., Moss, P. and Pence, A. (2007) *Beyond Quality in Early Childhood Education and Care: Languages of Evaluation (2nd ed.)*. London: Routledge.

Dewey, J. (1939) 'Creative Democracy – The Task Before Us.' In J. Boydston (ed.) *John Dewey: The Later Works, 1925–1953, volume 14*. Carbondale, IL: Southern Illinois University Press. (Original work published 1939.)

Fortunati, A. (2006) *The Education of Young Children as a Community Project: The Experience of San Miniato*. Azzano San Paolo, Brazil: Edizioni Junior.

Giudici, C., Rinaldi, C. and Krechevsky, M. (eds) (2001) *Making Learning Visible: Children as Individual and Group Learners*. Cambridge MA, and Reggio Emilia: Project Zerro and Reggio Children.

Hoyuelos, A. (2004) 'A pedagogy of transgression.' *Children in Europe 6*, 6–7.

Istituzione of the Municipality of Reggio Emilia and Reggio Children (2010) *The Infant-Toddler Centers and Pre-schools of Reggio Emilia: Historical Notes and General Information*. Reggio Emilia: Istituzione of the Municipality of Reggio Emilia and Reggio Children

Malaguzzi, L. (1993) 'For an education based on relationships.' *Young Children 11/93*, 9–13.

Malaguzzi (undated) Poem, untitled. Available at http://pah2.golding.id.au/theChild, accessed on 30 March 2011.

Morin, E. (1999) *Homeland Earth: A Manifesto for the New Millennium*. Cresskill, NJ: Hampton Press.

Moss, P. (2009) *There Are Alternatives! Markets and Democratic Experimentalism in Early Childhood Education and Care*. The Hague: Bernard van Leer Foundation.

Rinaldi, C. (2005) 'Is a curriculum necessary?' *Children in Europe 9*, 19.

Rinaldi, C. (2006) *In Dialogue with Reggio Emilia: Listening, Researching and Learning*. London: Routledge.

Turner, T. and Wilson, D.G. (2010) 'Reflections on documentation: A discussion with thought leaders from Reggio Emilia.' *Theory into Practice 4*, 5–13.

Unger, R.M. (2005) *What Should the Left Propose?* London: Verso.

Vecchi, V. (2004) 'The multiple fonts of knowledge.' *Children in Europe 6*, 18–21.

Vecchi, V. (2010) *Art and Creativity in Reggio Emilia: Exploring the Role and Potential of Ateliers in Early Childhood Education*. London: Routledge.

CHAPTER 10

Radical Democratic Education and Emancipatory Social Pedagogy: Prolegomena to a Dialogue

Michael Fielding

Possibilities for dialogue

Burgeoning interest in social pedagogy provides an important breath of fresh air in current discourse about education in England, not only because it reminds us of the always important, though too often elided, distinction between education and schooling, but also because it invites a renewed look at the traditions of pedagogic thought and practice that take seriously the nature of the relationship between teacher and students and also between the individual and the wider social, communal and political contexts which frame their present and future flourishing. Social pedagogy may have the potential for stimulating interest and remaking connections with important educational traditions and practices that have been overlooked and neglected in the current neoliberal climate with its focus on education in its narrowest sense.

What particularly excites me about the growing dialogue between mainland European traditions of social pedagogy and UK-based traditions of education and schooling is, first, that it is a renewal rather than a beginning. Certainly, many progressive and socially oriented approaches to education in its broadest sense share an overlapping heritage. As Walter Lorenz reminds us, 'The international genealogy of such fundamental community-oriented pedagogical concepts…at an immediate practice level stretches from Rousseau and Pestalozzi to Froebel and Montessori to include also figures like William Morris and John Dewey' (Lorenz 2008, p.634). From the 1920s to the 1970s, these traditions were at the heart of teacher education provision in colleges and universities and provided, together with the enduring commitment, if diminishing influence, of the New Education Fellowship and its journal *New Era*, the intellectual and practical backdrop to many of the radical pioneers in both public and private sectors during that time. Even the anarchist, libertarian, socialist and Marxist critiques that had a more prominent flowering from the late 1960s to the mid-1980s defined their advocacy in part against what they saw as the ameliorative waywardness of the progressive assumptions that neoliberalism was to systematically destroy, for quite other reasons, in the ensuing decades.

But I am also excited by the explicit acknowledgement of the importance and necessity of quite different traditions of social pedagogy, of the proper and inevitable plurality of approaches, which presume and advocate very different relations between the individual and society that lie at the heart of its fundamental intentions and aspirations. This recognition and valuing of plurality invites an equivalent acknowledgement within the field of formal education in general and radical education in particular (see Petrie 2003, 2010; Petrie and Cameron 2009).

As writers such as Lorenz (2008) remind us, the origins of social pedagogy lie in the historical conjunctures facing Germany in the 19th century. These included, on the one hand, social dislocation created by urbanisation and industrial revolution and, on the other hand, the political need to construct a national identity without suppressing the inevitable diversity incorporated within the new German state. The emerging disciplinary field of *Sozialpädagogik* thus took as its central rationale 'the linked tasks of preparing individuals for communal and societal life, and, at the same time, bringing society as a community to orient its culture and social life towards the personal development and social needs of individuals' (Lorenz 2008, p.634). How those central intentions were understood and enacted depended, of course, on the historical and ideological influences of circumstance and tradition. While those on the left placed the onus on society to provide the appropriate conditions of individual flourishing, those on the right tended to argue for obligations on individuals to fit the wider needs of a stable society and, in its most extreme fascist forms, reduce the individual to an organic functionary of the state.

Within the field of radical education there are, of course, similar emphases and divergences. 'Radical' is a relative term, which defines itself against a perceived derogation or betrayal of fundamental beliefs and seeks both a return to and subsequent renewal of unadulterated purpose and commensurately authentic practice. Radical also invites transgression and transcendence of the status quo, to name and enact a quite different future in the present, and it is primarily in this sense that it is used here. Thus, radical *democratic* education, the definition I choose to adopt and explore in this chapter, not only draws on these foundational imperatives; it insists on the catalytic significance of democracy as a pervasive orientation in all aspects of the educational process, including the structural and cultural arrangements that both support and express its emancipatory aspirations. It insists on the importance of 'prefigurative practice', of living and learning radical democracy as it might be in the here and now of largely unsympathetic times.

To develop a fully fledged account of the commonalities, differences and potential synergies between radical democratic approaches to formal education and schooling and democratic, emancipatory approaches to social pedagogy must wait upon more expansive contexts and more reciprocally developed expertise. Nonetheless, while the intentions and ambitions of this chapter are necessarily modest, my hope is that there will be enough of interest to practitioners and academics to legitimate and encourage a permanently restless commitment to the transformative aspirations that underpin both traditions.

What follows is a particular account of radical democratic education, which draws its examples mainly, but not exclusively, from the public (i.e. state) system of secondary education in England, focusing iconically on the work of Alex Bloom, one of the most radical headteachers of a state secondary school England has ever seen (Fielding 2005, 2008). It is hugely influenced by the dialogue between Peter Moss and myself (see Fielding and Moss 2011 forthcoming); by my own experience as a teacher and deputy headteacher/principal in such schools, and as an academic; by my re-engagement with the radical traditions of democratic education with marginalised and/or troubled young people pioneered in my own country by people like Homer Lane (Bazeley 1928; Stinton 2005), David Wills (Bridgeland 1971, Chapter 12; Wills 1941), Howard Case (Case 1966, 1978) and Tony Weaver (Weaver 1988) and so insightfully articulated and analysed by Maurice Bridgeland (Bridgeland 1971) and in mainland Europe by such inspirational figures as Anton Makarenko (Goodman 1949) in the Soviet Union and Oskar Spiel (Spiel 1962) in Austria.

Having set out what I take to be some of the key features of radical democratic approaches to education and schooling, I then very briefly suggest a number of commonalities and solidarities with emancipatory traditions of social pedagogy in the hope that there is enough of substance to merit mutually beneficial recognition and the possibility of further dialogue.

The school as 'a consciously democratic community'

The emphasis I place on a radical democratic education and on democracy is important and contentious. It is important because, in an overt and grounded way, it takes seriously the underpinning rationale of education in democratic society, something that is too often presumed or marginalised in the lexicon of schooling in England. It is contentious, first, because democracy itself is properly and inevitably an internally dynamic and disputed notion. Second, it is contentious because how democratic aspirations are best realised in practice within the context of predominantly hierarchical institutions like schools is a matter on which there is likely to be significant disagreement, both at the level of theory and at the level of daily enactment. Third, all schools, however strong their commitments to a particular understanding of democracy, will have within their staff a number of individuals who do not fully share those commitments and sometimes actively oppose them; likewise, the students within the school and the communities from which they are drawn.

The further emphasis on *radical* approaches to democratic schooling narrows the field still further. Here we move from the largely familiar traditions of representative democracy towards those of classical or participatory democracy, to democracy as a way of living and learning together that provides multiple daily and weekly occasions for individual and communal deliberation and decision, for shared responsibility, joint celebration and the renewal of hope.

The framework I propose argues both for the need to take account of ten key characteristics of radical democratic school practice and for an intended and significantly achieved synergy between them. Unsurprisingly, they are seldom realised in full, but they are occasionally and for long enough for us to learn with and from them in and over time. Their exemplification of a 'prefigurative practice', of the practical realisation of radically different future ways of being in the complex and largely unsympathetic realities of the present, has an important role to play in challenging the bilious insistence of neoliberalism that 'there is no alternative', that the greed and mendacity of the market provides the zenith of human aspiration and fulfilment.

These ten key characteristics comprise:

1. a proclaimed democratic vitality

2. radical structures and spaces

3. radical roles

4. radical relationships

5. personal and communal narrative

6. radical curriculum, critical pedagogy and enabling assessment

7. insistent affirmation of possibility

8. engaging the local

9. accountability as shared responsibility

10. regional, national and global solidarities.

1. Proclaimed democratic vitality

One of the distinguishing features of radical democratic schools is their desire not only to emphasise the primacy of education as the most important *raison d'être* of schooling. It has also to do with their commitment to both education in its broadest sense and to the further explicit articulation of democracy as an orienting way of life: democracy as the end and the means, the purpose and the practice, of education. Such overt commitment is not something that can be lightly undertaken. As well as the personal particularities of those headteachers/principals who have been able to make such a commitment, the geographical, cultural, political, economic and historical location within which they find themselves has inevitably had a significant bearing on even the possibility of such an undertaking, let alone its chance of success in and over time.

For these kinds of reasons, to announce explicitly democratic intentions is not necessarily the first thing to be done, but in the few instances of radical democratic schooling within the English state education system, that bold and brave articulation has pride of place in the development of the school. Thus, for example, Alex Bloom, the great, radical pioneer headteacher of St George-in-the-East, in Stepney, one of the toughest areas of the East End of London, tells us that on 1 October 1945 he deliberately set out to create a 'consciously democratic community... without regimentation, without corporal punishment, without competition' (Bloom 1948, p.121). Tim McMullen and his successor, John Watts (Watts 1977), did much the same thing at Countesthorpe

Community College in Leicestershire in the early 1970s. The same is also true of the now largely neglected (but see Oser, Althof and Higgins-D'Alessandro 2008) work of Lawrence Kohlberg's Just Community School movement in the USA (Kohlberg 1980). The key point here is that education in and for deep democracy has to be both the starting point and what Elsa Wasserman, in her reflections on the relative success of Kohlberg's work, calls the 'central educational goal' (Wasserman 1980, p.268) of the radical democratic school for which I am arguing. There has to be a proclaimed, not just an intended, democratic vitality, albeit one that bears in mind the vicissitudes of context and circumstance mentioned earlier.

Likewise within the disgracefully forgotten radical therapeutic traditions of English education, which so powerfully exemplify the central aspirations of social pedagogy. Here – in, for example, Homer Lane's Little Commonwealth (Bazeley 1928; Stinton 2005) that inspired A.S. Neill's (Neill 1968) development of the General Meeting at Summerhill School; in David Wills's Lane-inspired work with disaffected and damaged young people over 30 years (Bridgeland 1971, Chapter 12); and with Howard Case's Epping House School, a state-funded radical residential school for 'maladjusted' pupils between the ages of 5 and 12 (Case 1966, 1978) – there is a marked commitment to participatory forms of democracy, not primarily as a political structure but as a form of democratic fellowship that provided the precondition and the *telos* of democracy's emancipatory human intent. Thus David Wills insisted that his own pioneering of a 'shared responsibility' approach over many years with different groups of 'wild, neglected, undisciplined, over-disciplined and "dis-social" children' had its justification not as 'an efficient method of governing (a school), but because of its therapeutic value… Shared responsibility is a corollary of the primary instrument which is the effort to make children feel they are loved' (Wills 1948, p.79). Democratic community, with, as we shall see in a moment, the daily meeting at its centre, is important because its explicitly egalitarian form enables a deep and demonstrable reciprocity, thereby providing both existential and practical testimony of the need for and presence of love.

2. Radical structures and spaces
The next three indicators comprise complementary aspects of the interpersonal and structural integrity of democratic living. They demonstrate the unity of means and ends, not only in matters of

organisational structure, but also in the relational dimensions of daily engagement, which underscore the importance of care, respect and creative encounter as the foundational dispositions of social justice.

Structurally, the radical democratic school will be expressive of education in its broadest sense, of education as fundamentally concerned with certain kinds of human encounter. In the words of the great Scottish philosopher, John Macmurray:

> [T]he first priority in education – if by education we mean learning to be human – is learning to live in personal relation to other people. Let us call it learning to live in community. I call this the first priority because failure in this is fundamental failure, which cannot be compensated for by success in other fields; because our ability to enter into fully personal relations with others is the measure of our humanity. For inhumanity is precisely the perversion of human relations. (Macmurray 1958, no page number)

One of the many consequences of taking this view seriously is the need for those within a school to know each other and care for each other as persons, for individuals to feel significant and for that sense of worth to be integrally bound up with the reciprocities and diversities of a creative, inclusive community. It is thus no accident that each of the three secondary school examples cited in the previous section not only paid overt attention to the relational foundations of education for which I am arguing, but also sought to realise them in practice through the size and organisational architecture of their daily work. St George-in-the-East had about 200 students and ten staff; Countesthorpe Community College broke the school down into a series of interdisciplinary mini-schools; and one of the best known of the Just Community Schools – Brookline – operated as a school-within-a-school within a larger institution. Just as atomistic notions of representative democracy will forever and inevitably be compromised by the failure of their intellectual and historical conception, so too will large schools, unless they are broken down into smaller units.

The radical democratic school is thus a school that takes seriously the challenge of size and the radical rethinking of curriculum, of interpersonal and physical spaces for learning, for teaching, for the shared construction of identities and the making of meaning. It will also be mindful of what might be called 'positional restlessness' – that is to say, a libertarian and egalitarian insistence on the openness of opportunity, on the need to unsettle patterns and dispositions of presumption, and the need to open up much wider and more generous vistas of possibility for all members of a school community. Such a school will pursue a range of organisational articulations of participatory democracy at the heart of which lies an insistence on a permanent and proper provisionality. At both adult and student levels, this will include a permanent unease with hierarchy and a strong desire to create transparent structures that encourage ways of working that transcend boundaries and invite new combinations and possibilities.

There will also be substantial emphasis on the spatiality of democracy, on interpersonal and architectural spaces that encourage a multiplicity of different forms of formal and informal engagement with a multiplicity of persons. In addition to shared lifespaces, such as residential camps, that schools such as St George-in-the-East insist on as a matter of entitlement, radical schools also encourage and ensure 'subaltern spaces' or spaces in which minority, marginalised or emergent groups can develop the confidence, capacity and dispositions that enable them to explore and name what is important to them and also gain the confidence and desire to engage with larger, different groups of people within and beyond the school community. Pre-eminent amongst these other groups is likely to be the general meeting within which the whole school community will reflect on its shared life, achievements and aspirations. Certainly this is true of all the examples given earlier – of St George-in-the-East, of Countesthorpe, of Brookline SWS, of Homer Lane, of David Wills and of Howard Case, in whose view 'The meeting is one of the foremost means of giving the child freedom to develop' (BBC TV 1967). Here, young people and adults make meaning of their work together, returning tenaciously and regularly to the imperatives of purpose, not merely to the mechanics of accomplishment.

3. Radical roles

Just as the structures and spaces within a radical democratic school open up new possibilities, so too do the roles of those who work within them. This includes, amongst other things, a delight and belief in radical collegiality (Fielding 1999), an intergenerational reciprocity that reflects deep-seated faith in the encounter between adults and young people as a potential source of mutual learning, not just in an instrumental, technical sense, but eventually in a wider existential and more fully educational sense.

Thus, in the re-emergence of the student voice movement over the past 15 years, student and staff roles have developed in a variety of significant ways hinted at by the sixfold patterns of partnership below.

1. students as data source – where staff utilise information about student progress and well-being (e.g. as a result of an annual survey of student opinion on matters the school deems important)

2. students as active respondents – where staff invite student dialogue and discussion to deepen learning/professional decisions (e.g. the inclusion of students in the appointment process for new staff)

3. students as co-enquirers – where staff take a lead role with high-profile, active student support (e.g. in joint staff–student evaluation of the school system of reporting to parents on their children's progress)

4. students as knowledge creators – in which students take a lead role with active staff support (e.g. students using photo-elicitation as part of their enquiry into the causes of low-level bullying that went largely undetected by staff)

5. students as joint authors – where students and staff decide on a joint course of action together (e.g. devising and conducting a jointly led Learning Walk (NCSL 2005), which researches and discusses an agreed area of interest or concern)

6. intergenerational learning as participatory democracy – where there are shared commitments to and responsibilities for the common good (e.g. through the development of school meetings).

Different kinds of engagement will, of course, go on simultaneously within a school. However, it is unlikely that partnerships typical of forms 5 and 6 are sustainable in settings other than those that overtly aspire to radical democracy. The key point is nicely made by the Brazilian social theorist Roberto Unger, who argues for the importance of what he calls 'role defiance and role jumbling' (Unger 1987, p.563) as a way of undermining presumption and opening up new vistas of possibility.

4. Radical relationships

Just as the roles are more fluid and more diverse, so within radical education the relationships between students and between adults and young people are not only less bounded and more exploratory but also more openly informed by the dispositions and dynamics of care appropriate to education in its broadest sense. One aspect of a radical democratic practice in relational matters is caught by the notion of 'restless encounter'. Here, in tandem with the development of radical roles, is the development of radically different relationships to those that normally hold sway in schools. Such relationships enable us to 're-see' each other as persons rather than as role occupants, and in so doing nurture not only a new understanding, sense of possibility and felt respect between adults and young people, but also a joy in each others' being and a greater sense of shared delight and responsibility.

Another consequence of this relational re-centring of the educational process is that it enables us to look again at taken-for-granted aspects of the teaching and learning process and come to value them more profoundly and, as a consequence, engage with them more overtly and more deliberately. My own advocacy of what I have elsewhere called 'the dialectic of the personal' (Fielding 2000, pp.406–409) is one which traces the mutually conditioning interplay between the technical skills and the dialogic dispositions of teaching and learning. Such an approach sees care and knowledge of persons as centrally important. It sees individual flourishing as intimately bound up with relations with others, not as a relational lubricant for a smoother running or more measurably productive organisation.

5. Personal and communal narrative

The notion of narrative is central to radical democratic education for at least two reasons. First, it is important both personally and communally because it connects in a fundamental way with one of the core processes of education, namely with the making of meaning. Education is first and finally about how we learn to lead good lives together, lives that enable us individually and collectively to survive and flourish. Without some means of re-creating a constant link to those profound matters of purpose, education becomes impossible and we have to make do with the thin and dispiriting substitutes of competitive schooling. Within the radical democratic school, there will be multiple spaces and opportunities for individuals, both young people and adults, to make meaning of their work, both personally and as a community. Indeed, the two are connected. The anthropology of the self presumed by most radical traditions of education is communal rather than atomistic. The anthropology of an inclusive notion of community is one that honours difference and presumes the sanctity of the individual person.

The second reason narrative is important has to do with the necessary connection with history, with the radical traditions of education towards which I gestured earlier. Not only does history have much to teach its contemporary inheritors in a cautionary sense, but it also provides many examples of counter-hegemonic significance and power that remind us not only of what has been but also that, despite neoliberalism's insistence to the contrary, there are future alternatives.

6. Radical curriculum, critical pedagogy and enabling assessment

At the heart of radical democratic education's approach to the formal and informal curriculum lie four imperatives. The first is a focus on the purposes of education, organising the curriculum around that which is necessary for a sustainable, flourishing and democratic way of life. The second has to do with the necessity of equipping young people and adults with the desire and capacity to seriously and critically interrogate what is given and co-construct a knowledge that assists us in leading good and joyful lives together. The third argues that while knowledge must transcend the local, it must, nonetheless, start with the cultures, concerns and hopes of the communities that the school serves. Last, while perhaps not a requirement of a radical curriculum, a consequence of taking these first three desiderata seriously leads to a curriculum that emphasises connectedness; that is holistic in approach and organised around interconnected and interdisciplinary themes or areas, rather than separate subjects; and that encourages integrated forms of enquiry with students and staff working in small communities of enquiry.

A critical pedagogy of a radical curriculum will not only develop a reciprocity of engagement and involvement with the immediate community, but also reach out to other communities, other ways of being, at a local, regional, national and international level. Encounter with and delight in difference within the context of democratic values is central to the kinds of radical curriculum and pedagogy typical of the radical democratic school.

When radical approaches to the curriculum have worked well, they have invariably been enabled by forms of assessment at both national and local levels that have had the flexibility to respond to the particularities of context and significant professional involvement of teachers in the assessment, moderation and examination process. At classroom level, they have incorporated high levels of peer and teacher involvement through assessment-for-learning approaches and additional community and family involvement through public, portfolio-based presentations.

7. Insistent affirmation of possibility

One of the most important confluences of the libertarian and egalitarian impulses that inform a radical democratic approach to education is their insistent, persistent affirmation of possibility. Energised both by rage against what Unger calls 'the abandonment of ordinary humanity to perpetual belittlement' and by profound belief in the 'constructive powers of ordinary men and women' (Unger 2005, pp.46, 63) to create new and better ways of being in the world, this generosity of presumption requires us to keep options open, to counter the confinement of customary or casual expectation. This belief in the 'powers of ordinary men and women' is a key feature of radical education. So, too, is the companion insistence on keeping options open, on resisting closure, on a generosity of presumption that assumes the best rather than the worst of young people.

Thus, at St George-in-the-East, as in many other schools within the radical democratic tradition, there was a substantial attempt to replace the debilitating influence of fear as the prime incentive to 'progress'. For the headteacher Alex Bloom, '(f)ear of authority [imposed for disciplinary purposes]; fear of failure [by means of marks, prizes and competition, for obtaining results]; and the fear of punishment [for all these purposes]' must be replaced by 'friendship, security and the recognition of each child's worth' (Bloom 1952, pp.135–6). Of the impediments mentioned, Bloom had a particular distaste for competition, arguing not only that it was unethical but that it tended to destroy a communal spirit. Indeed, a communally oriented school does not need the artificial stimulus of 'carrots and goads': in such a school, the children will 'come to realize the self that is theirs and respect the self that is their neighbour's. And because there are neither carrots nor goads, there will be no donkeys, for when children are treated as we would have them be, they tend to reach out accordingly' (Bloom 1949, p.171).

Finally, at St George-in-the-East, there was no streaming or setting. For those within the radical democratic traditions, not only are the presumptions of this kind of labelling false, but more often than not its administration is crudely wayward and its consequences deeply damaging (see Hart *et al.* 2004). For these and other reasons, an insistent affirmation of possibility denies the legitimacy of ability grouping, promotes emulation rather than competition, and prefers intrinsic motivation and communal recognition to the paraphernalia of marks and prizes.

8. Engaging the local

There are a number of reasons why a confident and expansive reciprocity between the school and its local community is of fundamental importance to radical democratic education. Some of these reasons are philosophical and have to do with a view of education as a lifelong process and the school as a site of community renewal and responsibility in which young and old explore what it means to live good lives together.

Other reasons for underscoring the nexus of the local are more pragmatic. Here, the community and the school are seen as reciprocal resources for broadly and more narrowly conceived notions of learning. If this is to become a living reality, it requires school and community to problematise institutional boundaries and thereby encourage a mutual re-seeing of presumed identities. They need each other more fully and more insistently if they are to thrive, both in the hurly-burly of the here and now and in the excitement of an organically shared and mutually shaped future.

Alex Bloom was at the forefront of developments to involve parents in a whole range of ways and the school was often both host to and the driving force behind local cultural and communal events. He also earned the love of the community in less formal ways – for example, by providing warmth and shelter at the school long before it formally opened for lessons in the morning; by ensuring good quality meals were served for all at lunchtime; by his deep knowledge of the families and the struggles they faced, and by his care and compassion for individuals – there are numerous accounts of students without adequate footwear being bought shoes by Bloom himself.

9. Accountability as shared responsibility

Within participatory traditions of democracy, accountability takes on a significantly different meaning and form to their representative counterparts. Radical democratic notions of accountability are better understood and enacted as forms of 'shared responsibility'. Understood in this way, accountability is morally and politically situated, not merely technically and procedurally 'delivered'. It makes a claim on our ethical and civic responsibilities, which cannot be adequately understood or provided for by an entirely delegated mandate (to experts or managers) which provides too convenient and too corrosive an absolution.

We cannot know what we are responsible for in anything other than a thin, box-ticking sense unless we return to shared educational purposes and from there co-author an account of core beliefs and the kinds of practices we believe will exemplify their realisation in an appropriately demanding and life-affirming way. Young people can and should be involved in such process, a good example being at Bishops Park College, Clacton, a school for 11- to 16-year-olds in England where, towards the end of its radical phase of development, it created a Research Forum comprising a core group of students, parents, governors, school staff and a small university research and development team. One of the key tasks it undertook was the co-authorship and development of a framework of aspirations and practices that formed the basis of the College's accountability framework (Fielding *et al.* 2006).

What is particularly pertinent to this context is the way in which relationships between adults and young people changed over time. Both began to see each other with new eyes. The shared desire to explore matters of some significance and work in new ways led, in many instances and on a number of occasions, not only to respectful and appreciative encounters and new understandings, but also to mutual advocacy of and delight in intergenerational working. It also produced a remarkable document which exemplified the kind of shared responsibility for which I am arguing.

10. Regional, national and global solidarities

Last, education in and for a radical democracy must learn the lessons of its own histories. Too often, brave, imaginative and important work has been lost or weakened by the failure not just to connect with the local, but by the failure to take the strategic imperatives of the radical democratic tradition sufficiently seriously. Regional, national and global solidarities need to be made real and telling by building reciprocal ideological, material and interpersonal support through values-driven networks and alliances which draw on and contribute to the dynamic of radical social movements.

Over a ten-year period Alex Bloom was, in significant part, able to develop one of the most overtly democratic, radical secondary schools England has ever seen because of the multiple solidarities, alliances and networks to which he both belonged and contributed (Fielding 2008). In addition to huge support from his local community to which I have already referred, the school was used by a range of teacher training colleges. Despite some opposition at local office level, Bloom was supported by some key figures in the higher echelons of the London County Council – for example, Hubert Child, at the time their Chief Educational Psychologist and later an eminent head of Dartington Hall, one of England's most prestigious private progressive schools. Bloom also addressed national conferences on the potential of the (then) new secondary modern schools and was strongly supported by leading educational figures such as James Hemming who was at that time a research officer for the Association for Education in Citizenship. The school frequently hosted a huge number of overseas visitors from countries all across the world, largely through Bloom's longstanding, active membership of the New Education Fellowship and the articles on St George's that appeared in its journal *New Era*.

Commonalities and solidarities

This chapter has sought not only to exemplify the contested nature both of formal systems of education and of social pedagogies, but also to celebrate Pat Petrie's reminder that 'Pedagogies do not necessarily reflect and promote a dominant position, they can also attempt to subvert it' (Petrie 2003, p.72). Radical democratic education and emancipatory social pedagogy share just such an oppositional and practical utopian standpoint. Both take seriously Sünker and Swiderk's insistence that 'The future of a substantial democracy (on a world scale) requires education and participation in communal life as a basic element of social life' (Sünker and Swiderk 2007, p.304). Both begin the practical instantiation of that advocacy through a commitment to 'prefigurative practice', to a practice which is, in the words of the Gramscian scholar, Carl Boggs, 'the embodiment within the ongoing political practice of a movement, of those forms of social relations, decision making, culture and human experience that are the ultimate goal' (Boggs 1977/1978, p.100). This orientation, which Peter Moss and I take as the cornerstone of our advocacy of a radical democratic education in and through the common school (Fielding and Moss 2011 forthcoming), is one which is mindful of Pat Petrie's reminder that social pedagogy and formal education are 'not powerful enough to tackle the roots of poverty and disaffection' (Petrie 2003, p.77). However, taking its inspiration from the New Left and the feminist resurgence of the 1960s and 1970s and from contemporary writers such as E.O. Wright and Roberto Unger, it insists, along with Sheila Rowbotham, that 'some changes have to start now else there is no beginning for us'. (Rowbotham 1979, p.140).

Building on and transcending the core legacy of progressive education, which critiques traditional notions of education and the nature of knowledge, affirms the centrality of democracy as a way of life and insists on the development of young people and adults as whole persons (Darling and Norbenbo 2003), radical democratic education's enactment of a transformative practice through the felt realities of the ten dimensions sketched earlier in this chapter has, I would argue, a great deal in common with emancipatory traditions of social pedagogy. There is, of course, much more that could and should be said. Within my account of the radical traditions of democratic education, there has been no exploration of, for example, the key place of physical work or of the arts in developing individual and communal practices and aspirations of transformation; nor has there been as full an exploration as I would have wished of, for example, the centrality of certain kinds of relationships that underpin the intergenerational learning.

These and other lacunae notwithstanding, my hope is that there is enough common ground and enough prospect of creative difference to prompt future dialogue between education and social pedagogy, and in particular between those in both fields who value highly their democratic and emancipatory traditions: dialogue for mutual learning, dialogue for building solidarities, dialogue for re-creating an emancipatory international movement that imagines and enacts an overtly democratic fellowship. So much of what emancipatory social pedagogy and radical democratic education aspire to is under threat from an economic and political world-view that insists there is no alternative to a status quo that is intellectually impoverished and morally destitute; together radical education and social pedagogy can better resist this dictatorship of no alternatives and create spaces to imagine, explore and build alternatives. In this vein, I end with the words of one of the great contemporary figures of European art and literature, John Berger. In his beautiful essay 'Against the Great Defeat of the World' he argues that:

> The culture in which we live is perhaps the most claustrophobic that has ever existed; in the culture of globalisation...there is no glimpse of an *elsewhere*, of an *otherwise*... The first step towards building an alternative world has to be a refusal of the world picture implanted in our minds... Another space is vitally necessary. (Berger 2002, p.214)

References

Bazeley, E. (1928) *Homer Lane and the Little Commonwealth*. London: Allen and Unwin.

BBC TV (1967) *Special Children – Special Teaching*. Broadcast 5 March 1967.

Berger, J. (2002) *The Shape of a Pocket*. London: Bloomsbury Publishing.

Bloom, A.A. (1948) 'Notes on a School Community.' *New Eva, 29*, 6, 120–121.

Bloom, A.A. (1949) 'Compete or Co-operate?' *New Era 30*, 8, 170–172.

Bloom, A.A. (1952) 'Learning through Living.' In M. Alderton Pink (ed.) *Moral Foundations of Citizenship*. London: London University Press.

Boggs, C. (1977/1978) 'Marxism, Prefigurative Communism, and the Problem of Workers' Control.' *Radical America 11.6–12.1*, 99–122.

Bridgeland, M. (1971) *Pioneer Work with Maladjusted Children: A Study of the Development of Therapeutic Education*. London: Staples Press.

Case, H. (1966) 'A therapeutic discipline for living.' *New Era 47*, 7, 131–136.

Case, H. (1978) *Loving Us: A New Way of Education*. Privately published (copy held by London University Institute of Education Library, Classmark zz SA6390).

Darling, J. and Norbenbo, S.E. (2003) 'Progressivism.' In N. Blake, P. Smeyers, R. Smith and P. Standish (eds) *The Blackwell Guide to Philosophy of Education*. Oxford: Blackwell.

Fielding, M. (1999) 'Radical collegiality: Affirming teaching as an inclusive professional practice.' *Australian Educational Researcher 26*, 2, 1–34.

Fielding, M. (2000) 'Community, philosophy and education policy: Against effectiveness ideology and the immiseration of contemporary schooling.' *Journal of Education Policy 15*, 4, 397–415.

Fielding, M. (2005) 'Alex Bloom: Pioneer of radical state education.' *Forum 47*, 2 and 3, 119–134.

Fielding, M. (2008) 'Radical student engagement: The pioneering work of Alex Bloom.' Paper presented at the European Conference on Educational Research, University of Gothenburg, Sweden (www.michaelfielding.co.uk).

Fielding, M. and Moss, P. (2011 forthcoming) *Radical Education and the Common School: A Democratic Alternative*. London: Routledge.

Fielding, M., Elliott, J., Robinson, C. and Samuels, J. (2006) *Less is More? The Development of a Schools-within-schools Approach to Education on a Human Scale at Bishops Park College, Clacton, Essex. Final Report to DfES Innovation Unit*. Brighton: University of Sussex.

Goodman, W.L. (1949) *Anton Simeonovitch Makarenko: Russian Teacher*. London: Routledge and Kegan Paul.

Hart, S., Dixon, A., Drummond, M.J. and McIntyre, D. (2004) *Learning without Limits*. Buckingham: Open University Press.

Kohlberg, L. (1980) 'High School Democracy and Educating for a Just Society.' In R. Mosher (ed.) *Moral Education: A First Generation of Research and Development*. New York, NY: Praeger.

Lorenz, W. (2008) 'Paradigms and politics: Understanding methods in an historical context: The case of social pedagogy.' *British Journal of Social Work 38*, 4, 625–644.

Macmurray, J. (1958) 'Learning to be Human.' Moray House Annual Public Lecture, 5 May 1958. Unpublished.

NCSL (2005) *Getting Started with Networked Learning Walks*. Nottingham: National College for School Leadership.

Neill, A.S. (1968) *Summerhill*. Harmondsworth: Penguin.

Oser, F., Althof, W. and Higgins-D'Alessandro, A. (2008) 'The Just Community approach to moral education: System change or individual change?' *Journal of Moral Education 37*, 3, 395–415.

Petrie, P. (2003) 'Social Pedagogy: An Historical Account of Care and Education as Social Control.' In J. Brannen and P. Moss (eds) *Rethinking Children's Care*. Buckingham: Open University Press.

Petrie, P. (2010) 'Children's Associative Spaces and Social Pedagogy.' In P. Foley and S. Leverett (eds) *Children and Young People's Spaces: Developing Practice*. Basingstoke: Palgrave Macmillan.

Petrie, P. and Cameron, C. (2009) 'Importing Social Pedagogy?' In J. Kornbeck and N. Jensen (eds) *The Diversity of Social Pedagogy in Europe Today*. Bremen: Europäischer Hochschulverlag.

Rowbotham, S. (1979) 'The Women's Movement and Organizing for Socialism.' In S. Rowbotham, L. Segal and H. Wainwright (eds) *Beyond the Fragments: Feminism and the Making of Socialism*. London: Merlin Press.

Spiel, O. (1962) *Discipline without Punishment*. London: Faber and Faber.

Stinton, J. (2005) *A Dorset Utopia: The Little Commonwealth and Homer Lane*. Norwich: Black Dog Books.

Sünker, H. and Swiderk, T. (2007) 'Politics of childhood, democracy and communal life: Conditions of political socialisation and education.' *Policy Futures in Education 5*, 3, 303–314.

Unger, R.M. (1987) *False Necessity*. Cambridge: Cambridge University Press.

Unger, R.M. (2005) *What Should the Left Propose?* London: Verso.

Wasserman, E. (1980) 'An Alternative High School based on Kohlberg's Just Community Approach to Education.' In R. Mosher (ed.) *Moral Education: A First Generation of Research and Development*. New York, NY: Praeger.

Watts, J. (1977) (ed.) *The Countesthorpe Experience*. London: Allen & Unwin.

Weaver, A. (1988) *Making for Peace: Patterns in Education*. London: Brentham Press.

Wills, W.D. (1941) *The Hawkspur Experiment*. London: Allen and Unwin.

Wills, W.D. (1948) 'Shared Responsibility.' In New Education Fellowship (ed.) *Problems of Child Development: A Contribution to the Understanding of Children's Needs*. London: New Education Fellowship.

CHAPTER 11

Social Pedagogy: Future Directions?

Peter Moss and Claire Cameron

The outsider view

In this concluding chapter, drawing inspiration from the preceding chapters, we reflect briefly about what future directions social pedagogy *might* take. Not 'will' take, as we lack sufficient confidence in our crystal ball to offer predictions. Instead, by saying 'might', we want to consider hopeful possibilities, including a social pedagogy that is democratic and emancipatory in its political values and practices, while bearing in mind, as several chapters have warned us to, that social pedagogy is not inherently inscribed with these values and practices, and that there is another speculative direction that might be taken which would lead to more dystopian prospects.

Writing as outsiders, from the insular perspective of England, a country with little or no established practice or profession of social pedagogy and distanced from many of the controversies around social pedagogy that have arisen in Continental Europe, our hopes risk being tainted and discredited by claims of naiveté and ignorance. On the other hand, neither are they burdened by the national preconceptions and preoccupations of countries where social pedagogy is deeply embedded in theory, practice, profession and policy. In Denmark, for instance, there are recurring questions asked about how generic and wide-ranging the profession of pedagogue should be and about the education for that profession. Was the 1992 integration of three pedagogue professions and educations into one generic profession and education, progress or pitfall? Post-1992, should we be talking about 'social pedagogical' or 'pedagogical' practice in that country? Or, to take another instance, much of the debate in

Germany is about the relationship between social pedagogy and social work and the increasing absorption of the former into the latter. Has the home of social pedagogy lost faith in the discipline?

We cannot, of course, entirely ignore such local debates, which often raise wider and vital issues. But we can, perhaps, capitalise on our position as outsiders, being able to stand back a bit from the local fray to consider possible future directions for social pedagogy; or, to be more precise, to sketch out one possible direction that we think especially interesting and important and which should at least be a main item for discussion on national and, indeed, European policy agendas: social pedagogy as a main player in work with children and young people, and also perhaps adults too. This raises the question of who, if any, the other main players might be, and here we will raise, for further discussion, the relationships between social pedagogic education and school education, and between pedagogues and teachers.

We also suggest that the development of social pedagogy to this important role in Europe could be a European project, the development of a European tradition by a European Union – perhaps giving Europe world leadership in the field of working with children (and others). This aspiration is based on social pedagogy's European roots and history. But we should remember that the United Kingdom (and indeed her English-speaking neighbour Ireland) is also European and shares little of these roots or history, though we have been at pains in Chapter 1, as Michael Fielding has been in Chapter 10, to emphasise some experiences and sensibilities in UK work with children and young people that might be termed social pedagogic. But despite these, the UK has been linked more to a network of other English-speaking countries, none of which has explicitly engaged with or adopted social pedagogy, although again some would draw parallels between certain traditions in these countries (e.g. the youth work tradition in the USA) and social pedagogy. Any discussion on the future of social pedagogy must, therefore, wonder why this separation has occurred and ask what the likelihood is of the Anglophone world adopting a social pedagogic approach or, put another way, what obstacles exist to adoption. This is the note on which we end our reflections.

Social pedagogy and working with children

From a German perspective, the future for social pedagogy might not look promising, as it is increasingly converged with social work and, in the process, gradually loses its distinctive identity to the point where it can be asked: Will social pedagogy disappear in Germany (Braches-Chyrek and Sünker 2009)? This, we might say, is at one end of the futurology spectrum, a rather gloomy outlook for social pedagogy despite the rich traditions of its past. We want to offer another and more optimistic perspective, a possibility only and no certainty, a 'might' not a 'will'. This future possibility is informed more by Danish experience, but also by some debates in our own country recently, which imply the need for a common orientation across all those working with children and young people, and expressed in the ambitions of the last (Labour) government for common outcomes across all services and a common core of knowledge and skills across all workforces in these services.

The prospect is for social pedagogy as a main player in work with children and young people across a wide range of settings. This might involve a social pedagogic orientation or perspective becoming part of the education, sensibility and practice of a wide range of workers across many services and settings, who would, however, still retain their distinctive occupational or professional identities. Or, more radically, it might involve the development of a pedagogue profession, with a common identity, that would become the core workforce across these same services and settings in a process of radical rationalisation and integration. Even more radically, and following the Danish example, this pedagogue workforce might come to assume a core role in workforces in services and settings for adults, putting working with *people* on to the policy agenda, including what common values, understandings and practices there might be in work across the life-course, while at the same time bringing into clearer focus what may be the distinctive features of work with different groups and in different settings. We might even envisage a situation of documentation and dialogue between pedagogues working with younger children, adolescents, younger adults and elderly people with disabilities, a form of cross-generational exchange that at present rarely occurs, but which could have enormous potential for enriching the lives of all concerned.

First, though, a word of warning. Everything, Michel Foucault admonishes us, is dangerous, which is a reminder that, however benign of purpose or kind of heart, everything has the potential to normalise, govern, regulate, discipline and dominate. Social pedagogy is no exception, and, as several contributors to this book have pointed out, the question of political purpose and objectives is critical. Social pedagogy is a living form, capable of adopting different guises and not immune from complicity in authoritarian regimes with dubious or obnoxious ideologies and purposes. This complicity in unsavoury ends can come about explicitly (as in Nazi Germany) or more implicitly by focusing exclusively on technique at the expense of politics and ethics. As Michel Vandenbroeck and colleagues put it in Chapter 3, 'Reducing social pedagogy to a method could turn it into a useful instrument to control social problems'(p.56). So the first thing to say about the future direction for social pedagogy is that it must be kept subject to critical thinking and evaluation, never losing sight, for example, of the relationship between knowledge and power and of the efficacy of 'human technologies' in governing the soul; and it must be treated as, first and foremost, political and ethical, not just a technical practice or a bundle of methods.

But having insisted on this important proviso, the chapters in this book also suggest the huge positive potential of social pedagogy, if allied to political and ethical purposes such as deepening democracy, pursuing emancipation and social justice, supporting inclusion, enhancing individual and societal well-being and valuing diversity. Its rich histories, traditions and practices and its generosity in accompanying so many people enables it to claim, if it chooses, to provide the basis for working across a wide range of sectors and services, not just for children but also for young people and adults. At a time when, in the United Kingdom at least, there is much talk about and effort put in to improving coordination across services and their workforces, adopting a holistic approach to working with children and others, and recognising well-being as a key concept in policy and provision, social pedagogy can put itself forward as a coherent and cohering theory, practice and policy, as relevant to work with toddlers as to work with adults with disabilities and capable, in all cases, of working with head, heart and hands. In their chapter for this volume, Gabriel Eichsteller and Sylvia Holthoff put the rationale for an optimistic and ambitious future for social pedagogy as a generic or life-course profession: 'social pedagogy is, therefore not limited to work with children; its principles extend to all human beings, which means that social pedagogues value and support parents and families and, more generally, people in the wider community'.(p.35)

Moreover, this is not unproven supposition. Social pedagogy in Continental Europe already plays an important part in many services, no more so than in Denmark where pedagogues can claim, with some justification, to be working with people from birth to 100 years of age, being the main group of workers in early childhood centres, free-time services for children outside school hours, residential care for children and young people, and a range of services for adults with disabilities (though their presence is far less in services for older adults). Such breadth of work, in contemporary Denmark or in our future scenario, raises important issues about the balance to be struck – in initial education and beyond – between generic and specialist knowledge and experience, and tensions remain in Denmark about the 'integration' since 1992 of three types of pedagogue education and profession into one. Certainly, there are many Danish voices to be heard arguing that the current generic education and profession is not sufficient for working with young people who are very disadvantaged or who display very challenging behaviour. This controversy relates also to the two traditions of narrow and broad pedagogy outlined by Inge Bryderup and Anna Kathrine Frørup in Chapter 5.

This questioning is provoked by a welfare state, many of whose services for children and young people are inscribed by social pedagogy and staffed by well-educated pedagogues. It is a debate from a position of social pedagogical strength. But, even in Denmark, schools remain primarily the domain of another profession, the teacher. So even if the rest of children's services – or, to be more precise, non-therapeutic and non-health services for children and young people – were to be placed on a social pedagogic basis, what relationship could or should there be with the most dominant and, some might add, most conservative of services and institutions: the school? To which the typically pedagogical answer has to be: it depends. It depends on the meaning, values and purposes of education and the image of the school.

A relationship of distance, and very likely tension, is highly probable where schooling is or becomes under neo-conservative pressures, an expression of 'education in its narrowest sense', a highly instrumental exercise of applying prescribed technologies to deliver standards or predetermined outcomes, mainly through processes of transmission and knowledge reproduction, knowledge here being understood as primarily and narrowly cognitive – what Loris Malaguzzi in Reggio Emilia called a 'small' pedagogy. This is the school dominated by a standards agenda set forth in a detailed curriculum organised around separate subjects and evaluated through arid and rigid regimes of testing. This is the school where learning and care are separated, expressed in the notion of 'childcare' as something to be 'wrapped around' the main school day. This is the school where democracy, rights and dialogue have little part in everyday life or broader governance. Under such circumstances, a democratic and emancipatory social pedagogy may well turn its back on the school, feeling completely out of sympathy with its purposes and methods, and put up the defences to fend off any attempts at encroachment. At best, an atmosphere of suspicion may prevail.

But the two chapters in this volume that focused on school-based education – Chapter 9 on Reggio Emilia and Chapter 10 on radical education – hold up the prospect of another, more fruitful relationship between school-based education and social pedagogy, what might be termed 'a strong and equal partnership' (OECD 2001, 2006). An embryonic version of this relationship, giving some indication of how such a partnership might operate, can be found in Sweden today. Here, free-time pedagogues (*fritidspedagog*), who formerly worked outside school in separate free-time centres, have become part of a 'whole day' school, incorporating free-time services within an extended school day. But rather than teachers and pedagogues working separately within the school, one in the classroom, the other in the free-time service, they work together in teams, with mixed-aged groups of children.

There are a number of concerns expressed about this new arrangement. Free-time pedagogues (and the pre-school teachers who also form part of the new teams) do not enjoy parity with school teachers, either in pay and other working conditions or in status. In these circumstances, pedagogues may find themselves expected to act as glorified teaching assistants, rather than as professional equals bringing their own perspective and practice to education, a relationship that undermines the concept of team working as well as underusing the capabilities of the pedagogue. Rather than providing opportunities for all team members to co-construct new and broad understandings of education and learning, there is a distinct possibility of reproducing a narrow and outmoded understanding.

However, such dysfunctional team working, based on unequal relationships, is not inevitable. Many free-time pedagogues have shown themselves well able to establish themselves as equal team members, asserting their professional identity and the educational value of their pedagogical work. The Swedish project of working with multiprofessional teams – teachers and pedagogues together – requires further study and, perhaps, more sustained development by government, schools and unions to make team work by equals a reality and realise fully the great potential of such teams (for further information, see Johansson and Moss 2010). But it provides one indication of how a new relationship – strong and equal – between teacher and pedagogue, school and other children's services *might* develop.

One precondition for constructing such a new relationship seems to be a rethinking and re-enacting of education. This entails schools turning away from education in its narrowest sense towards what has been termed 'education in its broadest sense', concerned with all aspects of the child's development and well-being; and an education, too, that adopts democratic values and children's rights, a holistic and rich image of the child, and a view of learning that foregrounds relationships, listening, dialogue and co-construction of knowledge. This might include, as Michael Fielding puts it in Chapter 10, 'a curriculum that emphasises connectedness; that is holistic in approach and organised around interconnected and interdisciplinary themes or areas, rather than separate subjects; and that encourages integrated forms of enquiry with students and staff working in small communities of enquiry.' (p.187) This process of rethinking education as the basis for new relationships between services and workforces also presupposes that other non-school services for children and young people maintain or adopt similar understandings, values and concepts; again not inevitable, but again also quite possible.

Where such an idea of education in its broadest sense comes to exist, then the potential would be far greater for a strong and equal partnership between education and social pedagogy, between teacher and pedagogue, between schools and other services and settings for children and young people. Indeed, arguably, it might become harder to know how and where to draw the lines between fields and professions, the similarities and indeed overlaps would be so great. In such (admittedly ideal) circumstances, what would distinguish the teacher from the pedagogue? While sharing much in common, would each have areas of specialism and expertise? If so, what would these be? Or would the logic of the situation suggest moving to one profession with a common initial education, but again with some degree of specialisation possible?

With education in many countries pursuing a relentless retreat towards narrowness, these questions may seem more than usually hypothetical. Yet looking at school-based education and social pedagogy, teachers and pedagogues side by side does provide one way of breaking the grip held on so much education by the dictatorship of no alternative – Paulo Freire's old banking concept of education, resurfacing in new clothes but still the same at heart. Education and social pedagogy accompanying each other, in dialogue and going deeper into past relationships, can stir memories of other educational discourses, of rich educational traditions, of radical education movements and experiences. They can provoke previously stifled questioning and revive deadened imaginations.

So one clear message for us from this book is the need to bring school-based education and social pedagogy into closer contact, to stimulate debate about the meaning and purpose of education, and to explore the potentialities for future relationships and for jointly working on the project of radical democratic education in its broadest sense. In proposing this, we share the hope expressed by Michael Fielding in Chapter 10 that:

> there is enough common ground and enough prospect of creative difference to prompt future dialogue between education and social pedagogy, and in particular between those in both fields who value highly their democratic and emancipatory traditions: dialogue for mutual learning, dialogue for building solidarities, dialogue for re-creating an emancipatory international movement that imagines and enacts an overtly democratic fellowship. (p.192)

Social pedagogy and Europe

Social pedagogy is the child (or perhaps, to recognise its diverse forms, we should say the children) of Continental Europe, spreading out from its German origins, to establish itself, in various ways and in many occupations, across many countries. In so doing, it has evolved diverse forms, reflecting more local conditions. But despite this diversity, social pedagogy retains (as Gabriel Eichsteller and Sylvia Holthoff put it in Chapter 2) 'shared conceptual foundations, a core of values and principles' (p.36). As such, it gives expression to the ideal of the post-war European political project – of creating a European political and economic entity that combines coherence and diversity: certain shared values, principles and rights that define a common European identity and citizenship, but which leave substantial room for national, regional and local variations.

For us in our outsider position, social pedagogy seems to be something about which Europe should be proud and which Europe should celebrate and develop further. This calls for historical work, to better understand the intra- and cross-national developments of this theory and practice, including a mapping of the complex flows of ideas and practices and the way they came to be interpreted and taken up in different societies; this calls for critical study, since, as we repeat again, social pedagogy can be dangerous and may also often claim more than it delivers in practice; this calls for comparative studies, to investigate shared and local understandings and practices, as the basis for dialogue and further learning; and it calls for work, cross-national and European, to ensure social pedagogy is a dynamic force, responsive to new perspectives, new knowledge and new conditions. Though our own country may have been and is still today on the margins of social pedagogy and, more generally, remains deeply ambivalent about its relationship to the rest of Europe, we would argue that the UK is a European country and can participate fully in a European-wide project to understand social pedagogy better, past and present, and to realise its potential more fully in the future.

An important question here is the role of the European Union. To date, social pedagogy has had at best a very marginal and fleeting recognition in the EU, through some funded research and other projects. By contrast, 'care' (especially 'childcare for working parents') and 'education' are high-profile and mainstreamed political concerns, with both seen as central to achieving major policy goals, such as increased employment, the achievement of a 'knowledge' economy and gender equality. The EU could, however, bring social pedagogy in from the cold by recognising its potentially important relationship to 'education', its wider potential than 'care', its contribution to creating the 'high-quality' employment much aspired to, and its role in strengthening the capacity of welfare states to foster individual and societal well-being and enhance social inclusion and democracy. Deploying its various powers and resources, the EU could adopt a strategic role in the development of social pedagogy as a key European response to contemporary social challenges, not least by supporting a high and sustained level of cross-national dialogue, training and research.

By our focus on social pedagogy here, we are not saying that social pedagogy is the only European tradition relevant to working with children and young people. There are, we are aware, rich traditions in the field of education which would similarly benefit from study and development at a European level; and (as suggested earlier), there is great potential in exploring the relationship between some of the traditions in education and social pedagogy. Nor are we saying that only traditions and theories and practices emanating from Europe are worthy of European attention.

What we are raising is an opportunity, but also an anxiety. The opportunity is to realise further the potential of a European tradition and resource. The anxiety is that instead of engaging with this tradition and resource, and the theories and practices of working with children (and others) to which they have given rise, Europe will turn its back. The anxiety is that instead Europe will be increasingly seduced or compelled to adopt standardised approaches, global norms and universal best practices, informed by decontextualised and highly positivistic research, and emanating largely from the English-speaking world, a place that has signally failed to open itself to dialogue and exchange about the diversity of ways of working with children and young people. This seems a good point to move on to our third and final theme.

Social pedagogy and the English-speaking world

As we have earlier noted, there is a growing awareness of and interest in social pedagogy in the United Kingdom, and this book is one expression of this movement. It would, however, have to be acknowledged that in other parts of the English-speaking world, awareness of social pedagogy is even less than in the UK. But what chances are there of social pedagogy forging a closer relationship with English-speaking countries, culminating in establishing a substantial presence? And are there particular features of these countries that may hinder this relationship?

Three features seem to us to create considerable hindrances. First, existing concepts and structures. The UK, but also much of the English-speaking world, has adopted what might be termed a 'care work' approach to many of the sectors and services where social pedagogy is to be found in Continental Europe. Thus the wide spread of 'childcare workers' in 'childcare services' for pre-school age children; 'childcare' or 'social care' workers in many services for school-age children, young people and adults with disabilities; and 'elder care' workers in services for older people. Before making a critique of this 'care work' model, we should make it clear that we think that care is a very important part of working with children (or anyone else) – but the operative word here is 'part'. Care is one component, inseparable from others. Moreover, in our view, care is best treated as an ethic – as in an 'ethic of care', a way of being in relation to others that is the subject of much feminist scholarship (see, for example, Sevenhuijsen 1999; Tronto 1993) – and not as a commodity or function around which services, workforces and policies should be organised.

So care matters hugely in working with people, but this does not require a 'care work' approach – that is, services and workforces defined primarily in terms of providing care. Not only is 'care' in this context far too narrow to ensure a holistic approach to working with children, or anyone else, but 'care' as a descriptor applied to services and workers invariably means work that has low status, low levels of education and low pay. Conceptualising work and services in terms of care is a recipe for low-quality employment and low-valued work: perhaps it should not be, but in reality it is, most likely because it expresses a particular understanding of the work: as something akin to what is done 'naturally' by women in the home, especially as mothers, and as such assumed to require little in the way of education, reflection or judgement when transferred to the public arena (Cameron and Moss 2007). Even when this quasi-maternal image shifts, with an acknowledgement of the need for a better-qualified care workforce, it often moves only up a notch to the image of a lower-skilled technician, with basic training in how to apply technologies to children consistently and without much need for thought and analysis of practice.

Any attempt to introduce a new discipline and profession to a country is bound to be daunting. Different traditions and cultures confront each other; new concepts and ideas need to be translated in ways that are meaningful to people in the host country; concerns among existing workers about losing out in transition will be rife. But this perhaps is not insuperable, especially given awareness of some historical common ground; some present interest in new thinking and ways of working; an appreciation that new thinking and ways of working can and must adapt to the environment into which they are being introduced, to create a national variant (as social pedagogy has shown itself well able to do in its spread across Continental Europe); and a transitional arrangement that gives existing staff access to the emerging new regime and values their prior knowledge and experience.

What may be more problematic is replacing a 'care work' workforce – low-value, low-cost substitute mothers and technicians – with a workforce of pedagogues – higher-value, higher-cost, reflective professionals. This is not only expensive, but it challenges many values and presumptions in society, especially about the complexity, demands and nature of working with children (or others) – and indeed about the nature and rights of children (and others). Of course, it is a moot point whether the 'care work' model is sustainable in the long term, premised as it is on an ever-increasing supply of women with low levels of education ready to work in low-status jobs for low pay; as levels of female education rise above men's, and better employment opportunities open up for educated women, that supply is more likely to wither than increase, unless topped up by new sources of low-cost labour, such as migrant workers.[1] A French labour market expert has cogently expressed the doubts that surround the future viability of work based on such assumptions: 'wherever the present standard for the category of job is "low qualified women around the age of 30", there will unmistakeably be a strong need to improve the quality of job so it will be acceptable to people with higher educational attainments. And if no improved professionalization of the job was achieved, then it will rapidly end up in a severe labour supply shortage' (Coomans 2002, no page number).

But there are other reasons why a social pedagogical approach and profession may meet resistance or downright rejection. A second feature that presents a hindrance to the spread of social pedagogy might be termed the Taylorism of work with children and adults. A response in the UK to the growing demand for (and growing cost of) labour in a wide range of 'human services' (not only 'care work', but also in schools and hospitals) has been to create ever more differentiated workforces, with increasing layers of workers each graded according to function and training, forming growing hierarchies, with the most qualified workers at the top, supervising and delegating to a swelling body of assistants below them. This development is based on two premises: first, that work with people can be divided into particular functions and activities, which can be evaluated for required competencies, then distributed and attached to suitably and differentially qualified persons in a process of fragmentation and specialisation; second, that this form of organisation is more 'efficient' and less costly. This is the logic of the widget factory, applied to 'human services' operated as 'businesses', and where, like a factory, the work is governed by fixed procedures and prescriptive rules, top-down management and division of labour.

Social pedagogy, as we have seen, adopts a different rationality, with different premises. It values the 'everyday', working holistically with people and through relationships. As Jytte Jensen describes in Chapter 8, physical care is considered an important element of the pedagogical relationships and necessary to working with the whole child, so not something to be delegated: 'Physical caring tasks themselves do not define what pedagogical work is, but how the tasks are performed does,

---

1   There is evidence that private employers are already turning to this solution to labour scarcities – for example, high-income parents employing nannies from low-income countries (cf. Hochschild 2000); and one in five care workers and one in three nurses employed by organisations providing older adult care in the UK being foreign-born (Cangiano *et al.* 2009).

so the tasks cannot be left to less educated staff... [Pedagogues] blow children's noses and take children to the bathroom, rather than delegating such tasks to various levels of assistant and confining themselves to pedagogical "leadership"' (p.149–150).

Faced by the complexity and contingency of human beings, social pedagogy asserts too the importance of trusting individual pedagogues to make situated judgements that draw on knowledge and experience, dialogue and reflection; work based on procedures and technical manuals may be suited to widget making, but not to working with people in all their singularity and given the inescapable and unpredictable contingency of life. On the same basis, it would question the efficiency of an approach to working with people based on fragmentation and compartmentalisation; any savings will be strictly short-term. The 'widget factory' approach, so strong in countries like the UK, is therefore neither ethical nor economical.

So a certain managerial approach, deeply embedded in services for children and others in the UK, and to a greater or lesser extent elsewhere in the English-speaking world, presents an obstacle to the spread of social pedagogy. But the managerial approach is parallelled by a third feature hindering social pedagogy's introduction to the English-speaking world: the marketisation and privatisation of services for children and others in the current phase of neoliberal capitalism. Influenced by the re-emergence of neoliberalism as a powerful economic and political discourse, the English-speaking world has led the way in recasting the provision of services as an entrepreneurial activity, involving private providers competing in a market place, competition seen as an infallible means to drive price and increase 'quality'. In this regime, the state's role is to regulate (to a greater or lesser extent), to provide some funding to those too poor or financially dependent to enter the market, to enable the market (through 'creating a level playing field') and to create a climate where markets and private provision become natural, self-evident ways of thinking about and providing services.

'Marketisation' and 'privatisation' may prove a hostile environment to the spread of social pedagogy in several ways. They introduce or reinforce strong pressures to drive down workforce costs, through, for instance, the growth of hierarchies, the differentiation of tasks, the application of standardised procedures and prescribed outputs, and the removal of workers from the protections of trade union membership and collective agreements. The residential home or nursery may want to advertise itself as having a 'qualified pedagogue' on its staff, as a selling point for potential customers, but it is unlikely to want to pay for half or more of its staff to be so qualified. Instead, the 'qualified pedagogue' will most likely find herself managing a workforce consisting of different grades of assistants.

But the potential incompatibility goes deeper. For a democratic, inclusive, emancipatory and holistic social pedagogy, committed to social justice and rights and attaching importance to dialogue, reflection and situated judgement – the sort of pedagogy we have highlighted in this book and which we see as providing hope for the future – does not sit comfortably in a profit-driven, competitive, privatised market system. Social pedagogy so understood is a theory, practice and profession for working with children and adults as citizens within public spaces that they access as of right and on an equal basis; it is a profession for practising the value of democracy for all, not enhancing the private profit of a small minority; it is a profession of collaboration and dialogue, not competition and managerialism.

We raise these issues not with a feeling of despair, but with a belief that those who find social pedagogy an important future direction for working with children (and others) should combine their enthusiasm, which we share, with a hard-headed evaluation not only of how social pedagogy may be dangerous but also of the very real obstacles to its spread. At the same time, the exercise can be a cause of hope. For it can nurture critical thinking about the dominant regime of markets, so making the familiar strange, and re-assert what any healthy democracy needs: the articulation and advocacy of alternatives. There may be many obstacles to social pedagogy in the UK and elsewhere in the English-speaking world, but to speak about it, to explore its meanings, to understand better how it is practised – all this makes it impossible to assert there is no alternative. It means, to use the expressive phrase of Nikolas Rose, putting a stutter in the meta-narrative of managerialism, markets and commodification.

We attempt, therefore, to avoid extremes of naive optimism and cynical pessimism. While we should be aware of the importance of structural and institutional forces and of the power of dominant discourses, we need not and should not allow this awareness to reduce us to fatalism and hopelessness. For, strong as structures, institutions and discourses may be, they are not all-powerful nor all-encompassing. There are always, as Erik Olin Wright reminds us, 'contradictions, limits and gaps in systems of reproduction which open up spaces for transformative strategies...[and] even when the spaces are limited, they can allow for transformations that matter' (Wright 2009, p.203). In similar vein, Foucault argues that, except in cases of slavery, there is no power without resistance and no subject of power who is not also an active agent. So while social pedagogy's future in the English-speaking world, or indeed in some countries where it is established, may not be assured, there is reason to believe it could be a future direction for working with children and adults – people – in a more democratic, more just and more sustainable world, which is perhaps the only hope for our future as a species.

References

Braches-Chyrek, R. and Sünker, H. (2009) 'Will Social Pedagogy Disappear in Germany?' In J. Kornbeck and N.R. Jensen (eds) *The Diversity of Social Pedagogy in Europe*. Bremen: Europäischer Hochschulverlag.

Cameron, C. and Moss, P. (2007) *Care Work in Europe: Current Understandings and Future Directions*. London: Routledge.

Cangiano, A. Shutes, I., Spencer, S. and Leeson, G. (2009) *Migrant Care Workers in Ageing Societies: Research Findings in the United Kingdom*. Oxford: COMPAS (ESRC Centre on Migration, Policy and Society). Available at www.compas.ox.ac.uk/fileadmin/files/pdfs/Migrant_Care_Workers/MCW%20report%20-%20final%20-%20website%20version.pdf, accessed on 1 November 2010.

Coomans, G. (2002) 'Labour supply issues in a European context.' Paper given at European Conference on Employment Issues in the Care of Children and Older People, Sheffield Hallam University, 21–22 June 2002.

Hochschild, A. (2000) 'Global Care Chains and Emotional Surplus Value.' In W. Hutton and A. Giddens (eds) *On the Edge: Living with Global Capitalism*. London: Jonathan Cape.

Johansson, I. and Moss, P. (2010) 'Reforming the school: Taking Swedish lessons.' *Children & Society*, doi: 10.1111/j.1099-0860.2010.00319x

OECD (2001) *Starting Strong: Early Childhood Education and Care*. Paris: OECD.

OECD (2006) *Starting Strong II: Early Childhood Education and Care*. Paris: OECD.

Sevenhuijsen, S. (1999) *Citizenship and the Ethics of Care: Feminist Considerations on Justice, Morality and Politics*. London: Routledge.

Tronto, J. (1993) *Moral Boundaries: A Political Argument for the Ethics of Care*. London: Routledge.

Wright, E.O. (2009) 'Elements of a theory of transformation.' Chapter 8 of final pre-publication draft of *Envisioning Real Utopias*. Available at www.ssc.wisc.edu/~wright/ERU_files/ERU-CHAPTER-8-final.pdf, accessed on 1 November 2010.

Contributors

Janet Boddy is Senior Research Officer at the Thomas Coram Research Unit, Institute of Education, University of London. With a background in psychology and expertise in parents and families, she is part of a team researching social pedagogy in children's services in European contexts and beyond.

Lieve Bradt is a PhD student at the Department of Social Welfare Studies at Ghent University, Belgium. Her research interests include restorative justice for young and adult offenders.

Inge M. Bryderup is Associate Professor at the Department of Education, Danish School of Education, University of Aarhus in Copenhagen, Denmark. She is a sociologist with a research record in the field of social policy, social pedagogy and children and young people in care, and she coordinates a masters programme in social pedagogy.

Claire Cameron is Professor of Social Care and Social Work at Anglia Ruskin University, Cambridge. She was previously Reader in Education at Thomas Coram Research Unit, Institute of Education, University of London, where she had been researching the children's workforce, children's services and issues of care and education since 1992. European studies have led to a deep interest in social pedagogy and its potential contribution to understandings of the relationship between professional practice and children's lives in services in the UK. She started the first MA in Social Pedagogy in the UK.

Filip Coussée is Assistant Professor in the Department of Social Welfare studies at Ghent University, Belgium, where his work focuses on social pedagogy as a perspective on social work and youth and community work with a strong cross-national and historical perspective.

Gabriel Eichsteller set up ThemPra Social Pedagogy with Sylvia Holthoff as a training and development social enterprise dedicated to supporting the development of social pedagogy in the UK. His background is social pedagogy, European social work and the sociology of childhood, which he studied in Germany, Denmark and the UK.

Michael Fielding is Emeritus Professor of Education at the Institute of Education, University of London. His work is well known in the fields of radical education, student voice, school leadership and professional learning, and brings a perspective strongly influenced by person-centred, radical democratic traditions of publicly funded education.

Anna Kathrine Frørup is an Industrial PhD student in the National Federation of Social Educators in Denmark and at the Department of Education, Danish School of Education, University of Aarhus, Denmark. Her research interests include knowledge and discourses within the profession of social pedagogy.

Sylvia Holthoff is a trainer and co-director of ThemPra Social Pedagogy, which emerged after she and Gabriel Eichsteller developed and delivered training in social pedagogic approaches for an initial project run by the National Centre for Excellence in Residential Child Care and the Social Education Trust. She completed her studies of pedagogy for people with special needs in Germany and is a specialist in experiential outdoor activities.

Jytte Juul Jensen is Assistant Professor at VIA University College, Pædagoguddannelsen Jydsk, Denmark, where she educates pedagogues. She is an expert in early childhood education and has conducted many studies including the Danish part of Care Work in Europe: Current Understandings and Future Directions.

Stefan Kleipoedszus is part of a team supporting the development of social pedagogy in the UK based at Thomas Coram Research Unit, Institute of Education, University of London. A social pedagogue and social worker by background, and currently completing his PhD, his research interests are around the historical origins of social pedagogy and the contextual foundations of social pedagogy in children's services in the UK.

Peter Moss is Professor of Early Childhood Education at the Thomas Coram Research Unit, Institute of Education, University of London. His academic interests include early childhood education and care, its relationship with compulsory schooling, and the interplay between gender, care and employment.

Pat Petrie is Professor of Education and Head of the Centre for Understanding Social Pedagogy (CUSP) at the Institute of Education, University of London. She researches social and educational policy and practice towards children in the UK and abroad, and her work receives international recognition.

Rudi Roose is Assistant Professor at the Department of Social Welfare Studies at Ghent University and Associate Professor at the Department of Criminology at Free University Brussels, Belgium. His main research topics are social work theories, social pedagogy and children's rights.

Michel Vandenbroeck is Professor in the Department of Social Welfare Studies at Ghent University, Belgium, where he is a specialist in early childhood education and issues of diversity and inclusion. He is also chairman of the Resource and Research Centre for Early Childhood Care and Education at Ghent University.

Subject Index

Author Index